Continuity and Ch Darussalam

This book analyses the processes of social and economic change in Brunei Darussalam.

Drawing on recent studies undertaken by both locally based scholars and senior researchers from outside the state, the book explores the underlying strengths, characteristics, and uniqueness of Malay Islamic Monarchy in Brunei Darussalam in a historical context and examines these in an increasingly challenging regional and global environment. It considers events in Brunei's recent history and current socio-cultural transformations, which give expression to the traumatic years of decolonisation in Southeast Asia. A wide range of issues focus on foreign, non-Bruneian narratives of Brunei as against insider or domestic accounts of the sultanate, the status of minority ethnic groups in Brunei and the concept of 'Brunei society', as well as changes in the character and composition of the famous 'water village', Kampong Ayer, as the cultural heartland of Brunei Malay culture and the socio-cultural and economic effects of the resettlement of substantial segments of the population from a 'life on water' to a 'life on land'.

A timely and very important study on Brunei Darussalam, the book will be of interest to anthropologists, sociologists, historians, geographers, and area studies specialists in Southeast Asian Studies and Asian Studies.

Victor T. King is Professor of Borneo Studies at the Institute of Asian Studies, Universiti Brunei Darussalam and Emeritus Professor of South East Asian Studies, University of Leeds, UK. He is the co-author of *The Modern Anthropology of South-East Asia* (Routledge 2006) and co-editor of the Routledge series *Modern Anthropology of South-East Asia.*

Stephen C. Druce is Programme Leader in Graduate Studies and Research at the Academy of Brunei Studies, Universiti Brunei Darussalam. He is the author of *The Lands West of the Lakes: A History of the Ajattappareng Kingdoms of South Sulawesi, 1200 to 1600 CE* (2009).

The Modern Anthropology of Southeast Asia

Editors: Victor T. King
University of Leeds

Michael Hitchcock
Goldsmiths, University of London

The books in this series address issues in processes of development, globalisation and change in Southeast Asia. Where appropriate they contextualise change and local responses to it by providing ethnographic materials on social and cultural forms and institutions. Although all the contributors to the series examine modern and contemporary issues in the anthropology of Southeast Asia, the emphasis in each book differs as authors choose to concentrate on specific dimensions of change and globalisation or work out particular conceptual approaches to the complex issues of development. Areas of concern include: nation-building, power and the media; technological innovations in agriculture and rural-urban migration; the expansion of industrial and commercial employment; the rapid increase in cultural and ethnic tourism; the consequences of deforestation and environmental degradation; heritage and identity; contemporary expressions of religious affiliation; the 'modernisation of tradition'; ethnic identity and conflict; changing gender relations; and the religious transformation of society.

Kinship, population and social reproduction in the 'new Indonesia'
A study of Nuaulu cultural resilience
Roy Ellen

Post-Conflict Social and Economic Recovery in Timor-Leste
Redemptive legacies
Andrew McWilliam

Continuity and Change in Brunei Darussalam
Edited by Victor T. King and Stephen C. Druce

Origins, History and Social Structure in Brunei Darussalam
Edited by Victor T. King and Stephen C. Druce

For more information about this series, please visit: www.routledge.com/The-Modern-Anthropology-of-Southeast-Asia/book-series/MASEA

Continuity and Change in Brunei Darussalam

Edited by Victor T. King
and Stephen C. Druce

Routledge
Taylor & Francis Group
LONDON AND NEW YORK

First published 2021
by Routledge
2 Park Square, Milton Park, Abingdon, Oxon OX14 4RN

and by Routledge
52 Vanderbilt Avenue, New York, NY 10017

Routledge is an imprint of the Taylor & Francis Group, an informa business

British Library Cataloguing-in-Publication Data
A catalogue record for this book is available from the British Library

Library of Congress Cataloging-in-Publication Data
A catalog record for this book has been requested

ISBN: 978-0-367-07640-5 (hbk)
ISBN: 978-0-429-02179-4 (ebk)

Typeset in Times New Roman
by Apex CoVantage, LLC

Contents

List of contributors vii
List of figures ix
List of tables x
List of maps xi

1 **Introduction: Donald Brown's Brunei, society and recent transformations** 1
VICTOR T. KING AND STEPHEN C. DRUCE

2 **Monarchy in Brunei: past, present and future** 7
OOI KEAT GIN

3 **'So near yet so far': Shaikh A. M. Azahari and 1962** 21
B. A. HUSSAINMIYA

4 **Hybrid pathways to orthodoxy: bureaucratisation, Sharia-compliant exorcism and the powers of Japanese water-crystal photography in Brunei Darussalam** 46
DOMINIK M. MÜLLER

5 **Inside or outside the mainstream? An ethnolinguistic study of the status of minority indigenous groups in Negara Brunei Darussalam** 67
NOOR AZAM HAJI-OTHMAN AND JAMES McLELLAN

6 ***Menteri darat* and incorporation: integration of Dusun society into the organisational structure of the Brunei sultanate** 90
PUDARNO BINCHIN

7 **The place of the Kadayan in traditional Brunei society** 117
ALLEN R. MAXWELL

8 Living on water: water settlements in Borneo 145
HANS-DIETER EVERS

9 Development, change and modernisation in Kampong Ayer over the last fifty years 152
HAJI TASSIM BIN HAJI ABU BAKAR

10 Prospects and challenges of heritage tourism at Kampong Ayer (water village) in Brunei Darussalam 165
SHAFI NOOR ISLAM

11 Epilogue: Brunei studies: 50 years and more 176
DONALD E. BROWN

Index 179

Contributors

Pudarno Binchin (PhD), formerly Curator of Ethnography, Malay Technology Museum, Brunei Museums Department; author, *Singing Siram Ditaan: Composition, Performance and Transmission of Epic Tales of Derato in Brunei Dusun Society* (2014).

Haji Tassim bin Haji Abu Bakar (PhD), Senior Assistant Professor and Director of the Academy of Brunei Studies, Universiti Brunei Darussalam; PhD, *Permasalahan Perpindahan Petempatan Penduduk dari Air ke Darat di Negara Brunei Darussalam, 1906–2006*, Universiti Malaya (2009); co-author, 'Dari Padian ke Tamu Kianggeh', *Borneo Research Journal* (2012).

Donald E. Brown (PhD), Emeritus Professor of Anthropology, University of California, Santa Barbara; author, *Brunei: The Structure and History of a Bornean Malay Sultanate* (1970), *Principles of Social Structure, Southeast Asia* (1976), *Hierarchy, History and Human Nature: The Social Origins of Historical Consciousness* (1988), *Human Universals* (1991).

Stephen C. Druce (PhD), Assistant Professor, Academy of Brunei Studies, Universiti Brunei Darussalam; author, *The Lands West of the Lakes: A History of the Ajattappareng Kingdoms of South Sulawesi 1200 to 1600 CE* (2009).

Hans-Dieter Evers (PhD), Visiting Professor, International Studies, Institute of Malaysian and International Studies (IKMAS), Universiti Kebangsaan Malaysia; Emeritus Professor of Development Planning, University of Bielefeld; Senior Fellow, Centre for Development Research, University of Bonn; co-editor, *Catalysts of Change in Chinese Business in Asia* (2013), *Beyond the Knowledge Trap: Developing Asia's Knowledge-based Economies* (2011); co-author, *Epistemic Landscape Atlas of Brunei Darussalam* (2013).

Ooi Keat Gin (PhD), Professor of History, Universiti Sains Malaysia; author; editor *Southeast Asia: A Historical Encyclopedia from Angkor Wat to East Timor* (2004, 3 vols); *The Japanese Occupation of Borneo, 1941–45* (2010); *Post-war Borneo, 1945–1950: Nationalism, Empire, and State-building* (2013); co-editor with Hoang Anh Tuan, *Early Modern Southeast Asia, 1350–1800* (2015), with Volker Grabowsky, *Ethnic and Religious Identities and Integration in Southeast Asia* (2017); editor of *Brunei – History, Islam, Society* *and Contemporary Issues* (2016); *Historical Dictionary of Malaysia* (2018); founder-editor-in-chief of the *International Journal of Asia Pacific Studies* (IJAPS).

Noor Azam Haji-Othman (PhD), Associate Professor, English Language and Linguistics and Dean of the Faculty of Arts and Social Sciences, Universiti Brunei Darussalam; author and co-editor, *The Use and Status of Language in Brunei Darussalam*, and 'The Language Situation in Brunei Darussalam' (2016).

B. A. Hussainmiya (PhD), former Associate Professor, History, Faculty of Arts and Social Sciences, Universiti Brunei Darussalam, and Visiting Professor, Southeastern University of Sri Lanka; author, *Sultan Omar Ali Saifuddin III and Britain: The Making of Brunei Darussalam* (1995), *Brunei Constitution of 1959: An Inside History* (2000).

Shafi Noor Islam (PhD), Assistant Professor, Geography, Faculty of Arts and Social Sciences, Universiti Brunei Darussalam; co-author, 'Mangrove Wetland Ecosystems in Ganges-Brahmaputra Delta in Bangladesh', *Frontiers of Earth Science in China* (2008); co-author, 'Deltaic Floodplains Development and Wetland Ecosystems Management in the Ganges-Brahmaputra-Meghna Rivers Delta in Bangladesh', *Sustainable Water Resources Management* (2016).

Victor T. King (PhD), Professor of Borneo Studies, Institute of Asian Studies, Universiti Brunei Darussalam (UBD); Emeritus Professor, School of Languages, Cultures and Societies, University of Leeds; author, *The Peoples of Borneo* (1993), *The Sociology of South-East Asia: Transformations in a Developing Region* (2011), co-author, *The Modern Anthropology of South-East Asia: An Introduction* (2006); co-editor of three Routledge publications: a four-volume reader, *Tourism in East and Southeast Asia* (2018), *Tourism and Ethnodevelopment: Inclusion, Empowerment and Self-determination* (2018) and a reprint with a new Preface of *Tourism in South-East Asia* (2019).

Allen R. Maxwell (PhD), deceased 2011; formerly Emeritus Professor of Anthropology, University of Alabama; PhD, *Urang Darat: An Ethnographic Study of the Kadayan of Labu Valley, Brunei*, Yale University (1980); 'Malay Polysemy and Political Power: Census Categories, Ethnicity and Citizenship in Brunei Darussalam', *South East Asia Research* (2001).

James McLellan (PhD), Associate Professor, English Language and Linguistics, Faculty of Arts and Social Sciences, Universiti Brunei Darussalam; author and co-editor, *The Use and Status of Language in Brunei Darussalam* (2016); co-author, 'Introduction: English in Brunei Darussalam', *World Englishes* (2016).

Dominik M. Müller (PhD), formerly Head of Research Group (Emmy Noether) and now Cooperation Partner, Max-Planck-Gesellschaft, Munich; Professor of Cultural and Social Anthropology, Friedrich-Alexander-University Erlangen-Nuremberg; author, *Islam, Politics and Youth in Malaysia: The Pop-Islamist Reinvention of PAS* (2014).

Figures

5.1 Language and dialect shift in Brunei 77
8.1 Donald Brown in his motorboat on the Brunei River, 1968 145
8.2 Measuring the size of water villages (example from Labuan) 148
11.1 From left to right: Donald Brown in cara Melayu; Carrie Brown with hawker (*padian*) at the ladder to their house in Kampong Ayer; Donald and Carrie in the Brunei Museum; and Donald and Carrie on the ladder to their house in Kampong Ayer, with on-looking neighbours, all 1967 176

Tables

5.1	Cognates for languages and dialects of Brunei	73
5.2	Ethnolinguistic vitality rating of languages of Brunei (on a scale of 0–6: higher figures indicate greater vitality)	78
7.1	Summary of 20th-century censuses of Brunei Darussalam	132
8.1	Size of water villages by state or province, 2013	149
8.2	Extent of water villages (sq. km.), Borneo	150
9.1	Total population of Kampong Ayer today	156
9.2	Basic facilities of Kampong Ayer today	157
10.1	The number of tourists visiting Kampong Ayer Tourism Gallery by region from January 2018 to March 2019	171
10.2	The total and average number of tourists visiting Kampong Ayer Tourism Gallery, 2018–2019	171
10.3	Total number of monthly tourists in Kampong Ayer from January to March 2019	171

Maps

8.1	Water villages around Borneo	149
9.1	Map of Kampong Ayer: Location of current kampongs and those that no longer exist	155
10.1	The geographical distribution of 42 water villages in Kampong Ayer (1980)	167
10.2	The geographical location and distribution of 34 water villages in Kampong Ayer (2016)	168

1 Introduction

Donald Brown's Brunei, society and recent transformations

Victor T. King and Stephen C. Druce

The first volume which celebrates Professor Donald Brown's seminal studies on the Brunei sultanate and evaluates his volume *Brunei: The Structure and History of a Bornean Malay Sultanate*, published by the Brunei Museum as a special monograph in 1970, and his subsequent publications on Brunei's history and social organisation is now followed by an expansion of this project. With the publication of the volume 50 years ago, we mark its jubilee anniversary. Brown's publications are now standard references for our study of the society, culture and history of the Brunei sultanate. Indeed, his work was pioneering in two respects: it was the first major attempt to understand and analyse the historical development and the key structural principles which gave order to the Brunei sultanate from the mid-nineteenth century, and secondly, it brought to public attention some of the rich primary resources on Brunei housed in the London archives to which B. A. Hussainmiya refers in Chapter 3 in this volume. The two volumes celebrating his work give extended recognition to his achievements and the 50 years or so (the 'jubilee') since he undertook the research and published his monograph.

Though other studies were undertaken after the publication of Brown's monograph, without his scholarly contribution we would have had no major points of reference before the declaration of the full independence of Negara Brunei Darussalam from the British Crown on 1 January 1984. Brown was also in Brunei in 1967 when His Majesty Sultan Haji Sir Hassanal Bolkiah Mu'izzaddin Waddaulah succeeded his father, Al-Marhum Sultan Haji Sir Omar Ali Saifuddien Sa-adul Khairi Waddien, the Seri Begawan, so it is a happy coincidence to mark and evaluate Brown's achievements at the time when Brunei celebrated the 50th jubilee of their Sultan's reign in 2017. The present Sultan's official coronation was held in August 1968 just after Brown had completed his fieldwork and departed from Brunei. Brown's research comprised a six-month period in the London archives from July to December 1966 and then for one month in May 1968, and field research in Brunei from early January 1967 to April 1968, funded by the London-Cornell project.

Such interest has been generated in celebrating and evaluating Professor Brown's work that we have had to devise a means to embrace this burgeoning scholarship. Therefore, this is a second volume, which connects us to more contemporary issues and brings us directly to Donald Brown's study of the sultanate's socio-political organisation, its nineteenth-century antecedents and the reconstruction of these, the transformations in Brunei, especially in Kampong Ayer as the epicentre of the polity's social and cultural identity, and the sultanate's relations with its surrounding populations.

The rationale for this volume is expressed and explained in our exploration of Brunei's early history, origins and cultural development in the first volume. We have set the scene for the second volume which brings us to the nineteenth century, and then some of the issues and problems which Brunei Darussalam currently experiences. We begin with setting the scene in Ooi Keat Gin's scene-setting chapter, which explores the underlying strengths, characteristics and uniqueness of Malay Islamic Monarchy in a historical context. These have sustained the Brunei sultanate over the past seven centuries and continue to direct developments and the future direction of Brunei in contemporary times. Issues raised by the national ideology are examined in relation to its relevance, strengths, weaknesses and sustainability; each is examined in the context of an increasingly challenging regional and global environment. He covers primarily the period that Donald Brown was concerned to understand in his socio-historical study.

Ooi Keat Gin, in his overview of Brunei history in Chapter 2, has provided the context for Brunei's pathway to an uncertain, post-Second World War future. It is also captured in B. A. Hussainmiya's Chapter 3 which examines an event, in Brunei's recent history, as an expression of what was a relatively minor occurrence in the traumatic years of the decolonisation of Southeast Asia. How do populations, subject to the dominance and direction of European powers, prepare for a future which has to contend with the 'Cold War', political independence and nation-building? Hussainmiya, a historian of Brunei who, during his extended tenure at Universiti Brunei Darussalam, produced substantial historical work on the sultanate including a biography-history of Sultan Haji Omar Ali Saifuddien III, the Seri Begawan (1995) (for which Donald Brown was involved as an advisor), has written on a sensitive subject in Brunei in his Chapter 3 on the Brunei Rebellion of 1962. He argues that, although the rebellion was easily put down by British Gurkha forces from Singapore, it might have been successful had the event been planned with greater foresight and precision, especially given the nature of the fledgling monarchical power and the multiple pressures facing a declining colonial power. The leader of the Brunei People's Party and the alleged promoter of the rebellion was Shaikh A. M. Azahari, who, despite his charisma and political acumen, had failed to grasp the reality of local and global power games that brought about his downfall and the failure of the people's movement which he spearheaded. Another aim of the chapter is to re-evaluate Azahari's role in the rebellion. Donald Brown's plans for research in Brunei were presented with some difficulties in the aftermath of the rebellion in that it was impossible for him to investigate the then politics of Brunei and the socio-political contexts within which the rebellion occurred.

Dominik Müller in Chapter 4 gives us a thoughtful and informed chapter entitled, intriguingly, 'Hybrid Pathways to Orthodoxy: Bureaucratised Exorcism, Scientisation and the Transcendental Powers of Japanese Water-crystal Photography in Brunei Darussalam'. To an outsider unfamiliar with Brunei, this title seems incomprehensible. It is not, and it investigates an arena of socio-religious and political processes that Donald Brown could not have anticipated in the late 1960s, though we assume that he might have suspected that Brunei would move in directions which approximate those which Müller proposes. Brown would also appreciate the ways in which Müller addresses the issue of foreign narratives of Brunei as against insider or domestic accounts of the sultanate and its recent socio-political transformations. Müller investigates the bureaucratisation of Islam in Brunei and its interlinkages with socio-cultural changes and explains in what ways the realisation of state-enforced Islamic orthodoxy produces locally generated meanings, while simultaneously reflecting broader characteristics of the contemporary global condition. The chapter first introduces a theoretical perspective on the bureaucratisation of Islam as a social phenomenon, intertwined with the state's exercise of classificatory power and related popular processes of co-producing, and sometimes appropriating, symbolic state power. Second, it outlines the historical trajectory of empowering Brunei's national ideology, *Melayu Islam Beraja* (MIB). It then explores social imaginaries and bureaucratic representations of 'deviant'-declared practices, before illustrating how these practices have become reinvented within the parameters of state power as 'Sharia-compliant' services to the nation-state. Simultaneously, national-religious protectionism is expressed in globalised terms and shaped by forces the state cannot entirely control. In the main ethnographic example, bureaucratised exorcism, Japanese water-crystal photography and scientisation fuse behind the 'firewall' of MIB. It is argued that these hybrid pathways to orthodoxy complicate the narratives through which they are commonly framed.

In Chapter 5, Noor Azam and James McLellan explore, through their ethno-linguistic study, the status of minority ethnic groups in Brunei. The trigger for their chapter is Brown's statement about the status of minority ethnic groups as 'of lesser significance' in Brunei. The initial focus of the chapter is on the distinction between those designated in the 1959 Constitution and the Nationality Act of 1961 as *puak jati* (indigenous groups), namely Brunei Malay, Kedayan, Tutong, Dusun, Bisaya, Belait and Murut (Lun Bawang), and those deemed non-indigenous, particularly the Iban and the Penan. It is proposed that the languages of all these groups may be considered as dialects of Malay for political purposes, whilst linguistically they demonstrate varying degrees of difference and distinction from core Brunei Malay language, termed 'Pan-Bruneian Malay' by Noor Azam. Whilst non-Bruneian 'outsider' researchers tend to view the minority languages as stigmatised and endangered in varying degrees, Bruneian 'insiders' focus more on the downplaying of differences for reasons of national unity and alignment with the national ideology.

Pudarno Binchin, as a prominent local Dusun scholar, serving a long career in the Brunei Museum, pursues the theme of social identity and incorporation in regard to Dusun social organisation in Chapter 6. Pudarno notes that Brown's study of Brunei's ranked society in the nineteenth century touched only briefly on the Dusun people, except in generalised passages related to the institutions of *menteri darat* (land chiefs) and *ketua kampong* (village headmen). Before the British took over Brunei public administration in 1906, the sultanate's links with the Dusun people were conducted through the appointment of *menteri darat*, the 'inland' chiefs – as opposed to the 'sea' chiefs (*menteri laut*) of the Brunei 'water villages'. These *menteri darat* were conferred with honorific titles such as *dato* and *orang kaya*.

Pudarno points out that historically, some Dusun elders were appointed as *menteri darat*, and as recognised 'leaders' of their people in relation to the sultanate, but these positions were controlled from above by the traditional Brunei sultanate's Malay officials (*kepala menteri darat*). The representatives of ethnic minority groups could therefore not occupy the higher offices above the *menteri darat*. Brown uses the term 'non-Bruneis' (in contrast to 'Bruneis') to demarcate this exclusiveness. Pudarno also refers to Brown's paper on Brunei superordinated positions in relation to other ethnic groups entitled 'Inter-Hierarchical Commissions in a Bornean Plural Society' (Brown 1973). In this paper, Brown explains the interactions between the Bruneis and other ethnic groups through the administrative link of 'inter-hierarchical' offices as 'the points of interpenetration of socio-political systems' of the Brunei sultanate in relation to non-Brunei communities. There were two types of inter-hierarchical offices: (a) inter-hierarchical positions occupied by ethnic Bruneis, and (b) inter-hierarchical positions occupied by subjects who were not ethnic Bruneis but who held positions in the Brunei sultanate's administrative hierarchy. Pudarno examines in detail the second category which relates to the role of the Dusun *menteri darat*.

Allen Maxwell's important Chapter 7 on the Kedayan/Kadayan argues that they have occupied a pivotal role in traditional Brunei society, but that, at the time that he published his paper in 1996 (reprinted here, with minor revisions), the position of the Kedayan, as a Malay-speaking people, closely integrated as agriculturalists into the structure of the sultanate, remained obscure. He rectifies this lack of research on the Kedayan by providing a detailed account of their importance in the Brunei plural society and the complementarity that they offered to the water-based, seafaring ethnic Bruneis, who relied on the Kedayan for basic foodstuffs. In an important sense, the Brunei Malays could not function as a separate ethnic group; they needed the Kedayan.

In his consideration of the relations between the Bruneis and Kedayans within the context of a plural society, Brown draws our attention to a difficult conceptual issue. In his monograph he decided initially that they were not part of what might be termed 'Brunei society' (1970: 16). Nevertheless, he did accept that conceptually they might be seen in some sense as forming a part of a wider Brunei social formation. He concluded that this issue 'will require further analysis before sound judgements may be made', and that the Kedayans 'pose a special problem in the distinction between Bruneis and non-Bruneis' (1970: 16, 20).

Sadly, Professor Maxwell died in 2011, but his article on the place of Kedayan (rendered Kadayan by Maxwell) in traditional Brunei society seems to us to be such an important contribution to our understanding of the social and political organisation of the sultanate and its relationships with its ethnic minorities that it had to be included (it is reprinted from *South East Asia Research* [1996] by kind permission of the Taylor and Francis Group).

The final set of chapters examines 'water villages' in Borneo, including Kampong Ayer and its iconic status in the global imaging of the Brunei sultanate. It was the location which Donald Brown chose for his residence with his wife Carrie in 1967–1968 and where he conducted his research on the Brunei Malays and their historical development. Hans-Dieter Evers's Chapter 8 on water villages in Borneo, based on his earlier paper (2015) places Kampong Ayer in a wider context; Evers identified 84 water villages in Borneo; he has added a brief introduction to his reprinted chapter to situate it in this volume and in the context of Brown's residence there in the late 1960s (Chapter 8 is reprinted with the kind permission of the Editor of the *Journal of the Malaysian Branch of the Royal Asiatic Society*).

In his survey of 'water villages' in Borneo, Evers demonstrates that these were and still are common features along the rivers and coasts of Borneo, but that the water settlements along the Brunei River are by far the largest in extent and in number of inhabitants throughout the Indonesian, Malaysian and Brunei districts and provinces. Using remote sensing data, Evers and his research team examined the extent of water villages and estimated their number of households and inhabitants which covered a total area of approximately 25 square kilometres and provided homes for 215,000 inhabitants. Sadly, Kampong Ayer has declined rapidly in numbers through resettlement and the development of the Kedayan and Brunei Rivers waterfront; recent estimates, though these are subject to modification, suggest that its population now totals less than 10,000, and a proportion of these are not long-settled residents but migrant workers from other parts of Asia. Kampong Ayer's claim to distinction as the largest 'water village' in the world is possibly now in doubt.

Pursuing this theme, Haji Tassim Abu Bakar in Chapter 9 then examines the changes in Kampong Ayer from the early part of the twentieth century as Brunei began to modernise under the British Residential system from 1906, which moved the administrative centre of the country from water to land and began to develop Brunei Town (Bandar Seri Begawan) as a commercial area. British Residents also encouraged the inhabitants of Kampong Ayer to resettle on land. Interestingly they had little success in the early years, and it was only in the 1950s that a marked movement to land-based housing began with the implementation of several resettlement schemes. Over the years these schemes were expanded, which led to increasing numbers of people leaving Kampong Ayer; some of them were forced to move because their homes were lost to sudden outbreaks of fire. An important consequence of this movement, together with the social and economic development of Brunei, has been the loss of important handicraft skills once practised by Kampong Ayer's residents and often linked to specific villages that no longer exist. In order to protect and sustain these disappearing craft skills, the government established the Brunei Arts and Handicraft Training Centre.

Kampong Ayer, therefore, now houses a very small percentage of the total population of Brunei, about 3 per cent, though it continues to represent a unique and iconic symbol of Brunei's past. From the 1980s, new housing and villages were constructed in Kampong Ayer for residents who lost homes in fires and wished to continue living on water. As part of Brunei's promotion of tourism, Kampong Ayer has also become one of the sultanate's most important tourist attractions. In Chapter 10, Shafi Noor Islam attempts to address and analyse the universal cultural value, heritage status and tourism activities at Kampong Ayer within the framework of a potential UNESCO World Heritage Site selection. The significance of culture, heritage and the community lifestyle of Kampong Ayer is assessed in examining the opportunities and challenges of tourism development and better management and conservation policies for Kampong Ayer. Given the recent transformations in Kampong Ayer, the desire to claim heritage status is seriously challenged. Nevertheless, the historical importance of the 'water village' is not in doubt.

Finally, Donald Brown has also provided a brief Epilogue to the volume, pointing to the vitality of the study of Brunei in recent years and some of its more general contributions to social science. In his own work, Brown's study of Brunei led him to ponder the nature of human society and culture and the ways in which history is thought about and recorded. Inter-ethnic relations and their conceptualisation comprises another field in which social science thinking arising from research on Brunei has been engaged. We leave you with an appropriate observation from Donald Brown: 'There is still much to do and say in Brunei Studies. Its robust future is assured, and I count myself privileged to have taken part in developing our understanding of Brunei's history, society and culture'.

References

Brown, D. E. (1970) Brunei: The Structure and History of a Bornean Malay Sultanate. *Special Monograph of the Brunei Museum* 2 (2).

Brown, D. E. (1973) Inter-Hierarchical Commissions in a Bornean Plural Society. *Southeast Asian Journal of Social Science* 1 (1): 97–116.

Evers, Hans-Dieter (2015) Ḳampung Air: Water Settlements on the Island of Borneo. *Journal of the Malaysian Branch of the Royal Asiatic Society* 88 (1): 79–86.

Hussainmiya, B. A. (1995) *Sultan Omar Ali Saifuddin III and Britain: The Making of Brunei Darussalam*. Kuala Lumpur: Oxford University Press.

Maxwell, Allen R. (1996) The Place of Kadayan in Traditional Brunei Society. *South East Asia Research* 4 (2): 157–196.

2 Monarchy in Brunei

Past, present and future*

Ooi Keat Gin

Preamble

Negara Brunei Darussalam (hereinafter Brunei), in Arabic meaning 'Abode of Peace', is the official designation of the Malay Muslim sultanate of Brunei, whose current ruler, Sultan Haji Hassanal Bolkiah Mu'izzaddin Waddaulah ibni Al-Marhum Sultan Haji Omar Ali Saifuddien Sa'adul Khairi Waddien (b. 1946), is amongst the world's top ten richest monarchs in terms of personal net worth. Sultan Hassanal Bolkiah is the 29th *Sultan* and *Yang Di-Pertuan of Brunei*, sovereign monarch and head of state respectively. Concurrently he holds the executive post of Prime Minister as well as other ministerial portfolios. Since its foundation in the fourteenth century, Brunei's monarchical system of governance not only has survived but has consolidated its power, character, and identity. The centuries-long continuity of the monarchy and its form of absolute and personalised rule was, and still is, based on the concept of *Melayu Islam Beraja* (MIB), or 'Malay Islamic Monarchy', an ideological and philosophical foundation that has proven to be stabilising and sustainable since independence from the United Kingdom in 1984.

A British colonial protectorate from 1888 to 1984, Brunei had relied heavily on its oil and petroleum resources. Diversification of the economy to assuage the overdependence on petroleum has been initiated since the 1990s. A form of royal paternalism ensured that citizens benefitted from state welfare and privileges literally from cradle to grave. Brunei offers an exemplary case of a viable and sustainable traditional monarchy in the modern era.

Brunei, with 5,765 sq. km. in territory split into two hanging teardrops straddling the north-east coast of Borneo, has a population of 436,620 (July 2016 est.) (Central Intelligence Agency, The World Factbook 2017). Demographically it comprises Malay (65.7%), Chinese (10.3%), other indigenous (3.4%), and others (20.6%), with religious adherence being Muslim (78.8%), Christian (8.7%), Buddhist (7.8%), and others, including indigenous beliefs (4.7%) (2011 est.) (Central Intelligence Agency, The World Factbook). The category 'Malay race' comprises indigenous Brunei Malay, Tutong, Belait, Dusun, Murut, Kedayan and Bisaya, and is collectively referred to as 'Bumiputera', literally sons of the soil. Though indigenous, the Iban, Melanau, and Penan are not classified as 'Malay' but as 'Other indigenous', hence not considered 'Bumiputera', and subsequently deprived of any benefits derived from affirmative action. 'Others' comprised mainly Europeans and Filipinos.

This chapter identifies the underlying strengths, characteristics, and uniqueness of MIB that has to a great extent sustained the Brunei sultanate over the past seven centuries and continued to engineer the kingdom's developments and future direction in contemporary times. Issues of MIB's relevance, strengths, pitfalls, and sustainability are examined and evaluated amidst an increasingly challenging regional and global environment.

History

The Malay sultanate of Brunei predates the erstwhile fifteenth-century Malay sultanate of Malacca. The official date for conversion to Islam and the emergence of a sultanate is 1368, but Brunei as a political entity probably dates from around the tenth century. Brunei's 'golden age' spanned the early fifteenth century to the seventeenth century, claiming an empire that allegedly commanded influence as far north as present-day Manila and island-wide Borneo. Malacca's fall to the Portuguese in the early part of the sixteenth century was a boon to both Brunei and Aceh whereby Muslim merchants shifted their trade to these ports. Inevitably during the sixteenth and seventeenth centuries, Brunei-Spanish relations were unfriendly over the Philippine archipelago with armed clashes. The sultanate of Sulu also contended with Brunei for hegemony over north-east Borneo and the southern Philippines (Ooi 2016; Saunders 1994).

Challenges from without and factionalism from within gradually sapped Brunei's vigour and strength, and by the mid-nineteenth century the sultanate appeared as a weak kingdom of a ruler barely secured on his own *takhta* (throne). Meanwhile, an English gentleman-adventurer, James Brooke (1803–1868), entered the stage; with raw bravery he ended an anti-Brunei rebellion in Sarawak and in return was proclaimed *rajah* (governor) of a territory slightly larger than Rhode Island. Brooke's successors, Charles (r. 1868–1917) in particular, and Charles Vyner (r. 1917–1946), expanded Sarawak's frontiers eastwards to cover an area almost equivalent to the state of Mississippi (Ooi 1997). Since the mid-1860s, Borneo's north-east portion referred to as North Borneo (present-day Sabah) had attracted European fortune-seekers and speculators seeking territorial concessions from the sultanates of Brunei and Sulu, that finally in 1881 was secured by the British North Borneo Chartered Company (BNBCC) (Tarling 1978).

Owing to the ambitious and predatory moves by Rajah Charles Brooke of Sarawak towards the sultanate of Brunei, the British government granted protectorate status to Brunei, Sarawak and British North Borneo in 1888. Brunei's integrity was further guaranteed when in 1906, a British Residency system (similar to that imposed on the peninsular Malay states from 1874) was in place whereby all executive authority rested with a British officer titled 'Resident' while the Sultan continued to reign and kept sovereignty over the Islamic faith and Malay customs and traditions (Horton 1984). During the Pacific War (1941–1945), Brunei came under a benign Imperial Japanese Army military administration, and the Sultan was unharmed.

The Residency resumed after the war until 1959, when internal self-government and executive power were handed over to the Sultan under the terms of the Constitution of 1959. The Constitution 'granted internal self-government *to the Sultan*, not to the people . . . [and] no elective majority on the Legislative Council and no direct elections' (Saunders 1994: 138; emphasis added). Elections were only held in 1962 whereby the Partai Rakyat Brunei (PRB, Brunei People's Party) secured all 16 electoral seats; 17 other seats were appointed. Hence, it was a hollow electoral victory as it was impossible for the PRB to ever form a government.

But delays in convening the Legislative Council, and the detention of PRB militants, prompted the PRB to launch an armed seizure of power referred to as the Brunei Rebellion (1962) (Abdul Harun Majid 2007). A state of emergency was declared, and under the protectorate obligations, British military forces swiftly suppressed the revolt. This unprecedented armed rebellion surprised all quarters, particularly the palace, and in turn confirmed Brunei's rejection of any form of union or federation with neighbouring territories, whether a proposed British Borneo Federation or the Federation of Malaysia. Decades thereafter, Brunei remained understandably mistrustful of its neighbours. Technically and legally, the sultanate retains a state of emergency as declared in 1962, whereby that declaration has been renewed every two years since.

Full internal sovereignty was attained in 1971. Then in 1979, a new Anglo-Brunei Treaty was signed whereby the sultanate finally took charge of its defence and foreign relations. Five years later, at exactly 12.01 a.m. on 1 January 1984, Sultan Hassanal Bolkiah at the capital Bandar Seri Begawan declared the independence of Brunei. In his *titah* (decree, proclamation) then, Sultan Hassanal Bolkiah specifically emphasised MIB's significance and prominence.

> Brunei with the will and mercy of Allah, glorified and exalted be He, will forever remain a *Malay Islamic Monarchy* which is independent, sovereign and democratic founded on justice, trust and freedom, and with the guidance and pleasure of Allah, Glorified and Exalted be He, will always strive to preserve peace and security, prosperity and happiness for my people.
>
> (Quoted in Muhammad Hadi (2016a), emphasis added)

Malay Islamic Monarchy (MIB): the concept

Therefore, as presented in the royal proclamation at independence, MIB is the fundamental basis of Brunei premised on three foundations. Firstly, Malay ethnicity that comprises the Malay language, culture, customs, and traditions, secondly, Islam as the principal religious faith, and thirdly, the sultanate as the monarchical form of governance. The three foundations or pillars – Malay, Islam, Monarchy – are mutually interrelated and complement one another.

The category ethnic Malay, to a large extent, is indivisible with Islam. But Malay ethnicity in Brunei includes several other indigenous communities: Dusun,

Bisaya (Bisayah), Murut (or Lun Bawang/Lun Dayeh), Ked(a)ayan, Tutong, and Belait, besides Brunei Malay. Other indigenes such as Iban and the nomadic Penan are excluded and officially classified as 'other indigenous'. Apart from the Brunei Malays who are invariably Muslims, other aforesaid native peoples are divided in their religious adherence: Muslims, Christians, or traditional beliefs (animism). Nonetheless, the Brunei elite, including the royal family, are Brunei Malay. Hence, the close linkages between 'Malay' and 'Islam', 'Malay' and 'Monarchy', and 'Monarchy' and 'Islam', are apparent and interwoven. None of the pillars can stand alone, to the extent that if one is removed, the entire structure will collapse.

Although proponents of MIB emplaced the concept, implementation, and practice to Brunei's early years of establishment, its legal references originated in the Brunei Constitution of 1959 whereby the Malay language was declared as the national language (Bab 82 [1]), Islam as the official religion (Bab 3 [1]), and the Sultan as the head of state and government (Bab 4 [1]). The next official proclamation of MIB was, as mentioned, in the royal *titah* at independence in 1984. Six years later, in July 1990 on the occasion of his 44th birthday, Sultan Hassanal Bolkiah formally enunciated the MIB concept (Saunders 1994: 187). Nonetheless, advocates emphasised MIB's deep roots in Brunei's polity and monarchy to around the mid-fourteenth century.

Historical genesis of MIB

The Secretariat Office of the Malay Islamic Monarchy Supreme Council of Brunei Darussalam, in a series of articles in the *Borneo Bulletin*, the major English daily newspaper, drew public attention to the early beginnings of MIB in identifying the concept's genesis to the founding rulers of the country. For instance, 'The birth of Brunei Darussalam became the commencement of the MIB concept and up to this day, it is still the basis of the nation's ideology' (Muhammad Hadi 2016a). Moreover, MIB played a pivotal role in Brunei's heyday as an empire.

> SULTAN Muhammad Shah adopted the Malay Islamic Monarchy (MIB) as a governmental and authoritative foundation in the Brunei Empire in the 1360s. With MIB as the bedrock of the country's philosophical and spiritual values, combined with his skilled leadership and the loyal support of his followers, it became the driving force in Brunei's glorious expansion from the early 15th Century to the 17th Century.
>
> (Muhammad Hadi 2016b)

It was claimed that Awang Alak Batatar, an ancient Bornean culture hero who apparently existed in the mid-14th century when he embraced Islam, took on the title Sultan Muhammad Shah. Sultan Muhammad Shah's reign was believed to be 1363 to 1402 (see Brown 1970: 134–135; Saunders 1994: 43).

Furthermore, there is an element of divine sanction as Sultan Hassanal Bolkiah 'had decreed that MIB is a gift from Allah the Almighty', and elsewhere stated, 'It is believed that MIB is a gift from Allah the Almighty' (Muhammad Hadi 2017,

2016a). During the Prophet Muhammad's (s.a.w.) (the Arabic phrase ṣallā Allāhu ʿalayhi wa- ala ālihi wa-sallam, lit. 'blessings of God be upon him and his family and peace', rendered as s.a.w.) birthday celebration on 2 October 1990, the reigning monarch publicly pronounced MIB to be Allah's Will (Saunders 1994: 187). In incorporating the divine element, it delivers a caution: that MIB's position is unassailable, and that any deviation, whether in practice or implementation, is taken to be a transgression of the Will of Allah the Almighty.

When MIB was officially sanctioned in 1990, it was as a national philosophy. Courses in MIB were mandatory in all educational institutions from elementary to tertiary. Established in 1990, the Akademi Pengajian Brunei (APB, Academy of Brunei Studies) at Universiti Brunei Darussalam, a multi-disciplinary centre for study and research for all aspects of Brunei, was tasked with formulating MIB courses and modules for schools and colleges. Subsequently, the MIB concept increasingly transformed itself into a national ideology (FEER 1993: 89). Not only was MIB utilised in moulding the thinking of young citizens, but equally or more importantly, it was used as a justifying pivot of the role of the Sultan as protector and guardian of the Islamic faith and Malay customs and culture (Saunders 1994: 187–188).

In tracing it to the founding of the sultanate, relating it directly to expansion and empire, alluding to its divine sanction, and its transformation from a national philosophy to national ideology, MIB is well-entrenched as the philosophical and ideological foundation and moral compass amongst the peoples of contemporary Brunei. Emphasis is placed on MIB's unshakeable and irreproachable status in the past, in present times, and undoubtedly in the foreseeable future (Vienne (de), 2015).

Workings of MIB: past and present

In looking at MIB in practice and implementation in the past and currently in the early decades of the twenty-first century, the focus is on five elements, namely power, character, and identity on the one hand, and viability and sustainability on the other. Collectively, an understanding and comprehensive picture of the workings of MIB will emerge.

Power

Basically, MIB invested the Sultan with absolute power. Simply, as the 'Sultan' and 'Yang Di-Pertuan' of Brunei Darussalam, ruler and head of state respectively, Sultan Hassanal Bolkiah holds the highest offices of the sultanate. His power is protected by the Constitution of 1959, and the Constitutional Amendments of 2004 further enhanced his absolute powers:

> the 2004 constitutional amendments including new legislation [were] designed to entrench the Sultan as an absolute sovereign. The new amendments clarified the powers of the Sultan, giving him supreme authority.
>
> (Tey 2007: 270)

Under the Constitution of 1959, the Legislative Council had at least an advisory role in giving consent before any law could be legislated. This role, however, was abrogated in the 2004 amendments. Moreover, the latter did away with elected members to the Legislative Council which had only appointed members and which meets annually to approve formally the national budget. Consequently, the Legislative Council's existence appeared superfluous as all legislative powers rested with the Sultan.

Conveniently, the Constitutional Amendments of 2004 placed the Sultan above the law, beyond legal reproach in both his official and personal capacity (Tey 2007: 270). As far as political, executive and legislative power is concerned, contemporary Brunei represented a classic example of absolute monarchy like Imperial China (until the 1911 Revolution) and Siam (until the 1932 Revolution).

Besides the aforesaid command of state power by the Sultan, MIB further strengthened the throne in religious terms. In the Islamic context, the ruler is believed as such:

> *As-Sultān dhillullāh fi'l-ard*, meaning, "The Sultan is the shadow of Allah on earth". A Hadeeth (narration) attributed to the Prophet (s.a.w.), and which was reported by Al-Bazzaar in his Musnad from Abu Hurayrah, and by At-Tabaraani from Abu Bakrah, and by Ibn Khuzaymah and by Al-Bayhaqi in Shu'ab Al-Eemaan from Ibn 'Umar.
>
> (IslamWeb English 2017)

Therefore, loyalty and obedience to the Sultan is likewise to Allah as all Muslim faithful should exercise in present times, and in the hereafter.

Additionally, MIB draws from the traditional Malay injunction that forbade disloyalty to the ruler.

> *Sebenar taat setia dan pantang durhaka adalah satu konsep yang sangat penting dalam kebudayaan Hindu, tetapi Sejarah Melayu mewarnainya dengan unsur-unsur Islam. Taat setia kepada rajanya bukanlah kerana raja adalah dewa atau titisan dewa, melainkan kerana perjanjian yang dibuat antara Sri Tri Buana, raja Melayu pertama, dengan Demang Lebar Daun [raja Palembang]. Di bawah perjanjian ini, Sri Tri Buana bersumpah tidak akan memberi aib kepada rakyat Melayu; sebaliknya Demang Lebar Daun juga bersumpah bahawa rakyat Melayu tidak akan mendurhaka dan memalingkan mukanya dari rajanya, jikalau jahat sekali pun budi pekertinya.*
>
> (Liaw 2011: 442)

> True devotion and fidelity are very important concepts in Hindu culture, but the *Sejarah Melayu* coloured it with Islamic elements. The loyalty to the king is not because the king is a god or goddess, but because of the agreement between Sri Tri Buana, the first Malay king, with Demang Lebar Daun [king

> of Palembang]. Under this agreement, Sri Tri Buana vows not to disgrace the Malays; Demang Lebar Daun also swears that the Malays will not disobey and turn their faces from the king, if it is evil indeed.

Furthermore, the traditional relationship between ruler and subjects is described in this analogy.

> *Dalam wasiat raja juga senantiasa ditegaskan perhubungan yang erat antara raja dan rakyatnya. Rakyat diumpankan sebagai akar dan raja pohonya. "Jikalau tiada akar, pohon tiada akan dapat berdiri." Karena itu raja-raja hendaklah selalu berlaku adil dan memelihara rakyatnya.*
>
> (Liaw 2011: 442)
>
> In the royal will as well, a king always emphasized the close relationship between him and his people. If people are the roots, the king its tree. "If there is no root, no tree will be able to stand." Hence, kings must always be fair and nurture their people.

In Brunei, it was and still is, the common practice of providing largesse to the ordinary citizens of the sultanate in terms of free education up to tertiary level, subsidised housing, generous pensions to civil servants, absence from any form of taxation (personal income tax, goods and services tax, or value-added tax), and free medical and healthcare. The Brunei government is the largest employer, with the oil and gas industry sectors as the second largest consumer of labour. The GDP – per capita (PPP, purchasing-price-parity) stood at USD$79,700 (2015 est.), 13th highest in the world (Index Mundi 2016).

Crude oil and natural gas comprised approximately 65% of GDP and 95% of exports, with Japan as the main export market (Index Mundi 2016). Hence, drawing substantially from its income from exports of mineral fuels and organic chemicals of USD$7.08 billion (2015 est.) in contrast to imports of mainly machinery and mechanical appliance parts of $4.84 billion (2015 est.), it enabled the distribution of rents to its populace. If the economy has favourable returns, the support of the population appears to be affordable and sustainable. Brunei's ruler fittingly abides by the Malay tradition of '*selalu berlaku adil dan memelihara rakyatnya* (always upholds justice and nurtures its people)'.

Character

Brunei adopted MIB as a national ideology in drawing on its historical antecedents as a means of justification and legitimacy of its absolute monarchy, though a traditional system of governance that has long been discarded in the modern context. In tracing and identifying MIB to the first indigenous founding ruler of Brunei who embraced Islam, namely Sultan Muhammad Shah (1363–1402), the intention is to emphasise the ideology's long historical past. This ancient linkage is further enhanced when coupled with the claim that the third ruler was a blood relative of the Prophet (s.a.w.).

> Brunei continued its regional prominence during the reign of the third Sultan of Brunei, Sultan Sharif Ali (1425–1432). He was an Islamic scholar from Ta'if (Hejaz, South Arabia) and it was believed that he was a descendant of the Prophet Muhammad (pbuh, the Arabic, *'alayhi as-salām*, that translates as "peace be upon him"), through the lineage of Sayyidina Hassan, the Prophet's grandson.
>
> (Muhammad Hadi 2016b)

Blood relations with the Prophet (s.a.w.) lent immense prestige to the royal lineage. Hence, MIB possesses distinct religious credentials in the interrelationship between Islam and the Monarchy.

The interconnectedness of the triad of Malay, Islam, and Monarchy is succinctly encapsulated by Haji Abdul Latif Haji Ibrahim:

> [The three pillars of MIB] must be seen through a holistic approach of interdependency since each pillar cannot stand on its own without the others. In the context of Brunei Darussalam, what is a Malay without Islam as his spiritual power and the monarchy as his authority? What is a monarchy without Malay as the mass force to uphold its legitimacy and Islam as the basis of its vision towards a harmonious and prosperous nation under the guidance of Allah? What is Islam without the Monarch as *Khalifah* (viceregent) of God on this earth and leader of the Muslim Ummah with the Malay as the dominant force politically?
>
> (Abdul Latif Haji Ibrahim 2003, quoted in Schwartz 2016)

The three 'pillars' are integral to one another, and collectively contribute to the sustenance and legitimisation of the Brunei sultanate. Haji Abdul Latif Haji Ibrahim in a nutshell revealed that MIB 'has been projected as the only viable concept to be adopted by Brunei not only to uphold the cultural and religious identity of Brunei Malays but more significantly to procure the survival of the monarch itself' (Abdul Latif Haji Ibrahim 2003, quoted in Schwartz 2016).

Therefore, the nationwide embedding of MIB is undertaken among the citizenry, from schoolchildren to civil servants to the business community to military personnel. Fealty to the Sultan is continuously emphasised in MIB lessons in the classrooms, at public seminars, or in workshops. The combination of both Islamic injunctions and Malay socio-cultural traditions and customs ensures that the Brunei populace confirms their unquestioning and undivided allegiance to the Sultan.

Identity

Brunei's identity is encompassed within the national ideology of MIB. As the only Malay Muslim sultanate in contemporary times which directly holds the reins of power in governing a nation-state in contrast to constitutional monarchies as in the nine Malay Muslim sultanates of Malaysia, Brunei held fast to this distinctive identity of Malay monarchical political power and socio-cultural attributes of 'Malayness'. Brunei has in fact institutionalised the common attributes of Malayness, notably the Malay monarchy, Malay language, Malay culture, traditions, and customs, and Islam (Chong 2008: 60).

Brunei as a nation-state not only embraced MIB as a national ideology and identity but also is 'known globally as a country that preserves its heritage and culture by *living it* instead of archiving it in museums and in historical books' (Muhammad Hadi 2016a, emphasis added).

Viability

Apart from PRB's attempted coup in 1962, the viability of MIB in both its role as national ideology and national identity has been proven particularly apparent from the ascension of the current monarch in 1967. The Malay-only Brunei National Democratic Party (BNDP) that demanded a system of governance of parliamentary democracy under a constitutional monarchy was short-lived; in less than three years of its establishment in 1985, BNDP was de-registered, and its President and Secretary-General were held without trial for some two years (see Horton 2004).

Sultan Hassanal Bolkiah has fashioned a viable and workable monarchical system of government. Characterised by conservatism, paternalism, and centralisation, this form of governance appears to be appropriate and suited for the Brunei context. In the post-independence period, the sultanate prudently undertook the task of institution-building to meet the demands of governing a modern nation-state. The establishment of a ministerial form of government notwithstanding that Sultan Hassanal Bolkiah concurrently holds various posts including Prime Minister, Defence Minister, and Finance Minister. In 2015, he also assumed the position of Minister of Foreign Affairs and Trade.

Besides relying on support from the royal and traditional elites, Sultan Hassanal Bolkiah judiciously harnessed the talented educated-elite to serve in important positions in the government. His first-born son, Haji Al-Muhtadee Billah Ibni Sultan Haji Hassanal Bolkiah Mu'izzaddin Waddaulah (b. 1974) was proclaimed Crown Prince in 1998 and next in succession to be the 30th Sultan of Brunei. Crown Prince Al-Muhtadee Billah was elevated in 2005 to Senior Minister at the Prime Minister's Office and often took on the duties as Deputy Sultan when his father was abroad.

A generous cradle-to-grave state welfare system serves the citizens. Allegiance of the people is directed to the person of the Sultan, not to the government or the Constitution. Personalised rule is at the crux of the monarchical form of government. At the same time, Sultan Hassanal Bolkiah must also appear to be 'with-the-people'.

> The converse, that the ruler must also be accessible, was a tradition introduced from Islam. This occurred when the Sultan made informal visits to kampongs [villages] and government departments, or held 'meet the people' sessions. . . . [W]hen he attended Friday prayers at the main mosque and the

> faithful pressed around him to kiss his hand. . . . [A]t Hari Raya . . . when the Istana [palace] was thrown open to the populace to pay their respects to the Sultan and to members of the royal family.
>
> (Saunders 1994: 190)

Sustainability

The sustainability of MIB that has been utilised as an agent not only of legitimacy of the absolute monarchy but also of the monarchy itself seems to serve well for Brunei into the twenty-first century. In the absence of political participation and limited freedoms, the comprehensive welfare state has, to a large extent, catered to the needs of the populace. Thus far, the overdependence on hydrocarbon resources and the limited outcome of economic diversification has yet to present insurmountable challenges despite various hiccups in the global economic market, particularly fluctuating oil prices.

Meanwhile, the sustainability of MIB also relies on the non-Malay and non-Muslim sectors of the population. The non-Malay population, particularly the Chinese (10.3%), other indigenous (3.4%), namely Ibans in particular, and also Melanau and Penan, might feel alienated from MIB's emphasis on 'Malaydom'. The non-Malay population is also the bulk of the non-Muslim peoples of the sultanate. Communities of Christian (8.7%), Buddhist (7.8%), and indigenous beliefs (4.7%) account for 21.2% of the overall demography. The 'Islamic' element in MIB might not sit comfortably with non-Muslims. Although non-Malay and non-Muslim are minorities, their numbers are not insignificant.

Up until the present, non-Malays and non-Muslims seemed to be accepting of the ideology of MIB. No overt opposition has yet surfaced. Any dissent or recalcitrant voices, however small, in this age of communication and rapid interconnectedness (social media, internet) will certainly emerge and be heard. None, however, has been detected from any quarter of Brunei society.

Feedback obtained by the Secretariat of the Supreme Council of MIB in recent years drawn from numerous activities 'concluded that the overall understanding, practice and appreciation of MIB in the community of Brunei, consisting of civil servants, uniformed personnel, chiefs, headmen and grassroots villagers, youth, students and rural communities are at an acceptable level' (Muhammad Hadi 2017).

Of variables from within, and challenges from without

Close to the end of the second decade of the twenty-first century, only a handful of Islamic monarchies remain in the governing seats of their respective nation-states. Brunei's monarchical form of government, a Malay Muslim monarchy, has remained viable and sustainable from the mid-fourteenth century to the present. At the heart of this long-lasting monarchical system of governance is the ideological concept of MIB which continues to justify and legitimise the Brunei sultanate.

Barring any untoward developments, the royal succession is confirmed with the Crown Prince as the heir apparent. Whether Crown Prince Al-Muhtadee Billah will be as capable and adept as his father in governing the sultanate depends greatly on his personality and leadership style in handling and addressing the following variables from within, on the one hand, and challenges from without, on the other. The variables from within overlap with one another and are here listed in no particular order of importance or preference.

- Diversification of the economy to move away from overdependence on hydrocarbon resources, a declining asset.
- Cultivation of high returns from foreign ventures and investments to offset the revenues from hydrocarbon resources.
- Balancing the up-and-coming middle-class educated elite and the royal and traditional elite in terms of distribution of political positions and power.
- Judicious utilisation of domestic human resources in order to be less dependent on foreign labour, particularly in specialised fields in the oil and gas industry, agriculture, and service sectors.
- Thoughtful management of the welfare state in the delivery of social services and public goods to the populace.

The variables from without are as follows.

- The decrease in the ever-volatile prices of oil and gas resources that might seriously compromise the sultanate's earnings and wealth.
- Fundamental Islamist anti-monarchical elements which might instigate subversion and/or even an overthrow of the monarchy, as in the Iranian Revolution (1978–1979).
- Liberalism and forces of modernity which might undermine the social fabric resulting in agitation for change.

Brunei's vulnerability lies in its dependence on its oil and gas revenue. What is currently facing counterparts in West Asia, namely the oil-dependent Gulf states in the last five years and still being experienced in contemporary times, should be seriously considered.

> After years of strong economic growth, fueled by high oil and gas prices and massive government-funded infrastructure projects, most of the economies of the six-member Gulf Cooperation Council (GCC) began to slow back in 2014.
>
> That year, oil and gas prices slumped, from around \$114 a barrel in the summer of 2014 to about \$60 a year later – and a final low of less than \$30 in early 2016. With all the GCC economies highly reliant on revenues from oil and gas to fund their states, such a slump had major repercussions.
>
> (Gorvett 2018)

Consequently, drastic adverse implications were felt.

> In the United Arab Emirates, GDP growth went from 3.8% in 2015 to only 0.8% in 2017, according to official preliminary figures. Saudi Arabia and Kuwait moved into recession, the first seeing its economy shrink by 0.7% last year and the latter, by 2.9%.
>
> (Gorvett 2018)

The sudden drop in state revenues caused governments of the Gulf states to turn to borrowing in order to fund public expenditure. This in turn brought heavy financial burdens in national debts.

> With such drastic reductions in revenue, governments also began borrowing more heavily, with public debt rising across the GCC.
>
> This has impacted Bahrain and Oman most of all, with debt now approaching 100% of GDP in Bahrain, while in Oman, the ratio of debt to GDP went from about 5% to more than 40% between 2014 and 2017.
>
> (Gorvett 2018)

National debts are crippling in both the short and long term and have compromised future growth and development. A turn-around could occur only if the source of revenue – in the context of the Gulf states, namely oil and gas – receives an increase in value and prices. If not, a downward spiralling effect will set in, and the more the debts bring down the state, the more difficult it is for the latter to recover.

In such a dismal scenario, political instability begins to arise, an upsurge in social unrest due to cut-backs in benefits and subsidies, and even economic collapse. No doubt before the economy disintegrates, international financial organisations such as the International Monetary Fund (IMF), the World Bank, the Organisation for Economic Co-operation and Development (OECD), and others might offer recovery packages as in the past cases of Thailand during the Asian Financial Crisis (1997–1998) and Greece during its financial crisis (from early 2010) (for Thailand, for instance, see Chalongphob Sussangkorn 1999, and in the case of Greece, Wallace 2018).

Conclusion

In the case of Brunei, the aforesaid five internal variables could be adversely affected in the event of the eventuality of one of the most crucial variables from without, notably, the decrease in the price of oil and gas and declining reserves which will seriously affect the sultanate's economy to the extent of threatening the sustenance of the welfare largesse. In such a situation, reliance on foreign labour, whether skilled or non-skilled, and the dependence of the citizenry on social services and public goods will no longer be sustainable.

If the diversification of the economy away from overdependence on hydrocarbons and gaining high returns from foreign ventures and investments are successful, then Brunei could continue to sustain its welfare system. Otherwise, the middle-class educated elite might push for reforms and a different political system.

It is a challenge for the present Crown Prince. The political will needs to be strong and sustainable in order to consider all options in moving away from dependence on hydrocarbon resources. A diversified as well as resilient economy is essential in facing an increasingly globalised world. As sultan, he will hold all power literally in his hands. How judiciously he wields *all that power* shall determine his and his sultanate's future.

Note

* The present study was initially presented at an American Association of Asian Studies (AAAS) panel themed 'Modern Monarchies in Asia: A Comparative Perspective', convened by Professor Katherine Bowie at the International Convention of Asian Studies (ICAS), Chiang Mai, Thailand, 20–23 July 2017.

References

Abdul Harun Majid (2007) *Rebellion in Brunei: The 1962 Revolt, Imperialism, Confrontation and Oil*. London: I. B. Tauris.

Abdul Latif Haji Ibrahim, Haji (2003) *Issues in Brunei Studies*. Bandar Seri Begawan: Akademi Pengajian Brunei, Universiti Brunei Darussalam.

Brown, D. E. (1970) Brunei: The Structure and History of a Bornean Malay Sultanate. *Brunei: Monograph of the Brunei Museum Journal* 2 (2).

Central Intelligence Agency, The World Factbook (2017) Available at: www.cia.gov/library/publications/the-world-factbook/geos/bx.html (accessed 24 June 2017).

Chalongphob Sussangkorn (1999) *Economic Crisis and Recovery in Thailand: The Role of the IMF*. Paper presented at the Conference on Asia on Economic Recovery: Policy Options for Growth and Stability, organised by the Institute of Policy Studies, 21–22 June, Singapore. Available at: www.researchgate.net/publication/242759210_Economic_Crisis_and_Recovery_in_Thailand_The_Role_of_the_IMF (accessed 31 October 2018).

Chong, Terrence (2008) *Globalization and Its Counter-Forces in Southeast Asia*. Singapore: Institute of Southeast Asian Studies.

FEER (1993) *Far Eastern Economic Review 1993 Yearbook*. Hong Kong: Dow Jones & Company.

Gorvett, Jonathan (2018) Gulf Grapples with 'Silent' Economic Crisis. *Asia Times*, Middle East Economy, 21 August. Available at: www.atimes.com/article/gulf-grapples-with-silent-economic-crisis/ (accessed 31 October 2018).

Horton, A. V. M. (1984) *The British Residency in Brunei, 1906–1959*. Hull: Centre for South-East Asian Studies, University of Hull, Occasional Paper No. 6.

Horton, A. V. M. (2004) Brunei National Democratic Party (BNDP) (1985–1988). In Ooi Keat Gin (ed.), *Southeast Asia: A Historical Encyclopedia from Angkor Wat to East Timor*. Santa Barbara, CA: ABC-CLIO, pp. 274–275.

Index Mundi (2016) CIA World Factbook; updated on 8 October. Available at: www.indexmundi.com/brunei/economy_profile.html (accessed 28 June 2017).

IslamWeb English (2017) Available at: www.islamweb.net/emainpage/index.php?page=showfatwa&Option=FatwaId&Id=174979 (accessed 28 June 2017).

Liaw Yock Fang (2011) *Sejarah Kesusastraan Melayu Kelasik* [*History of Classical Malay Literature*]. Jakarta: Yayasan Pustaka Obor Indonesia.

Muhammad Hadi Bin Muhammad Melayong (2016a) MIB, Living Foundation of Every Bruneian. *Borneo Bulletin*, 10 October. Available at: http://borneobulletin.com.bn/mib-living-foundation-every-bruneian/ (accessed 26 June 2017).

Muhammad Hadi Bin Muhammad Melayong (2016b) Brunei's Golden Period of Expansion – (MIB Series). Secretariat Office, MIB Supreme Council, 24 November. Available at: http://bruneiresources.blogspot.my/2016/11/bruneis-golden-period-of-expansion-mib.html (accessed 26 June 2017).

Muhammad Hadi Bin Muhammad Melayong (2017) Malay Islamic Monarchy: Practice and Appreciation. *Borneo Bulletin*, 27 March. Available at: http://borneobulletin.com.bn/malay-islamic-monarchy-practice-appreciation/ (accessed 27 June 2017).

Ooi Keat Gin (1997) *Of Free Trade and Native Interests: The Brookes and the Economic Development of Sarawak, 1841–1941*. Kuala Lumpur: Oxford University Press.

Ooi Keat Gin (2016) Borneo in the Early Modern Period ca. Late Fourteenth to ca. Late Seventeenth Centuries. In Ooi Keat Gin and Hoang Anh Tuan (eds.), *Early Modern Southeast Asia, 1350–1800*. London: Routledge, pp. 88–102.

Saunders, Graham (1994) *A History of Brunei*. Kuala Lumpur: Oxford University Press.

Schwartz, Benjamin (2016) Holy Political Power Batman! Faith and Authority in Brunei and Beyond, International Relations and Foreign Policy Analysis Made Simple, 18 February. Available at: https://ramenir.com/2016/02/18/holy-political-power-batman-faith-and-authority-in-brunei-and-beyond/ (accessed 28 June 2017).

Tarling, Nicholas (1978) *Sulu and Sabah: A Study of British Policy towards the Philippines and North Borneo from the Late Eighteenth Century*. Kuala Lumpur: Oxford University Press.

Tey, Tsun Hang (2007) Brunei's Revamped Constitution: The Sultan as the Grundnorm? [online]. *Australian Journal of Asian Law* 9 (2), August: 264–288. Available at: http://search.informit.com.au/documentSummary;dn=271327048484939;res=IELHSS (accessed 28 June 2017).

Vienne (de), Marie-Sybille (2015) *Brunei: From the Age of Commerce to the 21st Century*. Singapore: NUS Press.

Wallace, Tim (2018) Greece Escapes a Financial Tragedy. *The Telegraph*, Business, 5 May. Available at: www.telegraph.co.uk/business/2018/05/05/greece-escapes-financial-tragedy/ (accessed 29 October 2018).

3 'So near yet so far'

Shaikh A. M. Azahari and 1962*

B. A. Hussainmiya

> The Brunei revolt of 8 December 1962 was a trivial, almost Gilbertian, little uprising, yet it provided the sparks which were in due course to be flamed into the conflict between Indonesia and Malaysia.
>
> J. A. C. Mackie (1974: 111)

Introduction

Donald Brown's grasp of history is as remarkable as his knowledge of anthropology. Even before he finally decided to move to Brunei in December 1966 for his field research to collect material for his doctoral thesis, he had already spent a considerable time in the British Public Record Office to scour Brunei-related historical documents to obtain a prior understanding of Brunei history. His monograph (Brown 1970) was an anthropological treatise, a first of its kind for Brunei, and, more importantly, a valuable pioneering work on a history of Brunei written with much insight and perspective. Since then Brown has pursued his interest in the history of modern Brunei as well by publishing several research papers, including editing some critical UK Public Records Office (PRO) documents pertaining to Brunei's period of the British Residency. In that sense he was the first scholar to work on Brunei colonial papers, followed later by people such as A. V. M. Horton, Nicholas Tarling and others who have since utilised the PRO documents more intensively.

The subject I am dealing with in this chapter was not strange to Brown. In fact, he arrived in Brunei when the embers of the failed 1962 rebellion still smouldered. Chapter 9 of his 1970 monograph titled *History of Brunei* (130–163) traces the history back to early periods and the founding of the Brunei kingdom and ends with a brief reference to the 1962 rebellion and its aftermath. At the time Brown carried out his research, I am sure that with the exception of some gossip and orally transmitted information in addition to journalistic writings on the rebellion, there was little in the way of documents for him to probe more deeply into this episode. At any rate, the subject of the rebellion remained too sensitive for public probing for long after due to the nature of the closed society of Brunei and the restraints imposed by the country's special branch.

Ever since I began my research on the period of Al-Marhum HRH Sultan Haji Omar Ali Saifuddien III (1950–1967), my interest was kindled on this epoch-making event that directed Brunei's future in reinforcing a strong if not absolute monarchy that we witness today. My chapter therefore is a sequel from where Brown left off, albeit his main focus was on Brunei's hierarchically ordained social structure; by the same token, it calls for a thorough revision of Brown's pioneering observations vis-à-vis an 'ascendant monarchy' of Brunei (see Stockwell 2004: 785). It is in this context that the details I have delved into in this essay are critical to understanding Brown's initial contribution to the evolution of Brunei's historical monarchical system and their ramifications, both before and after the rebellion, which led to many evolutionary changes to Brunei's society originally analysed in Brown's 1970 publication.

The rebellion

In the early hours of Saturday, 8 December 1962, there broke out an armed insurrection in Brunei, a tiny oil-rich sultanate and a British-protected state in Southeast Asia. The armed rebels, almost all of them local Malays, easily ransacked the Seria oilfield area and many key installations of Brunei Town, while their counterparts simultaneously staged attacks on police stations and key installations in the 4th and 5th Divisions of Sarawak, including Limbang.[1] The surprise attacks gained quick initial successes, but as might be expected, the protecting power, Great Britain, invoking the British-Brunei Agreement of 1959, moved swiftly and suppressed the outbreak in a few days.[2] That single event changed the progressive march of history, snuffing out the opportunity to establish a popular government in the sultanate, and instead paved the way for the ascendancy of the Brunei monarchy (Stockwell 2004).

The rebellion not only is an enigmatic episode in Brunei history but is still perceived in Brunei as a somewhat sensitive, even taboo matter; that notwithstanding, there has been a recent spate of publications on the subject by both local and foreign writers. While being useful contributions on a little-known topic, these writings offer few revelations, especially on the identity of the mastermind behind the revolt. No formal court enquiry was held in the aftermath of the rebellion, let alone systematic internal investigation into the role of its ringleaders whose actions resulted in the loss of lives and damage to property. In the end no one faced convictions and, except for a few rebels who were incarcerated without charge, most were released periodically not long after the event. Therefore, the Brunei rebellion raises many questions for modern historians.

Why, for example, did the Partai Rakyat Brunei (PRB, Brunei People's Party) risk its political advantages soon after the people had overwhelmingly voted for them in the District Council Elections of August 1962 which won them all the 16 elected seats on the 33-seat Legislative Council? Did its leader, Shaikh A. M. Azahari, mean to establish a client state under the aegis of Sukarno's Indonesia? Were the British intelligence services involved in engineering the revolt, as some conspiracy theorists would suggest? What was the then Brunei Sultan's stand on this affair? Although many documents exist in the London PRO, the fact that some critical files are still in embargo means the topic remains open for speculation.[3] The Brunei National Archives do not contain any records of significance. Possibly the Special Branch Files (Brunei and Singapore), which are not available for public scrutiny, contain valuable clues. Oral interviews conducted by the author with persons involved in the insurrection produced little insight as the responses by the interviewees, some of whom spent periods in detention for their alleged role in the rebellion, were fairly predictable due to self-censorship as well as post-facto rationalisations by the parties involved. Thus, writing soon after the revolt, a perceptive American observer, Willard A. Hanna, predicted, 'the full story of the Brunei insurrection will not soon be told' (Hanna 1964). The waiting is not yet over.

Many subsequent explanations surrounding the rebellion are no more than post-facto justifications. A good example is the book *Pertumbuhan Nasionalisme di Brunei* (2004)[4] by a former PRB stalwart, Haji Zaini Haji Ahmad, who justified the rebellion from the current perspective placing a premium on undivided loyalty of the Brunei subjects to their Sultan. The former Brunei Foreign Minister, His Highness Haji Mohamed Bolkiah (2007) wrote a cryptic-styled book on the rebellion and does not refer to the PRB or the leaders by name. Another work by a Bruneian author is Harun Majid's *Rebellion in Brunei* (2007), based on his master's thesis in London, but it repeats the themes, sources and facts from the work of others on the same topic. The book *Sultan Omar Ali Saifuddin and Britain: The Making and Brunei Darussalam* (Hussainmiya 1995), was the first to deal with the Brunei rebellion in detail while also highlighting the career of and assessing Shaikh Azahari, the principal rebel suspect. A recent book by Eileen Chanin (2013) mostly focuses on the Limbang attack by the rebels and does not make any major contribution to the subject.

The local writings on the rebellion tend to emphasise unduly the role of Azahari, the main protagonist, and his machinations as the primary mover of the rebellion.[5] More neutral writings claim that Azahari is a mere scapegoat to divert attention from the manipulations of British intelligence officers (Stockwell 2004: 799). Greg Poulgrain (1998), who had talked to Azahari at length,[6] has given valuable insights into his motivations and actions. Dubbed variously as an opportunist, fanatic and self-seeker in British official reports, Azahari is made to bear the brunt of the blame for the outbreak of the rebellion. Until his death, he maintained that he did not start the rebellion but had to go along with it once his brother, Shaikh Othman Mahmud, a Brigadier in the Tentera Nasional Kalimantan Utara (TNKU, National Army of North Kalimantan), informed him about it in Johor on 5 July. Circumstantial evidence aside, the truth will never be known as to who was the mastermind behind the whole saga. This chapter is not so much about finding out who started the rebellion, but it examines the role of Shaikh Azahari and probes why he failed to achieve his avowed goals of independence for Brunei within the framework of an independent United Northern Kalimantan State (NKKU, Negara

Kesatuan Kalimantan Utara) under a constitutional monarchy led by the Brunei Sultan. It would also be useful to assess his role vis-à-vis Cold War politics in Southeast Asia.

I

Having been variously termed a rebellion, revolt, uprising and insurrection, in retrospect it was a hopelessly botched attempt by wistful revolutionaries that within its first twelve hours was both won and lost. Commenting retrospectively on its outcome, an American political analyst was perhaps justified in dubbing the affair as a 'Teapot Rebellion' (Ness 1962).[7] It was never destined to succeed, and like the business undertakings of its chief protagonist, Azahari, it fizzled out almost as soon as it started. Azahari's belief that there would be simultaneous anti-Malaysia uprisings in Sarawak and North Borneo, as well as his illusory expectations of support from the Chinese-dominated Sarawak United People's Party, and perhaps from the large transient Indonesian population in the Tawau district of North Borneo, never materialised. In reality, the rebellion was staged almost entirely by Brunei Malays and their immediate kith and kin in the adjacent districts of Sarawak and North Borneo. Nevertheless, some believe that the rebellion came close to success. For example, Lord Selkirk in a dispatch to Whitehall wrote, 'the rebels thought . . . [the revolt] was a pushover and it very nearly was'.[8] Brigadier Smith, a military expert, affirmed that the rebels' plan was 'well considered'; and had it really been put into effect 'before British forces were able to arrive in strength from Singapore, then the story of Brunei and the Confrontation that followed would have been very different' (Smith 1985: 48). Also, the rebellion is crucial to understanding the forces at work that froze the democratic process set in motion during the early years of the reign of HH Sultan Haji Omar Ali Saifuddien (r. 1950–1967).

Several hypotheses have been put forward as possible causes for the revolt. For example, Brackman gave a list of issues that generated discontent in many strata of Brunei society at the time: abuse of religious power, hostility towards Europeans and Chinese, exploitation by the oil industry, nationalism and awareness of Britain's diminishing influence (1966). Means argues that the revolt was not anti-British, anti-Sultan, or anti-court, but was 'against anyone opposing Brunei's recovery of Sarawak and North Borneo' while also commenting that the rebels 'were never very clear about their objectives" (1976: 308). Mackie cited several factors, including opposition to the Malaysia Federation, which the rebels saw as a plot to maintain a conservative regime and British neo-colonialism. The rebels also feared the loss of Brunei's oil wealth to Kuala Lumpur as well as being taken over by the better-educated peninsular Malays. They also dreamed of re-establishing Brunei's bygone empire. Mackie states that, 'all these attitudes – particularly the first – probably played a part; however misguided they might have seemed to outsiders (1974: 116). Mackie and others think that it was conceivable for Azahari to expect the Sultan's support for a rebellion, because 'they were united in opposition to the Malaysian idea' (1974: 113).

If viewed from the Brunei perspective, the issues involved were far more complex than outside observers suggested. The two studies by Poulgrain (1998) and Menon (1988: 135–174) give considerable attention to the Brunei revolt characterising it as a struggle between an emerging democratic idealism and the Sultan's traditional right to absolute power. Sympathetic to the point of view of the rebel leaders themselves, their findings scarcely attempt to investigate the role played by Brunei's monarchy in ensuring a stable transition from British protectorate status to monarchic rule. Zaini Haji Ahmad in the first edition of *Pertumbuhan Nasionalisme* (1989) attempts to offer a readable account, but his narrative is overly influenced by his role as an insider in the PRB. On the other hand, Pehin Jamil's (Head of the Brunei's History Centre) account of the rebellion in his *Liku-Liku Perjuangan* (Jamil al-Sufri 1992) lays the entire blame on those who sought to limit the power of the Brunei monarch and his ruling elite.[9] Pehin Jamil's subsequent work, *8 Disember: Dalangnaya Siapa?* (8 December: Who Was the Mastermind?) (Jamil al-Sufri 2003), is a further attempt to discredit Azahari and to label him as a communist lackey. Interestingly, Prince Mohamed Bolkiah's book, *Remember, Remember: The 8th of December* (2007), does not refer to the theme of communism. Harun Majid's book *Rebellion in Brunei* (2007) also does not refer to the ideology of communism as the explanation for the events. Both my work (1995) and Stockwell's valuable article on royal ascendancy in Brunei (2004) placed the rebellion in the context of British colonial policy and the desire of the late Sultan to reinforce his dynastic rule unhindered and unchallenged. This chapter addresses Azahari's policies and role in the rebellion in order to understand the strengths and weakness of the failed rebellion.

The early career of Azahari

Azahari bin Shaikh Mahmud (A. M. Azahari) was born on 28 August 1928 in Labuan.[10] His father was of Arab descent (hence the title Shaikh), but his mother was a Brunei Malay.[11] Educated in English at the Brunei Town Catholic mission school (later St. George's School), he was one of the young talented Brunei men chosen to be trained abroad by the Japanese (during their occupation between 1941 and 1945), who dispatched him to Bogor in Java to study veterinary science. He left for Java at the age of fifteen, against the wishes of his parents.[12] While he did not complete his formal training in Java, he remained there and in 1947 joined the Sekolah Ekonomik, where he studied commercial subjects for two years.[13]

In Java Azahari met Mohammad Hatta and became involved in the Indonesian independence struggle against the Dutch colonialists. In Bogor he developed a comradeship with Achmad Zaidi of Sarawak, and they began a quest to gain independence for the British-controlled North Borneo territories.[14] Azahari joined the war against the Dutch after Sukarno and Hatta made their unilateral declaration of Indonesian independence on 17 August 1945 and took part in the battles of Palembang and Surabaya (Ahmady Hassan n.d.: 63). In mid-1945, he joined the Badan Keamanan Ra'ayat, the precursor to the Indonesian army under General Sudirman.[15] From 1946 to 1950, Azahari remained in Purwakarta, southeast of

Jakarta, contributing to the Indonesian struggle by setting up an intelligence network to monitor Dutch activities.

When Indonesia won independence in 1949, Azahari's attention turned to Brunei affairs. He declined several offers to serve in Purwakarta, including an opportunity to be a Chief Police Officer in Jakarta. A veteran from Indonesia's liberation struggle, he returned to Brunei sometime in October 1952.[16] News of his impending return to Brunei alarmed the British authorities (Poulgrain 1998: 85–86), due to his background as a nationalist fighter in the Indonesian struggle for independence.[17] The British Resident E. E. F. Pretty tried to prevent his return in early 1951, but the educated and smart Azahari attracted the attention of the Brunei Sultan, who seems to have welcomed him as a resourceful person to serve the state.[18] His silver-tongued oratorical skills and his Arab ancestry also earned him esteem among ordinary Bruneians. He was particularly revered among Brunei's young men for the part he had played in an independence struggle, and he shared with them his exploits during the Indonesian revolution.[19] British oil interests worked hard to sow seeds of suspicion about Azahari's motives in the mind of the Sultan.[20] Importantly, the British Malayan Petroleum Company (BMPC) considered Azahari's presence in Brunei a threat to its economic interests and portrayed him as a 'communist' troublemaker and a promoter of Indonesian interests.[21]

For his part, Azahari had mastered the blueprint from the Indonesian revolution for a textbook-style plan of action for an anti-colonial struggle. First, he sought a 'cause' for mass mobilisation against colonial interests. Second, he formed underground cells to train activists. Third, he guided his close associates to infiltrate the local security establishment, namely the police. Fourth, he introduced rudimentary trade union action, chiefly to disrupt the workings of the BMPC, the most important artery in the economic life of Brunei. Fifth, when the slightest repression occurred, he roused the masses to come out openly to demonstrate against the alleged injustice of the British administration. Finally, he accepted that if he could not achieve a transfer of power by peaceful means, he would emulate the Indonesian model by an armed struggle to seize power. However, in his vision to attain independence for Brunei, there remained a conflict between his professed loyalty to the Brunei monarchy and his hatred of the colonialists, who supported the Sultan's regime. In other words, he could not raise a banner against the Sultan as part of an anti-colonialist struggle. Anyone in his position had to realise the importance of the Brunei monarchy as the supreme symbol of Malay unity. Besides, the Sultan was not only the sovereign but was in principle the source of all authority for the British administration as well. Thus, Anthony Abell, the British High Commissioner, reported to the Colonial Office in 1953, 'I do not think that Azahari will at the present time find any great following for his avowed aim of turning the Sultan off his throne and making Brunei a republic'.[22] The BMPC workforce became the testing ground for Azahari's early radical political activism. According to BMPC reports that implicated direct Indonesian support[23] for political activities of Azahari in early 1953, 'the threat itself was ominous enough, as it envisaged mobbing the police stations, taking over arms stored there, and subsequently rounding up the entire European community!'[24]

The government was not hesitant to employ strong-arm tactics to contain protests at their earliest manifestation. Thus, over the BRUFICO affair and the fiasco that followed, in which the Resident's office was besieged by a 200-strong mob of his followers,[25] Azahari and seven protestors received jail sentences for unlawful assembly and disturbing the peace. Seven protestors received a one-year sentence, while Azahari's was halved to six months. While Azahari was still in jail, his mass appeal grew stronger and an incipient underground movement (*Gerakan bawah di tanah*) began to take shape. According to intelligence reports, 'while Azahari was in prison, an attempt was made to organise a revolt, which was to take over the police stations, release Azahari, and start a provisional government under his leadership'.[26] Again for offences committed under unlawful assembly, three of his associates were jailed for one to two years, namely Mohammad Haji Manggol[27] (who had already spent a three-month prison term for his involvement in the 23 January unlawful assembly case in Brunei Town), the brother of Mohd. Haji Manggol and Jais Karim[28] received one-year sentences.[29] After his release, from 1953 to 1956 Azahari began to concentrate on business activities, travelling often between Singapore and Malaya.[30]

The birth of the PRB

The massive 1955 electoral victory of the Alliance Party under Tunku Abdul Rahman in Malaya and the rising demand for *Merdeka* (Independence) inspired Azahari's political ambitions. He attended the UMNO assembly in Kuala Lumpur in late 1955 and was pleased to hear Tunku's plea for a united voice of not only Malaya but also their Northern Borneo neighbours[31] of Sarawak, Brunei and North Borneo. Interviewed by *Utusan Melayu*, Azahari agreed that the Federation must sponsor a united front to demand independence and the incorporation of Northern Borneo into the Federation of Malaya.[32] On the other hand, the Tunku's pro-British rightist politics did not seem to interest Azahari, who aligned himself with the left-leaning Partai Rakyat Malaya (PRM) headed by Dr Burhanuddin Helmy and Ahmad Boestamam, who were strongly anti-British and promoted an expanded Indonesia-Malay homeland.[33] Azahari's early attempt to form a branch of the PRM in Brunei in January 1955 was aborted, due mainly to disagreement among the local leaders and the government's refusal to recognise the party.

The UMNO, whose constituency lay among a working-class population with little or no literacy, could not be the role model for a left-leaning Azahari. His supporters came largely from the ranks of the oil workers, fishermen, rural agriculturists, the daily wage-labourers and the like who were easily attracted to his anti-colonial rhetoric.[34] Compared to Azahari, who had some English education, most of the leaders of the PRB were less educated and less sophisticated.[35] *The Brunei Annual Report* of 1956 superciliously described the PRB as having a very limited following among the 'educated classes', being drawn largely from the working class and dismissed ex-government servants who saw in the party a means of expressing their discontent. In comparison, UMNO's leadership was essentially an ultra-right to conservative, English-educated, aristocratic to upper-middle-class, propertied group that did not sponsor radical social change (Turnbull 1981: 246). Tunku Abdul Rahman, its leader, was himself a scion of a Kedah royal family. In retrospect, Zaini Haji Ahmad remarked that had Azahari decided to form a branch of UMNO in Brunei, it would have received patronage from the colonial administration and enabled Azahari to rise to the helm, even bringing early independence in the trail of Malaya's success (Zaini Haji Ahmad 1989: 52).

Since 1955, Azahari had cultivated friendship with Che'gu Harun Mohammed Amin, alias Harun Rashid, a long-term resident in Brunei.[36] It was Che'gu Harun who in 1955 first introduced Azahari to the left-of-centre Malayan leaders, Dr Burhanuddin Helmy[37] and Ahmad Boestamam (Zaini Haji Ahmad 1989: 50; Ahmad Boestamam 1972: 50).[38] On 11 November 1955, Azahari attended the launching in Perak of the Parti Rakyat Malaya (PRM), under the leadership of Ahmad Boestamam. The PRM appealed to all the Malays of the archipelago to unite against the colonial rule and to set up a 'Malay Homeland'.[39] Their creed appealed to Azahari more than did UMNO, as he wanted an independent Brunei to eschew neo-capitalism when he adopted Socialist-Nationalist-Democracy as his motto, and thus name his party the 'Nationalist Socialist Party'. However, he quickly heeded advice from one of his mentors, an Englishman who sensed Azahari's futile ambition.[40]

In the end Azahari formed the Partai Rakyat Brunei (the PRB, or Brunei People's Party); the first of its kind in British Northern Borneo, on 15 August 1956, which instantly attracted membership from about 10,000 local Bruneians. The party's manifesto opposed 'all forms of colonialism in the political, economic and social spheres' and requested independence for Brunei through constitutional means. In this planned new system, they promised to safeguard and maintain the position of the Sultan as a constitutional monarch. It would also strive for a Malay nation comprising all states in the Malay Archipelago. In the economic sphere, it would fight for workers' welfare and the equal distribution of the state's wealth.[41] Azahari and his associates held discussions with the High Commissioner Anthony Abell, the British Resident J. O. Gilbert and the UK Commissioner General in South-East Asia, Malcolm MacDonald (Zaini Haji Ahmad 1989: 55–56).[42] As advocates of democratic traditions, the administrators must have considered the PRB a healthy development. Azahari was also thus accepted by all quarters as the best choice for party leader. Despite his anti-colonialist sentiments, Azahari showed deference to the British administration. In his first speech to the PRB gathering, Azahari emphasised that 'we do not hate the British at all. On the contrary we respect and love them as our "guru" [teachers], particularly if the English Government recognise our rights'.[43] Unlike the Malayan Federation, Brunei had more in common with the politically backward adjacent territories of Sarawak and North Borneo.

II

The events following the founding of Brunei's first political party had two dimensions. The first relates to domestic politics, and the other impinged upon Cold War politics in Southeast Asia. Domestically, the PRB's rise gave legitimacy to British efforts to promote representative governance from the bottom up. In May 1953, the Sultan had already announced his intention to launch the first written Constitution for Brunei. The process of drafting an agreeable Constitution and its promulgation took a lengthy six years (Hussainmiya 1995, 2000). Constitution-making in Brunei was a long, drawn-out affair on account of conflicting and irresolvable expectations of power-sharing on the part of the monarch and the colonial government, and with the addition of the PRB factor. In contrast, in the Federation of Malaya, the sultans and the elected political leaders sat around the table to reach a common understanding under the aegis of the British. In Brunei, however, it was a different scenario. The Sultan continued to resist proposals by both Azahari supporters and British promoters of the Constitution to dilute the royal powers so as to turn the Brunei Sultan into a constitutional monarch. Brunei's case was an unprecedented phenomenon in the British history of decolonisation.[44] It might have been easier to solve the issues had Brunei asked in one voice for self-government. Instead, there was a three-corner tussle for power involving the Sultan, the British administration and the PRB. According to its British promoters, the Constitution was intended to be a stepping-stone for the creation of a new democratic order before their responsibility as the protecting power ended. As for the Sultan, his primary objective was to transfer power into his own hands while remaining safely ensconced under British protection. The PRB, on their part, clamoured for a greater share of power under the proposed Constitution and wanted to take a lead in the new legislative and executive councils, which were to replace the obsolete State Council system that had been functioning since 1907.

From the very beginning the PRB was wrong-footed in the business of developing limited representative institutions in Brunei. Under the Local Councils Enactment of 1956, the party was offered a chance to take part in the (nominated) Local Councils, which they flatly refused.[45] In Singapore and Malaya, the local council elections of 1952–1953 had advanced the careers of many budding politicians (Von Vorys 1975: 108–111). In Sarawak, too, similar local councils had operated quite successfully since 1952. In Brunei, the locals were to be nominated by the Sultan in the four District Councils and a separate Town Council for Brunei Town. There were two main reasons why the PRB refused to take part in local council affairs. First, it opposed the principle of nomination as it characterised 'another symptom of colonialism' because the nominated could not speak freely.[46] Second, Bruneians loathed paying taxes and dues, which Sarawak had imposed on its people following the introduction of the local councils. The traditional government officials, such as village headmen and *penghulus*, felt that the powers of the councils would circumscribe their prerogatives and duties. The opposition to the introduction of local government developed to such an extent 'that there was no alternative but to defer the application of this local Government legislation'.[47] The failure of this limited democratic experiment at this stage had far-reaching effects. If the PRB was at fault, then the verdict of history would be that it had undermined a worthy opportunity to advance Brunei politically. An impatient PRB was to pay a greater price in the future when it tried again to leap too many fences at once.

During negotiations for the Constitution, from 1957 until 1959 the PRB's fortunes ebbed. The Sultan would not give up his prerogatives as the country's supreme ruler and made sure that his supremacy was in the provisions of the new Constitution. A main strategy was to transfer power into his own hands from the British Resident's control while the general administration would be passed on to a *menteri besar* (Chief Minister), similar to the practice followed under the traditional constitutions of the un-Federated Malay States, particularly Johor. The Sultan also wanted his own nominees and officials to be in a majority in the proposed Legislative and Executive Councils. He also did not agree to the election principles based on secret ballot and majority rule. His stubborn position ran counter to both the British expectations that a Westminster-type system might be established, as in other dependent territories, and the proposals put forward by the democracy-seeking Azahari and his party. As a sequel, the final Constitution took an inordinate period of six years and did not fulfil any of the PRB's aspirations.

After 1957 Azahari and his party experienced a successive string of failures. On a couple of occasions, he even resigned as chairman of the party, only to be re-elected by popular request. As for the British, Azahari's leadership and the PRB was a *sine qua non* if the political reforms in Brunei were to become a reality under an elected representative system of government. Obviously, the British did not wish to see the PRB's eclipse. In 1957 a desperate Azahari even warned that they might provoke the people of Brunei to revolt.[48] Whenever Azahari became depressed and threatened to quit politics, both J. O. Gilbert, the British Resident, and Anthony Abell, the High Commissioner, were concerned. To them Azahari was the only reasonable politician with whom the British could deal, and so they discouraged him from quitting. 'I am afraid . . . there are even less reliable people waiting to step into his shoes. However, he is I think the only person who can hold the party together', wrote Abell in a confidential dispatch to the Colonial Office.[49] But the British administration walked a tightrope in not lending active support to Azahari's cause for fear of alienating the Sultan's goodwill.

The PRB engaged a British lawyer, Walter Raeburn, in May 1957 to present their case in a well-argued 'Merdeka' memorandum to the Colonial Office that enshrined representative rights and electoral principles. It did not influence the negotiations, however, and during the London negotiations between the Sultan and the British government in September 1957, Azahari literally had to gate-crash into the Colonial Office, uninvited; but his mission to establish a popular government was doomed to fail.[50] As a principal facilitator of the constitutional talks, the High Commissioner Anthony Abell had to exercise caution and strike a balance between the Sultan's proposals and the persistent demands of the PRB for full elections. Abell rejected proposals from the PRB which were then considered extreme, such as a ministerial form of government that would allow the untested PRB leadership to take power prematurely. After his last failed mission, Azahari was said to have been completely deflated, even talking of giving up politics and concentrating on his various businesses,[51] which were also faltering at this time. Meanwhile, the Sultan distanced himself from the PRB and reminded the agitators that Bruneians should not 'be too optimistic, proud or boastful to think that we are strong enough to stand on our own' (Hussainmiya 1995: 236). Countering the PRB's propaganda, he proved that he was no puppet of the British government and emphasised that none could ask for the independence of Brunei, because 'Brunei is not a British Colony' (ibid.: 236).[52]

The Brunei Constitution was finally promulgated on 29 September 1959. The PRB's voice had been muted, and the final document fell far short of their expectations. Whereas the British hoped, as Stockwell comments,

> that a written constitution would act as a check on an absolute monarch and his courtiers who by 1958 ignored and even ridiculed the British resident, His Highness used the device, in much the same way as had Sultan Abu Bakar of Johore in 1895, in order to reassert monarchical authority against British interference.
>
> (Stockwell 2004: 795)

In the end the final constitution made provision for the hierarchy of government, with His Highness the Sultan and Yang di-Pertuan as the supreme executive authority of the land, followed by a Privy Council (*Majlis Mesyuarat Di-Raja*), Executive Council (*Majlis Mesyuarat Kerajaan*, which later became the Council of Ministers, *Majlis Mesyuarat Menteri-Menteri*) and Legislative Council (*Majlis Mesyuarat Negeri*).

The Legislative Council, the principal law-making body in the country, was to consist of eight ex-officio members – the two Wazirs, the *menteri besar*, State Secretary, Attorney General, State Financial Officer, the Religious Adviser and another official to be designated by the Sultan. In addition, there would be six officials, three unofficial members the Sultan would nominate, and sixteen elected members chosen from among the elected District Councillors. Elections to District Councils were to be held not later than two years after the date of the promulgation of the new Constitution. Pending the elections, in the interim period the Sultan would appoint all members for a period of two years.[53] The Sultan might address the Legislative Council at any time upon any matter he saw necessary. He could by proclamation (published in the gazette) prorogue or dissolve the Legislative Council or any committee thereof. Each new Legislative Council had a maximum life span of five years from the date of first meeting but, if the need arose, might be dissolved sooner. The Constitution was a blow to the PRB's aspirations. Denouncing it as an instrument of colonialism, the party said that the Constitution gave Brunei not self-government but self-administration.[54] In the PRB's view, the proposed Brunei Constitution would benefit not the common people, but only the British and a privileged few Bruneians. Yet, the now-impotent PRB could do nothing but protest through press releases.

Nevertheless, in the interim Legislative Council, the Sultan nominated Azahari as a member, which he accepted out of deference to his Sultan. The Sultan appointed a Brunei-Malaysia Commission in early January 1962 to report on the opinion of the people (the equivalent of the Cobbold Commission sent to Sarawak and North Borneo for the same purpose). The Brunei Legislative Council became a forum for debate on the Malaysia issue, although the *menteri besar* kept reminding members that the Malaysia question could not be decided in the council as acceptance or rejection of the proposal to join Malaysia was the Sultan's prerogative. Although most members were silent on the issue, a few individuals were loudly critical of the government's attitude. Immediately after being sworn in on April 16, Azahari introduced a resolution on his Kalimantan Utara proposal which was soundly defeated, whereupon he described the council as undemocratic and 'the kind of colonial legacy that turns people into communists, even though they are not communists at heart'.[55] With that came Azahari's exit forever from 'representative' politics. After resigning, a dejected Azahari lamented, 'I am downhearted and despondent that my work as a nationalist . . . appears to be of no avail under the present system . . . in Brunei'.[56]

III

Although the PRB was seemingly lying low after the promulgation of the Constitution, this was the period when the party became increasingly radicalised due to the frustration felt by its rank-and-file. It consisted of leaders with various backgrounds nurtured by strong anti-colonial feelings. Chief among them was H. M. Salleh, a Malay-educated schoolteacher who went to prison on charges of collaboration with the Japanese when the British returned to re-establish their government over Brunei at the end of the Pacific War. Salleh was the most radical of all and loathed by the British administration, but Azahari, who was considered a moderate, got the better of him in political leadership of the PRB. In 1958, when Azahari's delegation returned empty-handed from their trip to meet Colonial Office mandarins, Salleh raised the banner of revolt during the Party Congress held in 1958. The party therefore consisted of differing shades of opinion and levels of activism, including those who would resort to the bullet if the ballot box failed. H. B. Hidup, a party vice-president, was a key trade union activist in the early 1950s and there were the Manggol brothers, who went to prison for sedition after forming underground cells. Then there was Yassin bin Affendi, Secretary General of the party, another radically minded member who went to Labuan in the early days for clandestine military training. Among the moderates was Haji Zaini Haji Ahmad, whose father was an important state functionary educated in the UK and a supporter of the Sultan. There was also Hapidz Laxamana, a scion of a landed proprietary family who easily rallied the workers to the Brunei United Workers Front, popularly known as the 4Bs (an acronym for *Barisan Buroh Bersatu Brunei* in Malay, United Brunei Labour Front), which consisted of four different bodies that was officially registered on 27 October 1960.[57] As for Azahari, he strived to maintain unity in his party by accommodating the conflicting aspirations of his followers. The members of the aforementioned United Brunei Labour Front also supported the PRB. It pledged to stand by all agitation made by the PRB, which it predicted would come to power after the elections.[58] The situation was indeed getting out of control as the PRB stepped up verbal attacks on the government: 'There is no administration in the world so weak. We urge the Government to improve things . . . the first time we will be patient, the second time we give warning, and the third time we give a slap', threatened Azahari.[59] As a former stalwart of the PRB explained, the party advocated an approach of 'Anarchy, chaos and new order' that 'involved the creation of a "power vacuum" by violence and once created, a revolutionary group would take over the machinery of the government in the midst of a confused society', wrote Zaini bin Haji Ahmad (1987: 16). Thereafter, the PRB launched an underground campaign and formed in mid-1961 an army that came to be known as Tentera Nasional Kalimantan Utara (TNKU, the National Army of North Kalimantan). While evidence is inconclusive about its origins, formation and modus operandi, as its name suggests, the army was to be built upon the nationalist urgings of all those who favoured a North Kalimantan State. Ideally, members were to be drawn from all three British Borneo territories.

The Brunei elections and the rejection of the Malaysia proposals

Some other contentious factors delayed the approval of the first Brunei Constitution. One of these was the British-sponsored proposals for a federation between the three Northern Borneo territories of Sarawak, North Borneo and Brunei. Strange bedfellows as they were, both the British and Azahari were on the same side in promoting the idea of a United North Borneo Federation. The British believed that such a federation would protect British Borneo from a 'potentially acquisitive Indonesia', would level social and economic developments in the territories concerned, and, more importantly, act as a prelude to the formation of a future Federation of Malaya and Singapore.[60] Azahari's party manifesto envisaged the setting up of a United North Kalimantan State under the Brunei monarch's leadership, taking into consideration the common bonds and social-cultural links that bound the three states. The Brunei Sultan, Omar Ali Saifuddien, however, opposed the idea. He shunned the proposals because he did not want his state to lose its identity or become subservient to a Sarawak administration, as seconded officers from Sarawak had largely run Brunei, including the Resident since 1948.[61] The more the Colonial Office promoted the concept of 'closer association', the greater the popular support enjoyed by the PRB among its rank-and-file. As an ideological replacement for British colonial rule, support for Kalimantan Utara was drawing together an incipient 'Borneo' nationalism. In fact, until late 1957 the Colonial Office had held back from openly pursuing the Borneo-Federation idea, since the PRB had already proposed it in their manifesto of 1956. The crisis-point came when Tunku Abdul Rahman finally announced his Malaysia plan in May 1961, which would include all three of the Borneo states. The PRB refused to come to terms with this development and all hell broke loose, which pushed the PRB towards the path of an armed rebellion, which is the main thrust of this chapter.

The road to the rebellion

Azahari's political orientation made him inclined towards his socialist-minded Malayan colleagues and mentors. He opened various channels of communication with people, countries and organisations aligned to anti-capitalist ideologies. During 1961–1962, Azahari's several trips abroad, particularly to Indonesia, Kuching and Singapore, brought him into close contact with Partindo (Indonesia Party), the Sarawak United Peoples Party (SUPP) and the Barisan Sosialis (Socialist Front)[62] respectively. Each of these political parties had been accused of alleged links with the Partai Komunis Indonesia (PKI, Indonesian Communist Party), Malayan Communist Party (MCP) and Sarawak's Communist Clandestine Organisation (CCO). Thus, deliberately or inadvertently, Azahari's politics drew him into the Cold War politics shaping decolonisation in Southeast Asia, particularly when he aligned himself with forces that were supposedly communist-oriented through ideological commitment to Soviet Russia and Mao Zhe Tung's China. Although Azahari was not a communist, because of these links he easily became a target for his detractors, especially those with oil interests in Brunei who tried to portray him as a communist sympathiser as at various times he had threatened to nationalise state assets, as the communists had done in states such as Russia, China and Cuba.

Azahari's increasing rapprochement with Indonesia alarmed the British authorities. Azahari counted on Indonesian support for money and training of the TNKU troops, and moral support from the Philippines. He had been visiting Indonesia since 1959 and made contacts with some of his former revolutionary colleagues who empathised with his cause to snuff out British colonialism in the region.[63] Several PRB senior members had also been ostensibly attending meetings and conferences in Indonesia. According to a British report, a senior PRB leader went to Jakarta in mid-August 1961 to enlist support for Azahari and that nearly all the party members of importance were in Jakarta in October of that year.[64] On 23 February 1962, a party delegation attended the congress of Partindo, an Indonesian party dominated by the PKI.[65]

In Brunei, the elections promised under the 1959 Constitution were delayed under various pretexts. The main stumbling block was the question of finalisation of the electoral list to determine the nationalities who came under the Sultan's authority. Eventually, a new Nationality Enactment came into force on 1 January 1961, following which the much-awaited elections to elect the representatives for the District Councils (a sort of electoral college to select representatives to Brunei's Legislative Council) took place in August 1962. Using the opposition to the Malaysia issue as its main election manifesto (Mohamad Yusop 1998: 57–73), the PRB achieved a massive electoral victory, winning 22 out of the available 23 seats.[66] It was a sweet revenge for the party over the British and the 'monarch-aristocrats' group, whom the PRB accused of delaying the elections to find ways to reduce the public appeal of the PRB and its opposition to Malaysia. The victory proved the undisputed popularity of the PRB and established its right to represent the people of Brunei in the elected bodies at both the district and national levels (Zaini bin Haji Ahmad 1987: 28).

The PRB victory had profound implications for the future of Brunei in general and the Malaysia proposal in particular. During its Fifth Annual General Assembly held in January 1961, the PRB announced that it would call for independence in 1963 if it won a large majority in the elections, and it demanded a British-styled cabinet form of government.[67] All the minor parties that supported Brunei joining Malaysia had been badly routed in the elections. The Malaysia issue divided societies not just in Brunei but also in the neighbouring states. Under a common ideological banner several organisations from these states joined hands to oppose the Malaysia plan, accusing it of being a neo-colonialist scheme to perpetuate British strategic interests in the region. The leading opponents were the Socialist Front in Singapore, formed in June 1961 after breaking away from Lee Kuan Yew's People's Action Party (PAP), the Malaya Socialist Front and the SUPP in Sarawak, which strengthened the PRB's call to thwart the formation of Malaysia. While the Brunei Sultan was sitting on the fence, supporting neither the pro-Malaysia parties nor its opponents, the PRB devised its own strategies to gain power. Referring to the rising anti-Malaysia fever, an editorial in the *Borneo Bulletin* commented on 'the danger . . . that, for the first time in Brunei's history, there may be an open rift between the administration headed by His Highness and the people. The signs are apparent [that], feeling is now running high on this issue and that the Brunei Government must tread carefully – and democratically'.[68]

The very brief history of the Legislative Council under PRB domination can be studied almost entirely against the background of the tensions brought up by the Malaysia issue. The Sultan, during his 46th birthday speech to the council on 23 September, informed them that he was accepting the merger in principle.[69] Relentless, the PRB members in the Legislative Council kept up the pressure to adopt several anti-Malaysia motions while demanding a proposed Federation of North Borneo States and asked Britain to grant complete independence to Brunei by August 1963. The Legislative Council sessions were postponed three times on various pretexts by the government to thwart the PRB's anti-Malaysia proposals. Rumours were in the air that a government-nominated member might vote in favour of the PRB motions, thus giving it the necessary majority.[70] Besides, the government was being pressured to grant instant democracy. In September 1962, Azahari wanted the Sultan to form a cabinet that included PRB members in recognition of the 55 popularly elected District Councillors.[71] Similarly, a senior leader of the PRB called for the 1959 Constitution to be scrapped and replaced with a new one based on the principles of democratic government.[72]

The PRB members submitted three motions to be tabled at the Legislative Council meeting scheduled to be held on 5 December 1962. The three motions dealt with:

1 Rejection of joining the Malaysian Federation.
2 Requesting the restoration of Brunei sovereignty over Sarawak and North Borneo and the installation of the Sultan as constitutional monarch of the North Borneo Federation.
3 Requesting that the British government grant independence no later than 1963.

The Speaker disallowed the motions because the Brunei Legislative Council lacked authority to discuss issues that fell within the purview of the British government under the 1959 Brunei-UK Agreement. Again, the Legislative Council sessions were postponed, first to 13 December and again to 19 December. Apparently, there was no statutory requirement under the 1959 Constitution to summon the new Legislative Council following an election,[73] as only the government (the Sultan) could summon the Legislative Council after elections. Besides the need to study the implications of the motions, the government was required to provide answers to more than one hundred questions raised by the PRB members elected to the council.[74] The PRB-dominated Legislative Council never met. Consequently, the other alternative started to take shape: for the TNKU to stage the attack instead of waiting for the ballot to resolve the impasse.

The 8 December rebellion failed to achieve any of its objectives. Brunei's slow advancement towards democratic government became an unrealistic dream. It also nailed the coffin on Azahari's grandiose scheme to become the Prime Minister of a Northern Kalimantan State that would have been headed by the Brunei Sultan as a constitutional monarch. Instead of continuing the democratic experiment, Brunei was flung backwards and embraced the path of a neo-traditional Malay monarchy. More important, in the immediate aftermath of the rebellion, the government imposed emergency rule, which remains in force to the present. Britain conveniently gave up her responsibility to establish Brunei as a truly democratic state and instead granted full independence on 1 January 1984 without any safeguards for a representative form of government. As Stockwell concluded, the rebellion, if at all, was one of the factors that helped maintain royal ascendancy in Brunei, which was set in motion during the reign of Sultan Haji Omar Ali Saifuddien III (2004).

Following the failure of the rebellion, Azahari and some of his associates did not have the courage to return to Brunei. Instead, they set up a government in exile that received the support of Malaysia and Indonesia. Malaysia continued to espouse Azahari's cause in the United Nations to the chagrin of the Brunei government until about 1975. But Azahari's luck ran out when Konfrontasi between Indonesia and Malaysia came to an end and diplomatic tensions eased between these two countries. The emergence of ASEAN also forged common links among the Southeast Asian nations. A much-disappointed man, Azahari, despite his yearning to return to Brunei like his other rebel compatriots, passed away as an exile in Bogor, Indonesia, in 2002. Nor did his counterparts, such as Lim Chin Siong, Syed Zahari and others in Singapore, prosper following the debacle of the rebellion. They too were incarcerated in prison under Premier Lee Kuan Yew's purge and were released only after many years of detention, dying without ever realising their dream of a socialist state.

Concluding remarks

No armed insurrection could have succeeded given the utter incompetence of the rebels who overestimated their strength and underestimated the might of their adversaries – the British Empire, the protecting power of both Brunei and its Sultan. At the start of the rebellion the TNKU arsenal consisted of no more than a couple of hundred shotguns, some pistols in the possession of its leaders, *parangs* (bush knives), axes, spears and bamboo sticks. A number of rebels wore 'magical' amulets in the belief that this would protect them from enemy bullets![75] But at the sight of blood or a colleague killed, they were ready to surrender or flee into the jungle.

In starting the rebellion prematurely, Azahari may have played into the hands of extreme elements in his party. As a leader of the party, he has to take the greater share of blame for the debacle, but local historiography is too quick, if not harsh, in condemning him and even accusing him of being a 'communist' (Jamil al-Sufri 2003; Ahmady Hassan n.d.). Similarly, the economic interests of the Brunei oil industry often played out the communist bogey to suppress Azahari's rise to power. In the wake of the global political crisis of the Cold War, as a socialist, Azahari stood little chance of being accepted as a pliant leader who would perpetuate British interests in the region. At the very beginning, it was in the best interests of the British to keep Azahari at bay and create a rift between him and the Sultan, although later they conceded Azahari's party a share of power in the proposed Constitution. A true Bornean nationalist at heart, Azahari did not wish to gain independence through British largesse by accepting the 'Grand Design' of the Malaysia Federation. Tunku Abdul Rahman's announcement in May 1961 created discomfort among the like-minded regional politicians who loathed the continuation of British capitalist and colonial interests. As is well known, the Malaysia proposals aided the emergence of new political movements in Singapore under Barisan Sosialis of Lim Chin Siong, and SUPP in Sarawak, which were both accused of having communist links, with whom Azahari was ready to cooperate to achieve his political goal of independence from British domination. However, Azahari never intended to establish a communist client state in Brunei, but in desperation he often threatened to seek one if pushed into a corner. During the rebellion, his fighters erroneously believed that arms and military support would flow from countries opposed to the American-British axis in the Cold War. The rebels' hope for overseas military assistance from Indonesia, as well as from the communist states of China, Cuba and Vietnam, was but a symptom of Cold War camaraderie (Mohamed Bolkiah 2007: 192). The only consolation came from the soothing words of comrade Nikita Khrushchev in a speech to the Supreme Soviet Assembly, in which he mentioned that Brunei, along with Hong Kong and Macau, were waiting to overthrow capitalist imperialism![76] From his Manila hotel at the height of the rebellion, Azahari claimed that he could send 100,000 Indonesian volunteers to fight alongside the rebels.[77]

If Azahari was working to gain constitutional power through the Legislative Council system, why did he agree to form an armed wing of the PRB – the TNKU? The TNKU was in fact intended as an adjunct to the political branch of the party, a common strategy of liberation struggles everywhere at the time. Azahari had been quick to admit that the formation of the TNKU was not just about starting a rebellion. For him, the underground army served as a nursing ground for an independent army network to defend Brunei's sovereignty in the event of the colonial government's departure. Furthermore, Azahari's liberation ideology of redistributing the income from the state oil resources had instant appeal to

Bruneians who felt many grievances against decades of British Residency rule that had failed to bring much progress to the state.

One final issue that deserves critical attention is the question of whether the Brunei Sultan, Haji Omar Ali Saifuddien, ever intended to join hands with Azahari in expelling the British from Brunei and become a Seri Mahkota Negara as constitutional monarch of the NKKU? In other words, was he a 'rebel' like others among Azahari's following? Such an implausible suggestion has been put forward by Azahari himself, both before and after the rebellion, and also by outside observers. The British version contended that the Sultan must have hedged his bets,[78] an impression repeated in the writings of some historians. Starner, for example, writes, 'it has been suggested in some quarters that there was perhaps a tacit agreement between Azahari and the Sultan, which the latter found it unwise subsequently to acknowledge' (1963: 523). Even the then British High Commissioner D. C. White's report implicated the Sultan in the rebellion.[79]

Soon after the rebellion broke out, the Sultan instantly condemned the actions of the rebels in his radio speeches on 8 and 15 December 1962. When he branded them as traitors (*derhaka*), it turned the tide in the course of the rebellion as many fighters lost the will to continue their struggle, since it appears that they had been led to believe that the Sultan was on their side. As Zaini Haji Ahmad, a former ideologue of the PRB, said:

> information gathered from the prisoners showed that the revolt was supposedly launched with the blessing of the Sultan. Its objective was to establish a government with the Sultan as its head. Such propaganda could easily influence the traditional people who were too fanatical towards the Sultan.
>
> (Zaini Haji Ahmad 1989: 269)

The Sultan, however, had walked a tightrope. He could not express his real inner opinion about whether or not to join the Malaysia Federation.[80] If he said that he did not like the plan, he would have thrown himself in with Azahari's camp, and this risked pushing both Britain and Malayan leaders to force unilaterally the hapless Sultan to accept the merger. If he declared openly that he was in favour of unification with Malaysia, then the PRB would have bulldozed its way forward in the Brunei Legislative Council and sought support from its socialist allies and even international bodies like the United Nations to defeat the Malaysia proposal. One of the staunchest rebels, Jassin Affandi, said in an interview that the NKKU would not have resorted to armed rebellion if only the Sultan had made his intentions clear about his dislike of the Malaysia plan at the time.[81] Perhaps there is much truth in this.

It was partly Azahari's inflexible attitude and over-confidence in his cause of establishing a people's government in Brunei, albeit under a constitutional monarchy, that led to the defeat of the rebellion, regardless of the arguments about who started it, and when it should have started. Both Azahari as well as his followers became losers in a political game that was played out not just within the borders of Brunei but also against the wider international setting of the Cold War, a situation which claimed many other victims in the region who opposed the formation of Malaysia. Azahari and his socialist colleagues in Singapore and Malaya failed to gain the power to realise their dreams of establishing libertarian governments away from neo-colonialism.

Notes

* A draft version of this paper was presented at the 3rd Nicholas Tarling Conference on Southeast Asian Studies, 'Exalted Heroes, Demonized Villains and Losers: Altering Perceptions and Memories of Leaders and Leadership in Southeast Asia, c. 1800–c. 2000', 12–13 November 2013, University of Malaya, Kuala Lumpur.

1 For a more recent account of the events in Limbang, see Eileen Chanin (2013).

2 Within three days, i.e., by noon on 11 December, the British had dispatched some 1,600 troops and recovered all the important installations. All hostages taken by the rebels were freed before the end of the month. Of the 2,700 rebels (estimated by the British as all but a handful of the TNKU) who either were captured or had surrendered, many were released by mid-May 1963.

3 Some examples of these documents are Colonial Office (CO) 1030/1071, File 7D, folio 300; CO 1030/1073, Part 2, folio 478, Part 7, folio 484; CO 1030/1074, Part G., Folios 521–522 and 542; CO 1030/1076, Enclosure 7, folio 7.

4 The 2004 publication is a revised edition of his book previously published under the same title in 1989, by Insan in Kuala Lumpur, which was adapted from his MA thesis submitted to the University of Malaya. The official Brunei History Centre sponsored the revised second edition. They encouraged Zaini to recant his previous explanations of the rebellion written from the rebels' perspective.

5 See Jamil al-Sufri, *8 Disember: Dalangnya Siapa?* (2003).

6 Poulgrain spent nearly six months at Azahari's home in Bogor, Indonesia, to interview him. In many instances he reproduced Azahari's version of the events rather uncritically.

7 For similar descriptions of the rebellion as a pathetic 'minuscule affair', see Phillip Darby (1973: 32).

8 CO 1030/1074, The UK Commissioner General in S.E. Asia to F.O., Telegram No. 369, 18 December 1962, para 6.

9 Pages 105–154 of this publication reveal interesting snippets on the Brunei rebellion, with some predictable post-facto rationalisations.

10 There is some controversy about this, and I am unable to verify the truth about his 'Brunei' birth. Many claim that Azahari was born on the island of Labuan and later asked to become the Sultan's subject by applying for registration. Azahari, however, vehemently denied this. He claims he was born in Brunei Town in a house where the Churchill Museum was later built. Personal interview, Bogor, 4 April 1994.

11 Azahari's grandfather, Shaikh Abdul Hamid, was of Arab descent. The title *Shaikh* refers to a leader and a holy person among the pilgrims, or Haji, who venture to Mecca.

12 Most of what follows regarding Azahari's career is based on information given by Azahari himself during my interview with him in Bogor in June 1994. Other useful sources by authors who interviewed Azahari are Poulgrain (1998) and Zariani Abdul Rahman (1992). Also useful is the summary resume prepared on Azahari in 1961 by D. C. White, the British High Commissioner. CO 1030/1075, 'A. M. Azahari', by D. C. White, 27 September 1961. Annexed in 'Brunei: Note by Colonial Office'. Colonial Office, 28 December 1961.

13 CO 1030/1075, 'A. M. Azahari' by D. C. White.

14 The late Achmad Zaidi, known as Tun Datok Patinggi Haji Ahmad Zaidi Adruce Mohammad Noor, was the Yang Di-Pertua of Sarawak (personal interview in April 1994 in Kuching). For his biographical details, see Sanib Said (1991).

15 For further details on this, see George McTurnan Kahin (1952).

16 Zaini Haji Ahmad (1989: 34) mentions that Azahari came to Brunei in mid-1951 having been invited by his brother Shaikh Mohammad to return home while he was still engaged in business in Lampong. This information, Zaini claims, came from Shaikh Mohammad himself, whom Zaini met in July 1980. However, British sources agree that Azahari arrived in Brunei around October 1952. CO 1022/396, Extracts of letter by H. Hales, Managing Director of the BMPC in Brunei to Dr. W. L. F. Nuttall, 11 February 1953, enclosure in Dr. W. L. F. Nutall to W. H. L. Monson (CO), 5 March 1953. This is further confirmed by D. C. White's account, which further stated that in 1950, at his father's request, Azahari was offered repatriation, but he refused. CO 1030/1075, 'A. M. Azahari', by D. C. White.

17 In September and October 1945 when British and Dutch troops landed near the Batavian port of Tanjong Priok, Azahari was involved in the protests and skirmishes against them.

18 This is Poulgrain's (1998) version. According to the British version, it was Azahari who refused repatriation, even when his father requested him to return.

19 In fact, most of the former colleagues of Azahari whom I interviewed in 1994, including Abdullah Ja'afar and Pehin H. M. Salleh, confirmed this point. These interviews were conducted to collect oral sources as part of preparation for my 1995 book, *Sultan Omar Ali Saifuddin III and Britain: The Making of Brunei Darussalam.*

20 As reported by Anthony Abell, the Governor cum High Commissioner in Brunei, Azahari was there, 'to stir up trouble, preaching an anti-colonial and pro-Indonesian creed [and] his persuasive tongue and superior education gained him considerable support among the young rank and file of the police and the junior grades of the Civil service' (CO 1022/396, High Commissioner Brunei to CO, Savingram, No. 32, 10 March 1953).

21 Ibid. Nuttall (Whitehall official) to Monson (CO), 5 March 1953. See also Notes from extract of letter from the Managing Director of British Malayan Petroleum Company Limited to Nuttall, 11 February 1953.

22 CO 1022/396, Anthony Abell to CO, Savingram No. 54, 13 May 1953, para 6.

23 Ibid. 'What is becoming apparent is that there is a shadow organisation trying to amalgamate the various factions in Brunei towards "nationalism" and the possibility cannot be overlooked that support may be coming directly from Indonesia'.

24 Ibid.

25 Hussainmiya (1995: Chapter 3) discusses the BRUFICO affair in detail.

26 CO 1030/1075, D. C. White's report on 'A. M. Azahari', 27 September 1961, Annexed in *Brunei: Note by the Colonial Office,* Colonial Office, 28 December 1962. According to a contemporary newspaper report, the three accused were allegedly members of a secret society that advocated the overthrow of the Brunei administration (*Straits Times*, 7 & 8 October 1953).

27 Mohd. Manggol bin Dato Seri Paduka Tuan Haji Manggol, born c. 1930, was sent to Labuan on a government scholarship to study in the Government English School. He once acted as a local guide to the BMA officials. He became a pupil teacher in 1947 and received training in SITC, Perak, Malaya, from 1948 to 1950, where he became an ardent follower of radical Malay nationalists, Ahmad Boestamam and Harun Aminur Rashid. Returning to Brunei, he became an early convert to the teachings of Azahari, whom he knew from his Labuan days. Mohd. Manggol went on to pursue tertiary education at Madras University from 1956 to 1961 and remained only as an external spokesman for the PRB cause. In 1961 he left for Indonesia to further his studies. While still a student at Gajah Mada University in Yogyakarta, he became a promoter of the Negara Kesatuan Kalimantan Utara (the Northern Kalimantan State) concept. He was the Foreign Minister in Azahari's government in exile after the failure of the rebellion but after that time their relations became strained. Manggol has lived in Indonesia ever

since, but recently returned to Brunei to develop his business interests. Personal interview held at Pusat Sejarah (Brunei History Centre), Brunei, 18 April 1994.

28 A policeman who became an active follower of Azahari and a leading PRB figure, he was arrested for his role during the rebellion and detained for more than a decade.

29 BA/0257/83 (SUK Series 3, Box 20), Item 94, Petition of Dato Seri Paduka Tuan Haji Manggol, Penghulu, Kampong Kilanas to H. H. the Sultan of Brunei, 8 October 1953.

30 Personal interview with Azahari, 7 April 1994. Azahari and his brothers, especially Sheikh Nikman, owned a business company known as the S. M. & Sons, which dealt in quarrying, contract works and transport.

31 For details, see Mohamed Sopiee (1974: 129–131).

32 *Utusan Melayu*, 31 December 1955.

33 For an account of extreme political movements in Malaya, see Firdaus Haji Abdullah (1985). For a detailed account of the Parti Rakyat Malaya and Malayan People's Socialist Front, see R. K. Vasil (1971).

34 Comparatively speaking, the Parti Rakyat Malaya (PRM), relied heavily upon the support of fishermen and rural workers (von Vorys 1975).

35 H. M. Salleh, the vice-president of the PRB, did highlight this fact in an interview with *The Borneo Bulletin* of 13 October 1956, when he said that the ten members of the executive committee, with the exception of Azahari, had very little to boast of by way of educational qualifications.

36 He had held the post of Superintendent of Education in Brunei from 1939 and was interned by the British in 1945 for allegedly collaborating with the Japanese. A product of the Malayan SITC, Harun Rashid inspired many Bruneians, especially during his tour of duty in Brunei, with nationalistic ideals. For a biography of Che'gu Harun, see Abdullah Hussein (1981).

37 Dr Burhanuddin Al-Helmy was a product of the distinguished religious school in Malaya, the Madrasah Al-Mashhor, Penang. He was a prominent Malay nationalist leader and one of the founder members of the Malay Nationalist Party of Malaya (MNP). In the aftermath of the Brunei rebellion of 1962, the Malaysian government interned him for his alleged connection with the PRB. Until 1966, he was the Chairman of the Pan-Malayan Islamic Party.

38 Dr Ahmad Boestamam was known previously as Abdullah Sani. He hailed from an aristocratic family in Perak in 1920 and was educated at Malay and English schools in the state. He was an active member of the KRIS movement and was a founder member of the MNP. He founded the Parti Ra'ayat of Malaya. On several occasions he was detained by the authorities for pro-Indonesian activities.

39 *Malay Mail*, 21 February 1956.

40 Anthony Burgess (John Wilson), in his autobiographical account of his brief experience as a schoolteacher in Brunei from 1958 until 1960, states that he knew Azahari rather well and that Azahari lived across from the school, the Sultan Omar Ali Saifuddien College, where Burgess taught. Apparently, Azahari had intended to, or actually at first did, name his party the Nationalist Socialist Party. When Burgess explained to Azahari the evil connotations of the label, he changed it to the Brunei People's Party (PRB) (Burgess 1987: 426).

41 BA/0257/83 (SUK Series 3, Box 20), Document No. 3/PRB/56, pp. 95–98. See also *Borneo Bulletin*, 28 January 1956 and 25 February 1956.

42 On 5 March 1956 during a meeting with Azahari, Sir Anthony Abell expressed 'sympathy with the wishes of the people of Brunei for having taken steps towards independence of their mother country' (Zaini Haji Ahmad 1989: 55).

43 Azahari's inaugural speech at the Partai Rakyat Sessions, 22 January 1956, quoted in Zaini Haji Ahmad (1989: 54).

44 For a comparative understanding of British efforts and the local reaction elsewhere in the Sheikdoms, see David Roberts (1985: 4).

45 A rudimentary local council system devised to supervise mainly matters of public amenities in the main townships since 1920. The Sanitary Boards, whose members were appointees of the Resident, had no statutory powers. BA/0032/86(SUK Series 2, Box 126), Resident's notification No. 5 of 1948, 5 January 1948; and No. 2 of 1948, 2 January 1948.
46 *Borneo Bulletin* interview with Azahari, 20 October 1956.
47 CO 1030/460, G. C. Whiteley's Minute to J. B. Johnston, 7 May 1957. Zaini Haji Ahmad, says 'it is important to note that at this juncture opposition to the local Government idea came from the people and not through political mobilisation. . . . The PRB was not registered yet [*sic*]'. By contrast, the Colonial Office definitely laid the blame on the PRB for opposing the Local Councils Enactment: 'We tried to introduce local Government as a basis for further constitutional advance. Azahari ruined it'. *Parti Rakyat* p. 10. Also, in CO 1030/464, J. B. Johnston's Minute, 30 May 1957.
48 *Suara Rakyat*, April 1957, p. 4.
49 CO 1030/460, Anthony Abell to J. B. Johnston (CO), Secret, 13 May 1957.
50 Azahari's three-man delegation (including Zaini Haji Ahmad and Jassin Affendi, the Secretary General of the Party) arrived in London on 18 September 1957. The London authorities did not give the green light for Azahari to proceed to London until the second week of September. Since August, his delegation had been holed up in a Singapore hotel waiting for news, sending desperate telegrams to the Colonial Office. Details in CO 1030/464; see G. C. Whiteley's Minute, 23 August 1957.
51 CO 1030/461, Anthony Abell to G. C. Whiteley (CO), 25 January 1957.
52 Ibid., 18 January 1958.
53 Ibid., para 3.
54 *Borneo Bulletin*, 12 December 1959.
55 *Borneo Bulletin*, 5 May 1962.
56 Borneo Bulletin, 5 May 1962.
57 The trade union legislation had still not been passed. CO 1030/1215, Official Communiqué of Brunei Labour Movement, 4 November 1960. Ibid. Minute of J. Holloway, 23 November 1960.
58 BA/2636/83 (SUK Series 3, Box 210), Proclamation by Barisan Buroh Bersatu Brunei as communicated to the Brunei State Secretary, 18 July 1961, Item 7.
59 *Borneo Bulletin*, 24 June 1961.
60 CO 1022/61, item 19, J. D. Higham's Memorandum, 20 January 1953, para 6. A British parliamentarian, Sir Robert Boothby, one of the five members of a visiting Commonwealth parliamentary team, in 1954 suggested, 'a confederation of these territories within the Commonwealth was "essential" for economic and strategic reasons, and even Burma could be asked to enter at a later stage'.
61 For details, see Hussainmiya (2000: chapter 2).
62 For a cogent account of the Barisan Sosialis from one of its founders, see Said Zahari (2001).
63 The best account of Azahari's Indonesian connections is presented in Poulgrain's 1998 publication, particularly chapters 3, 4 and 6.
64 CO 1030/932, The CO Brief on 'The Brunei Party Ra'ayat', January 1963, Enclosed in J. D. Higham to CRO, 19 February 1963.
65 Ibid.
66 It is understood that the PRB gained 31 seats unchallenged, and the remaining seats were won by ballot on the day of the election. The non-PRB candidate that won the last seat in the District Council was a private candidate in Temburong who joined the PRB after the election.
67 Ibid., 28 January 1961.
68 *Borneo Bulletin*, 1 September 1962.
69 N.d. *Titah KDYMM Paduka Seri Baginda Maulana Al-Sultan,* Government Press, Brunei Town, pp. 138–139.

70 See Abdul Rahman bin Karim (1963). The Legislative Council was finely balanced with (a) 8 ex-officio members, (b) 6 officials, (c) 16 elected members (all PRB) and (d) 2 nominated members. The nominated members were Mr. Linton of the Brunei Shell Company and Dato Temenggong Lim Cheng Choo. The High Commissioner envisaged that 'the voting of the Dato Temenggong is likely to be governed by the degree of intimidation the PR can bring to bear'. CO 1030/933, D. C. White to J. D. Higham (CO) Personal and Confidential, 27 October 1962.
71 *Borneo Bulletin*, 8 September 1962.
72 *Borneo Bulletin*, 22 September 1962.
73 BA/2502/83, (SUK Series 3, Box 202), Attorney General to State Secretary, 21 July 1962, Item 2, Para 3.
74 BA/13867/78, (SUK Series 3, Box 227), Pengiran Momin, Clerk of the House, to Raja Azam Kamaruzzaman, State Secretary, 3 December 1962.
75 When I met Azahari at his home in Bogor on 7 April 1994, he still seemed to hold his faith in magical amulets.
76 See C. W. Chuang's article in the *Malay Mail*, 24 December 1962: 'Even Tiny Brunei Did Not Escape the Attention of Azahari's Uncle: A News Post-mortem'.
77 *Straits Times*, 14 December 1962.
78 CO 1030/1075, The UK Commissioner General in S.E. Asia to the CRO, Unnumbered Saving (Confidential), 18 December 1962. According to Lord Selkirk, 'I think he [the Sultan] has had a severe shock which does not exclude the possibility that he hedged his bets', para 8.
79 CO 1030/1076, D. C. White to the Secretary of State, Personal Dispatch, No. 25, 20 December 1962, para 29.
80 See, for example, CO 1030/1075, The UK Commissioner General in S.E. Asia to the CRO, Unnumbered Saving (Confidential), 18 December 1962.
81 I owe this information to Dr Haji Yusop Damit, who interviewed him in 1995 to gather information for his PhD thesis submitted to the London School of African and Oriental Studies.

References

Abdullah Hussein (1981) *Aminurashid: Pembangkit Semangat Kebangsaan*. Kuala Lumpur: Dewan Bahasa dan Pustaka.

Abdul Rahman bin Karim (1963) Northern Borneo Nationalism: The Threat to Malaysia. *Eastern World* 16 (6): 14–16.

Ahmad Boestamam (1972) *Dr. Burhanuddin: Putera Setia Melayu Raya*. Kuala Lumpur: Penerbitan Pustaka Kejora.

Ahmady Hassan (n.d.) *Ke Mana Azahari*. Kedah: United Development Corporation.

Brackman, A. C. (1966) *Southeast Asia's Second Front: The Power Struggle in the Malay Archipelago*. London: Pall Mall Press.

Brown, D. E. (1970) Brunei: The Structure and History of a Bornean Malay Sultanate. *Brunei: Special Monograph of the Brunei Museum Journal* 2 (2).

Burgess, Anthony (1987) *Little Wilson and Big God*. London: Heinemann.

Chanin, Eileen (2013) *Limbang: 7 Days in December 1962 Rebellion*. Singapore: Ridge Books.

Darby, Phillip (1973) *British Defence Policy: East of Suez, 1947–1968*. London: Oxford University Press.

Firdaus Haji Abdullah (1985), *Radical Malay Politics: Its Origins and Early Development*. Petaling Jaya: Pelanduk Publications.

Hanna, Willard A. (1964) *The Formation of Malaysia: New Factor in World Politics*. New York: American Universities Field Staff, Inc.

Harun Majid Hassan (2007) *Rebellion in Brunei: The 1962 Revolt, Imperialism, Confrontation and Oil*. London: I. B. Tauris.

Hussainmiya, B. A. (1995) *Sultan Omar Ali Saifuddin and Britain: The Making of Brunei Darussalam*. Kuala Lumpur: Oxford University Press.

Hussainmiya. B. A. (2000) *The Brunei Constitution of 1959: An Inside History*. Bandar Seri Begawan: Brunei Press.

Jamil al-Sufri, Pehin Jawatan Dalam Seri Maharaja Dato Seri Utama Dr. Haji Awang Mohd. (1992) *Liku-liku Perjuangan Pencapaian Kemerdekaan Negara Brunei Darussalam*. Brunei: Jabatan Pusat Sejarah, Kementerian Kebudayaan Belia dan Sukan.

Jamil al-Sufri, Pehin Jawatan Dalam Seri Maharaja Dato Seri Utama Dr. Haji Awang Mohd. (2003) *8 Disember: Dalangnya Siapa?* Brunei: Asia Printers.

Kahin, George McTurnan (1952) *Nationalism and Revolution in Indonesia*. Ithaca: Cornell University Press.

Mackie, J. A. C. (1974) *Konfrontasi: The Indonesia-Malaysia Dispute, 1963–1966*. Kuala Lumpur: Oxford University Press.

Means, G. P. (1976) *Malaysian Politics*. Second edition. London: Hodder and Stouton.

Menon, Unnikrishnan (1988) Negara Brunei Darussalam from Protectorate to Statehood: The Ceaseless Quest for Security. Unpublished PhD thesis, Victoria University of Wellington.

Mohamed Bolkiah (2007) *Remember, Remember, 8th of December*. Bandar Seri Begawan: Brunei Press (Sdn. Berhad).

Mohamed Sopiee (1974) *From Malayan Union to Singapore Federation: Political Unification in the Malayan Region 1945–65*. Kuala Lumpur: Penerbit Universiti Malaya.

Mohamad Yusop (1998) The Malaysia Plan and the First Brunei Elections, 1962. *Journal of the Malaysian Branch of the Royal Asiatic Society* 71 (1): 57–73.

Ness, Gayl D. (1962) *Brunei's Teapot Rebellion: Despatch to Mr. Richard H. Nolte: CDN-21*. New York: Institute of Current World Affairs, December 22.

Poulgrain, Greg (1998) *The Genesis of Konfrontasi: Malaysia, Brunei, and Indonesia, 1945–1965*. Bathurst: Crawfurd House.

Roberts, David (1985) The Consequences of the Exclusive Treaties: A British View. In B. R. Pridham (ed.), *The Arab Gulf and the West*. London and Sydney: Croom Helm, pp. 1–14.

Said Zahari (2001) *Dark Clouds at Dawn: A Political Memoir*. Kuala Lumpur: Insan.

Sanib Said (1991) *Yang Dikehendaki: Biografi Yang Di- Pertua Negeri Sarawak: Tun Datok Patinggi Hj. Ahmad Zaidi Adruce Mohd. Noor*. Kuching: Persatuan Sejarah Malaysia.

Smith, Brigadier E. D. (1985) *Counter Insurgency Operations: 1. Malaya and Borneo*. London: Ian Allan.

Starner, Francis L. (1963) Malaysia and the North Borneo Territories. *Asian Survey* 3 (2): 519–534.

Stockwell, A. J. (2004) Britain and Brunei, 1945–1963: Imperial Retreat and Royal Ascendancy. *Modern Asian Studies* 38 (4): 785–819.

Turnbull, Mary C. (1981) *A Short History of Malaysia, Singapore and Brunei*. Asian edition. Singapore: Graham Brash.

Vasil, R. K. (1971) *Politics in a Plural Society: A Study of Non-Communal Political Parties in West Malaysia*. Kuala Lumpur/Singapore: Oxford in Asia.

Vorys, Karl von (1975) *Democracy without Consensus: Communalism and Political Stability in Malaysia*. Princeton NJ: Princeton University Press.

Zaini bin Hj Ahmad, Haji (ed.) (1987) *The People's Party of Brunei: Selected Documents*. Petaling Jaya: Institute of Social Analysis.

Zaini Haji Ahmad, Haji (1989) *Pertumbuhan Nasionalisme di Brunei (1939–1962)*. Kuala Lumpur, Malaysia: ZR Publications.

Zaini Haji Ahmad, Haji (2004) *Perumbuhan Nasionalisme di Brunei: (1939–1962)*. Second edition. Brunei: Asia Printers.

Zariani Abdul Rahman (1992) *Escape from Berakas! 1962 Brunei Revolt*. Kuala Lumpur: Al-Ahad Enterprise.

4 Hybrid pathways to orthodoxy

Bureaucratisation, Sharia-compliant exorcism and the powers of Japanese water-crystal photography in Brunei Darussalam*

Dominik M. Müller

Introduction

This chapter investigates the bureaucratisation of Islam in Brunei and its interlinkages with socio-cultural changes. It elucidates how the realisation of state-enforced Islamic orthodoxy produces locally unique meanings, while simultaneously reflecting broader characteristics of the contemporary global condition. The chapter introduces a theoretical perspective on the bureaucratisation of Islam as a social phenomenon that is intertwined with the state's exercise of classificatory power and related popular processes of co-producing, and sometimes appropriating, symbolic state power. Second, it outlines the historical trajectory of empowering Brunei's national ideology, Malay Islamic Monarchy (*Melayu Islam Beraja* [MIB]). It then explores social imaginaries and bureaucratic representations of 'deviant'-declared practices, before illustrating how these practices become reinvented within the parameters of state power as 'Sharia-compliant' services to the nation-state. Simultaneously, national-religious protectionism is expressed in globalised terms and shaped by forces the state cannot entirely control. Newly established Sharia-serving practices become culturally re-embedded, while also flexibly drawing upon multiple transnational cultural registers. In the main ethnographic example, bureaucratised exorcism, Japanese water-crystal photography and scientisation fuse behind the 'firewall' of MIB. These hybrid pathways to orthodoxy complicate the narratives through which they are commonly framed.

The cultural and political position of Islam in contemporary Brunei Darussalam (henceforth Brunei) is commonly portrayed as conservative and orthodox. Indeed, the authoritative Islamic Religious Council and its Legal Committee *de jure* follow 'the orthodox tenets' of Shafi'i Sunni Islam.[1] International media portrayals of Brunei as a vanguard of strict 'Islamisation' have become increasingly prominent since 2013. The government has undeniably formalised an increasingly restrictive regulation of Islamic discourse and practice since gaining its independence in 1984. Personal religious liberties are more constrained than in neighbouring countries, and the government aims to transform its citizenry into right-guided subjects adhering to state-controlled religious doctrines, justified with the aim of protecting its souls in light of Judgement Day.

However, generalised narratives of 'growing Islamisation' and 'orthodoxy' tell us little about the actual empirical realities, social meanings and local discursive embeddedness of Brunei's Islamisation policies, and how different actors position themselves towards and within these processes. Such narratives, and the often purely speculative self-referential knowledge-production on Brunei in international media, typically written by journalists who know little to nothing about Brunei society let alone having discussed their claims about Brunei *with Bruneians*, only perpetuate and further deepen what Donald Brown (1988: 81) described as a long-standing 'conflict between domestic and foreign accounts of Brunei' – in his case, referring mainly to Bruneian history, but valid also for anthropological accounts of the present.

Through a close examination of Bruneian discourses and social processes at the micro-level, this chapter ethnographically explores Islamisation policies in post-colonial Brunei vis-à-vis parallel socio-legal and cultural transformations. As we shall see, the social realisation of state-enforced orthodoxy is sometimes remarkably flexible and culturally hybrid. This not only challenges essentialising narratives but also has implications for our understanding of developments elsewhere that are framed in similar terms. Explanatory schemes of 'Sharia'isation' may obscure more than they reveal, and to generate a deeper understanding of the dynamics at play, researchers should examine them where they take place – in everyday life-worlds, ideally in interaction with involved actors. To be sure, where such researchers are non-Bruneians, and even where they are seeking close epistemic partnership with Bruneian academics and citizens (like I do), such an approach probably cannot entirely overcome the historically and politically deep-rooted 'conflict' of internal and external perspectives that Brown so rightly identified. For many (though not all) Bruneians, the notions of 'Sharia'isation' and religious 'purification' of Malay culture – which likely played a comparably little role when Brown conducted his doctoral fieldwork in the late 1960s – may simply capture the phenomena I describe. Yet, I would nevertheless insist that only micro-level approaches, aiming to 'speak nearby' (Chen 1992) in close exchange with Bruneian perspectives – without speaking *for* them – offer the most promising and ethically responsible option available in order to establish hopefully some middle ground 'between domestic and foreign accounts of Brunei' (Brown 1988: 81). As I will demonstrate, assumed Islamisation and growing orthodoxy should in my personal understanding be conceived of vis-à-vis their actual settings and micro-level manifestations – in other words, in light of how Bruneian social actors themselves put them to work and ascribe their own meanings to them, in simultaneously locally specific and deeply globalised ways. The closer we examine Brunei's Islamisation and the related powerful policies and societal trends of orthodox 'purification', the more our findings may challenge common assumptions about the phenomena these terms aim to signify.

I start by introducing theoretical considerations pertaining to the bureaucratisation of Islam as a social phenomenon that transcends its institutional boundaries, informs cultural changes and is inherent in the state's exercise of classificatory power. Second, I sketch the trajectory and institutional empowerment of Brunei's national ideology and bureaucratisation of Islam. I then ethnographically elucidate social imaginaries and bureaucratic representations of supernatural powers and deviant-declared practices, before illustrating how such practices become reconfigured within the symbolic parameters of state power, while simultaneously drawing upon multiple transnational cultural registers. In my main example, Sharia-compliant exorcism, Japanese water-crystal photography, market-inspired corporatisation, and the quest for scientific evidence-making fuse behind and across the 'firewall' of MIB. I will conclude that new orthodoxies become re-embedded in pre-existing symbolic vocabularies while simultaneously creatively appropriating transnational cultural flows in a manner that, in many ways, reflects the contemporary global condition. New cultural forms arising from such appropriations are likely transitory, like many hybridities that serve as 'unstable forms of mediation and distinction' (Hahn 2016) between dialectically intertwined local and global spheres. Yet, they demonstrate how the pathways to Brunei's state-enforced orthodoxy, at a deeper symbolic level, complicate narratives of Islamisation, purification and national-cultural protectionism through which they are framed.

Bureaucratic meaning-making, classificatory power and the bureaucratisation of Islam: conceptual considerations

This chapter departs from an anthropological perspective that conceptualises the bureaucratisation of Islam (henceforth BoI) as a social phenomenon that transcends its organisational boundaries, as categorical schemes of Islam diffuse into society and become appropriated by social actors and institutions (Müller 2018). In settings such as Brunei, where governments have empowered Islamic institutions to influence the direction of Muslim discourse, the BoI often penetrates deeply into public discourse and everyday life.

Therefore, the BoI is not simply a formalisation, expansion and diversification of Islamic institutions, or an attempt to control or politically neutralise religious actors, it also informs socio-cultural transformations, albeit without determining them. The BoI furthermore implies a *bureaucratisation of knowledge* and related processes of systematising and reflecting, which Eickelman calls an 'objectification of Muslim consciousness', resulting in 'a significant reimagining of religious and political identities'. Following this concept, Islam

> has implicitly been systematised . . . in the popular imagination, making it self-contained and facilitating innovation. Questions such as 'What is my religion?', 'Why is it important to my life?', and 'How do my beliefs guide my conduct?' have become foregrounded in the lives of large numbers of believers . . . These transformations also mean that 'authentic' religious tradition and identity are foregrounded [but also] questioned, and constructed rather than taken for granted.
>
> (Eickelman 2015: 605)

Accordingly, the BoI implies distinct epistemic modes of understanding and organising the world. These often fuse with other registers, such as marketisation (particularly at its symbolic levels), governmentality, the punitive turn (which is by no means merely grounded in Islamic settings) and other transnational flows, alongside symbolic discursive frames of the nation-state, which result in complex mediations and the negotiation of novel social meanings of Islam.

The BoI is entrenched in the empowerment of what Bourdieu, Wacquant and Farage (1994: 13) called 'state forms of classification' and their 'social frameworks of perceptions', 'understanding', 'appreciation' and 'memory', which are to varying extents popularly habitualised. Therefore, the state's classificatory power is not simply produced by state actors (in the term's conventional sense), but *co-produced and contested in society* (Müller 2018), while the boundaries between state- and non-state spheres are blurred. In certain contexts, non-state actors become state actors as well. Accordingly, symbolic power, of which state power and state-determined social classification are manifestations, 'presupposes, on the part of those who submit to it, a form of complicity which is neither passive submission nor a free adherence to it' (Bourdieu 1991: 50–51). Social actors (including bureaucrats themselves) position themselves diversely: they do not simply internalise state classification to a taken-for-granted, common-sensical level, or circumvent, pragmatically adapt, subversively resist or cautiously navigate between official and unofficial roles. They also ascribe their own meanings to and creatively re-signify hegemonic discourse, partly conditioned by their embeddedness in existing power-knowledge regimes. Although actors may submit to symbolic state power and participate in its social production, they may still inform some of its contents in originally unanticipated ways.

This chapter illustrates such everyday state-making with the example of a Bruneian Islamic healing centre that incorporates the symbolic language of state power. It specialises in exorcism, which had long been the domain of Malay supernatural specialists (*bomoh*) whose once-normalised practices have become bureaucratically classified as deviant (*sesat*) in the post-colonial state; growing segments of the population have internalised this position as common-sensical Islamic. In this context, the BoI affects cultural changes in the normative forms and practices of everyday life, but it also informs social agency and its creative realisations of the state. The agency behind establishing this healing centre problematises widespread notions about Brunei society being apathetic, which continue to dominate perceptions of the country.

Another conceptual point of reference pertains to paradoxical, uneven continuities in the government's path towards religiously purifying Malay culture, or what Herzfeld (1992: 35) calls 'the organic part played by symbols in creating the new order out of the old'. Transformations presented as radical shifts are, at certain levels, not always what they purport to be. Herzfeld (1992: 25–26, 42) used the example of sudden changes towards new state ideologies, such as Kemalist secularism in early 20th-century Turkey. In its proclaimed abandonment of public religious symbols, this 'non-religious' regime of 'secular modernisation' appropriated religion-like symbols into a new nationalist culture, although these were neither intended to appear nor consciously perceived as religious. While some forms change, 'others will probably persist, if not as external symbolic forms, then as structures of thought that will continue to provide an organizing framework for people trying to come to terms with change'. New normative projects 'batten on to an existing cultural vocabulary', allowing people to 'make their respective accommodations to this new order' (Herzfeld 1992: 57). In Brunei, where the omnipresent workings of spirits, sorcery, exorcism and consultation with supernatural specialists had long been a 'widely accepted symbolism' (to borrow Herzfeld's 1992: 58 wording), the state policy towards establishing an Islamic order in a complete (*lengkap*) manner became similarly re-embedded. Before going into detail, some contextual information about the BoI in Brunei needs to be provided.

Bureaucratised Islam and classificatory power in the 'MIB State'

Brunei has been conceptualised by its government as a non-secular Islamic state, and specifically a Malay Islamic Monarchy, since its independence in 1984. Sultan Hassanal Bolkiah (in office since 1967) embodies state power more than any other Southeast Asian leader. In addition to heading all ministries, he is the constitutional 'head of the official religion' (Article 3), i.e., Shafi'i Sunni Islam. He enjoys enormous popularity and, in Bourdieuan (Bourdieu, Wacquant and Farage 1994: 11–12) terms, personally forms the country's '(central) bank of symbolic capital'. Another politically stabilising factor is the oil- and gas-funded high living standards. There is no personal income tax, education and public medical services are free for all citizens and the state provides numerous social services, including large amounts of state-religious aid (*zakat*) for the Muslim poor and converts. Accordingly, the Sultan is officially and popularly referred to as a Caring Monarch (*Raja Yang Prihatin/Pemedulian*). The reciprocal relationship between the Sultan and the citizenry is also framed as representing a deep-rooted Malay principle according to which 'the ruler must be just, and the people must be loyal'.

The government seeks to instil the values of the official national ideology (*ideologi negara*, also 'national philosophy') *Melayu Islam Beraja* (MIB, Malay Islamic Monarchy) in society. MIB privileges Malay (*Melayu*) supremacy, *Islam* (as interpreted by the state), and the monarchy (*Beraja*) – this 'triangle' (Abdul Latif 2003: 206; Brunei Times 2013) defines the government's understanding of national identity, with Islam being officially superior among the three components. As a bureaucratic categorical scheme, MIB is the *leitmotif* of the state's exercise of classificatory power.

Officially, MIB has existed since the first Sultan converted to Islam in 1368 (on the construction of royal genealogy in local historiography, see Brown 1988: 79, 1984). In the 1984 Declaration of Independence, the Sultan proclaimed Brunei 'shall be forever a . . . Malay, Muslim Monarchy upon the teachings of (Sunni) Islam'. MIB became gradually institutionalised, and Brunei-specific notions of *Melayu*, Islam and the monarchy became translated into the language of bureaucracy. In 1986, an MIB Concept Committee was established. It was transformed in 1990 into the MIB Supreme Council (*Majlis Tertinggi MIB*, originally *Majlis Tertinggi Kebangsaan MIB*). Its Secretariat is hosted by the Academy of Brunei Studies (*Akademi Pengajian Brunei, APB*) at Universiti Brunei Darussalam. The

APB was established in the same year. This structure, a key site for MIB knowledge production and dissemination, still exists today. In 1991, compulsory MIB university classes were established. In 1992, MIB became a compulsory school subject (it had been part of curricula since 1986; Dewan Majlis 2014: 469). The contents of MIB teaching have been modified over time – regrettably, no study has yet systematically examined this doctrinal genesis.

The Supreme Council is defining, systematising and propagating the meanings of MIB, with the Sultan's *titah*s providing the main parameters. It prepares curricula and teaching materials, alongside publications and information for the national media. Systematic publishing began in 1994, although texts conceptualising MIB have existed since at least 1987. Its Secretariat reminds citizens of their obligations towards the MIB State (*Negara MIB*, Dewan Majlis 2014: 271). One of its leaders, Muhammad Hadi (2016), for example, argues that MIB's 'values . . . are innate for every Bruneian', a descriptive statement and normative expectation. Similarly, a former Minister of Education stated: 'Every individual is responsible for practicing, appreciating, and strengthening the concept of MIB' (Dewan Majlis 2014: 473). This exemplifies the centrality that MIB enjoys in government discourses about desirable national identity.

The government aims exclusively to define MIB – its 'interpretation must be protected' (Muhammad Hadi 2016, translation). MIB propagation has undergone various reorientations; it is now taught in a more interactive and activating manner, resembling transnational pedagogical trends. Learners should become 'multipliers'. In line with target-group adjusted marketing and evidence-oriented bureaucratic thinking – two transnationally powerful cultural forces – the Council tries to maximise quantified and measured 'success rates' (Dewan Majlis 2014: 472–473). In MIB teaching, transnationally inspired up-to-date methods are applied. Another new trend, as a former MIB lecturer explained, is to encourage 'critical thinking': learners should reflect critically upon how they can strengthen MIB. MIB teaching now also extends to previously less explored fields, such as environmental protection, which is considered essentially Islamic and Malay and simultaneously mirrors globalised eco-trends.

In the language of market-inspired governance, the Supreme Council operates with 'five-year working plans'. The 2015–2020 plan calls for expanding the MIB bureaucracy's 'human resources' and 'infrastructure', alongside other goals. The Secretariat distinguishes three propagation fields – educational sector, other institutions and the general public – and five target groups: government officers/staff, sub-district and village heads (as 'multipliers'), youth/pupils/students, the private sector and society at large. By educationally empowering these groups to themselves empower MIB in society, the authorities seek to *make* the BoI transcend its institutional boundaries: MIB should not simply be state-dictated and obeyed, but society should sincerely understand it and actively co-produce the state's classificatory power. As the Council also integrates other institutions and companies under its 'multi-agency approach', boundaries between state and society blur in many ways, and the MIB state takes a paramount interest in fostering a state-in-society understanding of good citizenship.

The Council organises extensive outreach activities, often co-organised with other agencies/companies and state media. Thus, Bruneian citizens are extensively exposed to the MIB discourse and its normative expectations. They are subject not only to control or disciplining mechanisms, but also to the everyday didactics and *meanings* of the MIB State's power/knowledge nexus. Even those who circumvent or resist the state's pedagogical aspirations can rarely evade being affected by its symbolic power and classification. For Bruneians younger than 40 – the generation that underwent MIB education, whom I call the MIB generation – being MIB citizens and being expected to present themselves as such, at least in official spaces, has to varying extents become habitualised. This is often accompanied by hidden transcripts, negotiations and insecurities, also among state actors; nevertheless, MIB discourse, which is integral to Brunei's BoI, deeply penetrates their life-worlds and subject formation.

Centralising Islamic discourse

Brunei has no public space for non-state Islamic organisations or voices. The Islamic bureaucracy enjoys the exclusive right to speak publicly and publish about Islam. Islamic scholars are, by definition, civil servants. Islam-related publications from abroad are carefully screened before distribution to counter falsifications and deviations. What Iik (2002: 88) noted almost two decades ago remains valid, namely that religious policies 'are discussed internally and . . . introduced slowly and quietly. Open religious . . . debates have never taken place'. Attempts to establish institutionally and promote alternative Muslim groups were quickly and effectively cracked down on, with many becoming bureaucratically classified as 'deviant teachings' (for detailed accounts from state-Islamic perspectives, see Norafan 2007, as well as the State Mufti Abdul Aziz Juned's (1992) insightful elaborations on banning the Bahai and other 'enemies of Islam', which, under certain conditions, in his theological assessment would deserve the death penalty as maximum punishment for persistent refusal to change their ways).

The MIB Supreme Council is entrenched in a wider bureaucratic assemblage of institutions enacting Islamisation and MIB-isation policies. Its most powerful actors include the Ministry of Religious Affairs (MoRA), the State Mufti Department, and the Islamic Religious Council (MUIB, *Majlis Ugama Islam Brunei*).

Initially called the Department of Religious Affairs, the MoRA was established by Sultan Omar Ali Saifuddin III in 1959. Its predecessor body was founded by Sultan Ahmad Tajuddin and served as the Sultan's 'Mohammedan religious adviser'. In 1954, Sultan Omar Ali Saifuddin III formed a consultative council for Sharia affairs; in 1955, he established the MUIB, which until today continues to serve as the 'chief authority' in 'all matters relating to religion' (RCKCA, Section 38) and belongs to the MoRA.

The MoRA's responsibilities include the building/maintenance of mosques, employing mosque personnel, compulsory Islamic education, pilgrimage matters, propagation, conversions (and supporting converts), alms (*zakat*), handling religious offences, doctrine (*aqidah*) control, *halal* certification, advice for families, prayer services and cemeteries. It also manages the Sharia judiciary. Among its sub-institutions are the *Pusat Da'wah Islamiah*, the Sharia Affairs Department, the *Aqidah* Control Unit, and numerous other offices classified into *jabatan, pejabat, bahagian, unit* and *institut*. The current Minister, Badaruddin Othman, was reportedly among the 'creator(s) of MIB' (Kershaw 2001: 19).

Like market-inspired religious institutions translating Islam into the language of bureaucracy elsewhere, the MoRA pursues a 'vision and mission' (*visi dan misi*). The 'vision' includes 'strengthening of the officiality (*kerasmian*) and practice of Islam as a straight and complete way of life', its 'mission' is to 'support and protect Islam and its officiality through an effective and dynamic administration'. Both aim at the 'development and prosperity of the state, based on Sharia Law, the Constitution, other laws, and the MIB philosophy' (Kementerian Hal Ehwal Ugama, translations).

The State Mufti Department works under the Prime Minister's Office. The Mufti is Brunei's chief interpreter of Islam. His office holds the exclusive authority of issuing *fatwas* (Islamic legal opinions, in Brunei officially translated as 'rulings') and transgressions are punishable up to imprisonment under the Syariah Penal Code Order 2013 (henceforth SPCO, Section 228). The State Mufti's *fatwas* are legally binding on Shafi'i Muslims, which Brunei Malays are legally expected to be, once the Sultan or MUIB order them to be gazetted (RCKCA, Section 43; SPCO, Section 228). Mocking or insulting these *fatwas* can result in imprisonment (SPCO, Section 220). Printing/publishing/selling/importing books containing instructions, positions or *fatwas* 'contrary to . . . any lawfully issued fatwa' by the State Mufti is punishable by jail terms or fines (RCKCA, Section 188). Spreading doctrines 'contrary to' state-interpreted Sharia Law is punishable with up to five years (SPCO, Section 207). Notably I am unaware of cases where any of such punishments have ever been enforced, rendering them largely symbolic.

The State Mufti Department's and Mosque Affairs Department's Friday prayer sermons, read in all mosques, frequently remind Muslims of their duty to loyally support the government under Shafi'i doctrines. The Sultan is the leader of believers (*ulil amri*) and *khalifah* (Allah's vice-regent). This points to his role's religious dimension, and its implications for state-desired good citizenship: 'the people sustain their obedience and loyalty to the ruler, as obeying and being loyal to the ruler is part of obeying Allah's commands' (Siti Norkhalbi 2005: 247).

The MoRA, the State Mufti Department and the MIB Supreme Council are authoritative in producing the BoI's doctrinal meanings. These are related to, but must be distinguished from, its social meanings that Bruneians of diverse backgrounds ascribe to and derive from official discourse.

The firewall of MIB and its supernatural counterforces

As Asiyah az-Zahra Ahmad Kumpoh (2011: 39) put it, in post-colonial Brunei, the 'status of religious tolerance . . . remained unchanged' but there have been 'cultural changes where activities . . . which did not conform to Islamic teaching could no longer be tolerated'. This may sound like a contradiction ('tolerance unchanged' vs. 'can no longer be tolerated'), but for hegemonic Bruneian discourse it is not. It addresses two locally powerful themes. The first is feeling misrepresented as intolerant/radical by outsiders, whereas actual Bruneian Islam ensures harmonious, peaceful relations with everybody. The second is the banning of long-standing supernatural traditions, which, in the now dominant view, is not a question of 'religious practice' or 'minorities' and thus potentially tolerable, but of protecting the essence of Islam and Muslim souls facing Judgement Day.

In 2015, the Sultan famously called MIB a 'firewall' against unwanted elements. These include crime, social ills and undesired foreign cultural flows invading Brunei if no 'firewall' separating positive and negative influences were in place. This new digital metaphor reiterates a long-standing view contrasting Brunei *Darussalam* (*Abode of Peace*) with threats from abroad, a theme in MIB literature from the start. Undesired 'external' elements are not just alternative readings of Islam, militant ideologies, non-Muslim missionaries, and 'immoral' or 'Westernised' behaviours – they also pertain to internal threats in the spheres of the supernatural, and they related once widely accepted symbolisms. One such tradition that Asiyah az-Zahra (2011: 50) mentions as no longer tolerable are '[c]elebrations at spirit shrines', such as 'powerful graves' (*kubur keramat*) (Müller 2018). In the era when Brown did his doctoral fieldwork in the late 1960s, such practices had still been socially normalised and mostly uncontroversial, as elderly Bruneians I spoke with confirmed. For example, Brown (1988: 81) noted that Bruneians 'know to be true . . . that some individuals (can) achieve invulnerability', and he was closely concerned with the thoroughly supernatural Bruneian myth of origin, Syair Awang Semaun (Brown 1980, 1988: 76–77, 81), which had been full of miraculous detail and religiously syncretic Southeast Asian symbolism. In that regard, however, the 'Brunei culture' Brown observed has changed in a far-reaching way, and the post-colonial state's bureaucratisation of Islam played a key role in this development.

The Islamic bureaucracy conceptualises the state as a protector of Muslim souls: It is *obliged* and accountable towards God to realise the Islamic principle of 'enjoining good and forbidding wrong'. Nowadays, the Malay mainstream similarly views many banned traditions as either deviant or outdated. This view was fostered by state-Islamic education, but it also takes inspiration from bottom-up trends. At the same time, however, as the Bruneian scholar Amin Abdul Aziz (2015: 9) rightly reminds us, the Bruneian (MIB) Islamic State's symbolic language continues to contain numerous syncretic (especially Indic) elements (see also Brown 1980), although their centrality gradually decreases, and their non-Islamic origins are normally not publicly problematised as potentially 'deviating' from orthodox purity. In some cases, however, royal regalia (*Alat-Alat Kebesaran Diraja*) such as two golden cats (*kucing emas*) previously attached to the throne, among other cases, have been abandoned, as the State Mufti's theological assessment (*fatwa*) concluded they would violate Islamic norms and may bring harm (Abdul Aziz 2017: 228–245, 349).

Beyond *keramat* shrine-worshipping, other deviant-declared practices are certain Malay customs (*adat*) such as wedding ceremonies, dances and dress. A Friday prayer sermon in 2015 told Muslims not to shake hands with members of the opposite sex who are not their spouses or direct relatives (*mahram*) – an instruction which is not enforced. In other fields, the bureaucracy takes action. One example is supernatural specialists/healers (*bomoh*). Their status has changed from 'an indispensable figure in a Malay village' whose culturally normalised existence was largely 'taken for granted' (Mohd Taib 1988: 157), to a shadowy criminal who engages in *syirik* (sin) and *khurafat* (forbidden superstition). Under MIB State forms of classification, 'bomoh-ism' (*perbomohan*) can, at least *officially*, no longer be tolerated. *Bomoh* as a social institution and certain individuals in particular have always been surrounded by ambivalence, due to their simultaneously fascinating and suspicious access to invisible worlds. This ambivalence, however, has been revalorised vis-à-vis policies aiming to govern individual practices and beliefs, and in ways that pay greater heed to the negative side of things. Thus, this socio-legal transformation pushed forward by bureaucratic actors is not a historical rupture *per se*, although the changes are dramatic.

Social imaginaries and bureaucratised representations of black magic

Notwithstanding these normative shifts, experiences of the omnipresent workings of sorcery (*sihir*) remain a social reality, and Brown's (1988: 81) observation that many Bruneians 'know to be true . . . that some individuals' can, for example, 'achieve vulnerability' by magic means remains fully valid, as this section will ethnographically illustrate. During a car ride in 2017, a married couple of two religiously observant Bruneians, whom I had known for years, shared some personal experiences with me. Neither were inclined to any deviance in the MIB State's sense, had temporarily lived abroad, and one had taught MIB before. Like many Bruneians, they had personally experienced the workings of sorcery and/or interferences by *jin*: 'I have seen it with my own eyes', Tijah told me. In her youth, she saw a fireball, caused by a form of sorcery called *ranggau*, in the sky. Others had seen it too, and her father told her to come into the house immediately. Such fireballs, she explained, are known to be the result of the workings of sorcerers (*tukang sihir*) – often non-Muslim Iban, but any sorcerer could learn it. Tijah recalled her father saying that when such a ball is nearby, a person will be harmed or die. The fireball would be related to a spirit controlled by the sorcerer, which must be fed with human lives. Tijah had seen such fireballs twice. Other interlocutors confirmed the concept.

Her husband, Mamat, stated that a generation earlier, such phenomena's cause, and protection against it, had been the *bomoh*'s domain. Thanks to 'better education', this was now known to be *syirik* (sin), especially by the younger generation, i.e., the MIB generation. Both emphasised that proper Islam, as they learned it, confirms the reality of sorcery, evidenced by the Qur'an and *hadith*. They, and other interlocutors, stressed that even Prophet Muhammad had once been under a spell. This reflects state-Islamic positions.

MoRA officers showed me two exhibitions of confiscated objects used by 'real' and 'fake' sorcerers in 2014. At first, all objects had been 'cleaned' by a MoRA *ustaz* – yet strange sounds came from the room after dark, and nobody would enter it at night. Officer Khairul also narrated how a MoRA scholar had 'tested' a confiscated talisman (*azimat*) for 'academic' purposes, and 'it worked, he was not able to cut into his skin!' Such experiments, he added, were dangerous for anyone's soul.

In the late 2000s, this theme room, entitled 'Objects Leading to the Deviation from the True Doctrine (*Aqidah*)' (translation), was opened within an exhibition at the MoRA's premises. It became the most popular room. The purpose was pedagogical; that is, to explain 'what is prohibited, what you cannot do, and cannot sell'. Khairul added, '20 years ago, Islamic education was not as strong as now'. Especially some elders would still trust *bomohs* and practice deviant traditions, although this would gradually change from the 1990s.

Some exhibited objects had been used to protect their owners from other people's magic, to increase business profits, for love magic and to become temporarily invisible or, resembling Brown's (1988: 81) previously cited example, invulnerable (*kebal*). There were protective bottles with mystical symbols, numbers and Arabic letters that offenders place above doors and cooking/eating bowls with inscribed chants/numbers, kept in restaurants to enhance revenues. Some restaurant owners had been elderly Malays 'who still believe in such methods'. However, elders would stop once they were 'strongly' exposed to the 'right information'.

Other objects are protective rings, often found in a 'suspicious mix'; for example, wrapped in yellow cloth, indicating usage for worshipping (*pemujiaan*). When such objects are found at post offices or border posts (often sent by/for foreign domestic helpers) or confiscated locally, they are sent to the MoRA for investigation. Some are 'harmless' and others are 'used for special purposes, although the owners themselves often don't exactly know what'. Normally, no legal action is taken, but they remain confiscated – the Islamic bureaucracy's main concern is educational, not punitive.

At the second exhibition, officers showed me pictures of a graveyard where photographs of a target person of sorcery had been buried, wrapped in underwear. They regularly find pictures in other settings. The usage of pictures for *sihir* worries many Bruneians: An officer from another institution later told me how friends recommended that he not have a photograph on Facebook as it could be used by enemies (informal conversation, Gadong, January 2017).

Arif, an *aqidah* control officer, explained that there are no written guidelines regarding what defines a 'good *bomoh*' and a 'bad *bomoh*' – theoretically, their 'practice can be good if it is not against Islam'. If a hospital is far away, a 'good *bomoh*' (who, Arif hastened to add, should rather be called *orang pandai*) might provide helpful herbs. However, even well-intentioned *orang pandai* would often unintentionally engage spirits/demons. I did not find consensus, among bureaucratic interlocutors or elsewhere, about what defines the difference between *bomoh* and *orang pandai*, and whether both, or all representatives of one of the two categories, are *necessarily* 'deviant'. The tendency was to view *bomoh* as generally deviant (reflecting the state-media's tone), and *orang pandai* undecidedly with mixed suspicion and admiration. Bruneian *bomoh* no longer call themselves *bomoh*, as the term has acquired a de-legitimising stigma. Some are called *Cikgu* or *Ustaz* (teacher), albeit in one recent case, a more daring underground healer called himself *Yang Keramat Agong* ('holding superior powers').

Arif estimated 'hundreds' of *bomoh* in Brunei, '70–80 per cent foreigners', mainly Indonesians. Local *bomoh* were mostly elders (*kampung* people), who learned 'from generation to generation', and whose often-unintended deviance was mainly about interacting with *jin*. No generation followed the family transmission pattern any longer. Local suspects in their 30s and 40s were often 'fake *bomoh*' engaging in financial or sexual exploitation.

For many students, exchanging supernatural stories is an everyday normality. Sometimes, these directly relate to symbols of state power. Ramlee shared with me rumours about a certain Prince having a room for his dagger (*keris*) collection that was haunted. One *keris* 'stood in the room', haunted by 'several spirits' causing troubled social relations. The Prince, following the narration, called an Indonesian 'good *bomoh*' who 'cleaned' the room, performed prayers and brought away the *keris*, refusing payment. Ramlee added that some people believed the Prince himself has 'powers'; 'he can walk up walls, like Spiderman!' Ramlee also shared a popular story that the Sultan's father could control the rain by twisting his moustache (informal conversation, July 2017). Similarly, some royal graves were once popularly considered 'powerful' (*keramat*). One, *Makam Di Luba*, is still rumoured to be haunted and occasionally visited by 'deviants'. The underlying popular imagination, however, obviously dates back to a time when the idea of royal status implying exceptional supernatural capabilities had once been generally accepted and unproblematic in Brunei, just like in Java and across the entire Malay world (compare Brown 1988: 84).

The main institution responsible for 'controlling' religious deviance is the MoRA's *Aqidah* Control Unit. It organises surveillance and faith rehabilitation, and it maintains a confidential 24-hour hotline. Formed in 1986, it has undergone several restructurings. Following public calls to report suspects, 38 *bomoh* were arrested in 2004 and 55 in 2005. Later statistics list smaller numbers, but each year suspected offenders have been identified.

I interviewed Razak, who offered himself to the authorities to observe a *bomoh*'s community. He explained his motivation as ethical. As the *bomoh* was harming his patients and disciples, reporting him was a civic duty. He thus, in a sincere spirit of governmentality, fulfilled the expectation to co-produce and strengthen the MIB State's classificatory power as a 'multiplier' in society.

Bomoh cases are normally settled outside of courts, through warnings and 'voluntary' re-education called counselling (*kaunseling*). Its legal basis has long been the RCKCA (Section 186, 'False Doctrine'). In 2014, Arif emphasised that, if enacted, the SPCO would make prosecution easier: Muslims worshipping 'any person, place, nature or any object, thing or animal in any manner' contrary to Islamic Law, or making '(a)n act or statement that shows faith to any object, thing or animal' possessing 'power', 'for example the ability to bring good luck, increas(ing) wealth, grant(ing) wishes, heal(ing) diseases and others', could be sentenced to imprisonment, fines and counselling. Muslims who claim that they 'or any other person knows an event or a matter that is beyond human understanding', contradicting Islamic teachings, face up to ten years' imprisonment, caning, and forced repentance. Advertising black magic is punishable by up to five years' imprisonment; attempted murder through black magic with ten years; fulfilled murder with the death penalty (Sections 152, 153, 206b, 208, 216). The SPCO is enacted in three stages, and severe punishments will be enforced only in the not-yet-enacted second and third.[2] Even then, there would be high procedural burdens and mechanisms to avoid the punishment, reflecting the traditional Islamic art of not punishing.

Sharia-compliant healing, water-crystal photography and the reconfiguration of deviant-declared practices

Parallel to the *bomoh*'s outlawing and social marginalisation, Brunei witnessed the rise of 'Sharia-compliant Islamic healing' and exorcism (*ruqyah syariah*/*pengubatan Islam*). State-*ulama* have long conducted such practices, but the most insightful example for my analytic purposes, and the biggest trend, is Darusysyifa' Warrafahah, an institution established in Brunei in 2007. Its model was the Malaysian Darusyifa', led by the late Haron Din, a former Islamic Studies professor and Spiritual Leader of the Islamic Party of Malaysia. Haron Din was Malaysia's most prominent expert of the invisible world: his books were bestsellers, his institution expanded and he was admired across religious-political divides.

Many Bruneians admired him too, including an aspiring small group of Bruneians who came in touch with him and wanted to establish a local branch. Haron Din repeatedly visited Brunei upon the Sultan's invitation and was bureaucratically 'cleared' to teach and speak publicly about Islam-related matters, which is remarkable, considering he was a foreign Islamist politician, and shows the respect he enjoyed among elites.

It took some time until the founders were able to establish the institution as an association through the Registrar of Organisations (ROS). This permission being granted to a *non-state Islamic organisation* is highly unusual. Haron Din was its supreme teacher, but pro forma it became an independent local organisation. Its 'governing committee' reports all activities to the ROS, and the organisational structure follows the ROS's obligatory pattern. The original group of founders consisted of 20 people, from both genders, of diverse educational and professional backgrounds, ranging from government employees, retirees, and private sector workers to housewives. Despite this diversity, they all were literate in reciting the Qur'an, as a founding member emphasised.

Brunei's DS offers a standardised one-year curriculum course on the 'basics of Islamic healing', using Haron Din's writings. Students learn purpose-specific Qur'anic verses, recitation patterns and 'ethics'. Their certificate (*tauliah mudawi/sijil pengijazahan*) entitles them to practise as volunteers at the centre and/or privately. In 2017, 700 people were actively involved. Patients also include non-Muslims, including Chinese Bruneians, guest workers, and, for example, a Japanese manager who hired Darusysyifa' after 'many disturbances' in his company. The number of certified Islamic healers (*perawat Islam*) and treated patients/places grew annually, as internal statistics illustrate. Darusysyifa' distinguishes *mudawi* (also *perawat*/'medical practitioner') and *musa'id* (also *pembantu perawat*/'assistant'). *Mudawi* undergo 90 hours of training.

Darusysyifa' categorises three treatment fields: 'Physical', 'spiritual/emotional' (*rohani/emosi*) and 'disturbances' (*gangguan*). "Disturbances" are caused by *jin* and/or sorcery, affect individuals or places/buildings and may result in possession (*kerasukan*) or 'hysteria' (*histeria*). They may also be manifested by poisoning, a classical *bomoh* tool. Sometimes, *jin* accompany people, while some consciously own and feed them, until 'in the end, the *jin* owns them' (interview with Darusysyifa' representatives, 11 October 2014). *Jin* ownership can also be hereditary. An indication of disturbances is difficulty in reciting Qur'anic verses that one normally knows. During exorcism, Muslim *jin* would often leave the body 'if they are told in Islamic terms, but not always!' Infidel *jin* (*jin kafir*) are considered even more challenging, but they can convert, which helps the exorcism. One should avoid speaking with them ('they lie the whole time'), but, if they wish to convert to Islam, they may require assistance.

Jin speaking through possessed patients happened 'twice each week' in 2014. More frequent disturbances are not manifested by alien voices. 'Often there is no clear identification of the cause: *jin*, *syaitan*, we don't want to know, what counts is successful healing!' In the Japanese manager's case, workers had seen legs flying and headless people ('like in the movies, it's the same!' a healer explained). Such scenes were 'very common'. Some solutions are immediate; some treatments take months.

When I visited the centre one evening in 2014, all ten treatment rooms were occupied. I witnessed a 'disturbance': Maryam's sister had tried to heal her 'by copying Darusysyifa' without knowing the right method, then a *jin* became involved', a healer explained. Black spots emerged on Maryam's skin, and she went to Darusysyifa'. A female healer exorcised Maryam, who made long buzzing noises before throwing up (the material outcome of which is normally disposed at a nearby river) when the *jin* assumingly left her body, a pattern the healer expected. I was told that because this is a dangerous moment, healers (and their families) must use protection. In its previous smaller building, spirits 'sometimes jumped from one person to the next'. Things improved after the clinic was enlarged, with partitions to provide enclosed treatment spaces.

After the exorcism, Maryam received a mixture of mashed herbal leaves and rice powder to shower with at home. Medicines can be purchased but are free for patients. In most other cabins, counselling took place for issues such as social/family problems (categorised as *rohani/emosi*), to be solved by Sharia-compliant rather than *bomoh* means. Many patients visited *bomoh* before they came, a healer stated. Common advice is to pray the *right prayers in the right way*, remember Allah and observe Islamic norms for social behaviour.

Darusysyifa' also exorcises state buildings, for example, the national hospital and an Arabic school for girls that had been closed following a 'mass-hysteria' in 2014. Some of this has been reported on by state-controlled media, where Darusysyifa' has a regular presence as a valued societal actor. Darusysyifa's first graduation ceremony in 2010 took place at a government building. In return, Darusysyifa' cleaned it. Disturbances had occurred, particularly after dawn: A solider 'heard somebody calling him, found somebody sitting at a table, asked why he had called him, suddenly the person was gone!' During the exorcism, 'a door opened and closed by itself, but not in the direction in which it would have been pushed by the wind, the other direction! Banners at the wall were shaking, a lamp stopped working'. After the exorcism, the 'disturbances' stopped (interview, 11 October 2014).

Controlling the invisible world (*dunia ghaib*) is sometimes a government affair, structurally and in specific cases. In 2010, for example, a 'mass hysteria' hit three schools during the examinations period. Even teachers and the school's cook were possessed, before Darusysyifa' and the Institut Tahfiz Al-Quran solved it. At one school, the 'hysteria' started when a 'student cried after seeing a spirit'. The press cited a teacher saying '[i]ronically, the spirit also made several demands. But the religious expert from Tahfiz Institute told us not to meet the demands as it was the voice of Satan'. The acting Minister of Education 'advised the school authorities to clean the restrooms, believed to be the favourite spot for the spirits and the school environment' (Borneo Bulletin 2010).

But Darusysyifa's engagement with state power goes beyond state-prescribed bureaucratic forms and cleaning jobs. When the first healers graduated, the Sultan himself launched a Darusysyifa' event at the Convention Centre. Prince Malik, the Sultan's son, became a Darusysyifa' patron. Princes Sufri and Jefri, the Sultan's brothers, also visited Darusysyifa' events. These visits expressed royal endorsement and provided the locally most powerful form of symbolic capital. Photographs in Darusysyifa' annual reports documented this legitimation of the highest order.

All Darusysyifa's graduation reports available to me share the following structure: A full-page portrait of His Majesty on the first page (in 2010 preceded by Qur'anic verses) and Prince Malik on the second. In 2013, the third page carried a text thanking Prince Malik and emphasising popular 'trust' in Darusysyifa', adding that 'the people' now turn away from *bomoh.*

In the 2010 report, a picture shows Haron Din standing next to the Sultan, the Crown Prince and Prince Malik, symbolising the foreign Islamic scholar's royal acceptance. A picture of the State Mufti on the same page symbolised the Islamic bureaucracy's equally crucial endorsement. In 2009 the Mufti, himself an author on Islamic healing, inaugurated the year's course with a speech. Some course events were held on the MoRA's premises, which underlines its blurring boundaries with the state's BoI. Darusysyifa' leaders I spoke with stressed their contribution to MIB and the Sultan's goal of Brunei as *Negara Zikir* ('a nation that always remembers *Allah*') under his Vision 2035.[3] Through such references to and cooperation with state power, Darusysyifa' performatively stages its conformity with the MIB State's normative expectations, expressed through powerful symbolic codes in a Brunei-specific cultural vocabulary. It is a *necessary condition* for its existence to co-produce the MIB State's classificatory power in society, yet its leaders also passionately believe in that project. But through the very act of establishing Darusysyifa', they not only reproduce state power but also inform some of its meanings in ways that were neither originally planned nor expected by the BoI's governmental architects, resulting from the creative agency of individuals who appropriate symbolic state power for their own purposes.

Unlike the earlier-cited MoRA officer, the Darusysyifa' interlocutors assumed that *bomohs* were 'always negative': 'for example, when they say a prayer, the last part is not correct, they always twist verses [through which evil powers become involved]'. Yes, 'white *bomoh*' and 'black *bomoh*' would exist, and some 'do not know they practise the wrong way', but 'in the end they are all the same, they use the powers of *syaitan* and *jin*'. Some certificate holders are ex-*bomoh*: 'Some admit it openly', but Darusysyifa' would not ask about 'earlier mistakes', following Haron Din's advice not to expose sins. They believed that the role of *bomoh* was declining due to Darusysyifa's work, state education and the MoRA's *dakwah*. As one representative stated enthusiastically, 'now there is an alternative!'

There is demand. A Bruneian told me how his father had practised traditional healing in the family before attending Darusysyifa's course to learn the 'proper' way. Just like former *bomoh*, people like him can purify and re-legitimise their work vis-à-vis hegemonic power/knowledge-structures, and simultaneously protect their souls.

However, MoRA's officers stated that 'not everything labeled Darusysyifa'' was unproblematic; for example, an arrested *bomoh* had falsely claimed holding a certificate. Even certified healers would 'not all practice the right way'. One had touched a woman, claiming a *jin* had possessed him. Another *bomoh* brought a real certificate to a *kaunseling* session. Some 'turn to the wrong direction again after a few years'. Darusysyifa' was not to be blamed, though, and the MoRA welcomes its work (interview with MoRA representatives, 8 October 2014). These transgressions indicate yet other modes of creating agency by (mis)appropriating state-approved symbolic codes; namely by (false) reference to Darusysyifa' and the authorising powers its certification system provides.

Darusysyifa' healers work voluntarily; their services are free. Patients 'can donate if they wish', 'as they like'. *Bomoh* and *orang pandai* typically use the same wording. Darusysyifa' is funded by donations but also sells products exposed to prayers (*dizikirkan*), such as herbs, coconut oil and honey. This, too, presents a paradox, uneven continuation of *bomoh* practices of praying into natural products such as water and oils, although Darusysyifa' views these as entirely different: one realises divine normativity through authentic verses, the other engages demonic forces, either through lacking education, or on purpose. Its best-selling item during my fieldwork was prayed-upon healing water, large boxes of which were stored at its premises.

Darusysyifa' representatives showed me a PowerPoint presentation visualising the powers of their healing water through microscopic photographs of water crystals. Darusysyifa' had sent frozen samples of different types to a Japanese water photographer, Masaru Emoto (1943–2014). Emoto was internationally renowned among esoteric circles for his water experiments. In academia, his work is widely dismissed as pseudo-scientific, to which he once responded it was merely art. For my interlocutors, it possessed academic character. This added yet another powerful vocabulary of legitimation inherent to the BoI: the quest for scientific evidence in the construction of facts, and its importance for convincing others.

Samples included average water, water exposed to '4444 prayers' (*selawat tafrijiyah*), water exposed to *zikir* prayers and *zam-zam* water from Mecca. Emoto assumes that water 'has a memory' that is acoustic and visual. Negative influences 'break the micro-crystals', but water also 'remembers' positive influences. Going beyond Emoto's interpretive frame, my interlocutors stated that water is a 'creation of Allah' (*makhluk Allah*). Going beyond more common orthodox Sunni discourse, but appropriating Emoto's ideas, they explained that water 'can hear' and 'has feelings'.

Emoto compared Darusysyifa's samples with others, including water exposed to heavy metal music. He was 'fascinated', they told me, and the pictures left little doubt: prayed-upon water exhibited the 'most beautiful' structures. Other samples had gradually fewer fine structures. The 'heavy metal'-exposed water was the 'worst', 'completely destroyed'. The crystals exposed to *zikir* prayers looked exceptional, but the *tafrijiyah*-exposed water (4444 prayers, including by Haron Din) went even beyond that: 'Emoto had never seen anything like that!' For Darusysyifa', Emoto's pictures and the PowerPoint presentation visualised the invisible and objectively proved the effectiveness of their prayers. The scientific character was also stressed at a Darusysyifa' symposium in 2013, which Emoto, Haron Din and the State Mufti attended in Brunei. Emoto presented a 'working paper' entitled 'The Science of Beautiful Water'. The written programme, which referred to him as 'Prof.' (he never held a university professorship)[4] described Emoto as a 'scientific expert' (*pakar saintis*) presenting 'scientific findings' (*hasil kajian saintifik*).

Pictures of water crystals decorated a wall inside Darusysyifa's building, next to pictures of herbs. The back cover of its 2013 graduation report also showed water crystals. These crystals, and the ideas attached to them, had become part of Darusysyifa's organisational culture, and of its culture of self-presentation towards outsiders.

Darusysyifa' sold *tafrijiyah* water for BND$0.70 per bottle ('some people now drink it every day'). It serves as a medicine, and for protection from harm or disturbances, which, in earlier days would have been done through talismans and/or related verses. To be effective, it should be used alongside particular prayers and firm belief. Outsiders may be puzzled by the fact that like Darusysyifa', *bomoh* always used water as a medium and prayed into it. From Darusysyifa's perspective, any equation, or claiming a continuity of 'structures of thought that . . . continue to provide an organizing framework' (Herzfeld 1992: 57), would be fundamentally misleading, with dangerous consequences.

Concluding remarks

As a social phenomenon, the BoI in Brunei is deeply structured by the MIB State's discursive substrate. Boundaries between state and society are *blurred* through educational means, and by non-state actors themselves who appropriate the state's powerful symbolic forms. Therefore, the BoI transcends its organisational boundaries and informs social and cultural transformations, as the state's bureaucratic schemes and symbols of power diffuse into society and become actively embedded in everyday life-worlds in a unique Brunei-specific way.

As the Darusysyifa case illustrates, such appropriations do not simply reproduce state power but also ascribe new meanings to it. The politics of orthodox purification become creatively re-embedded into pre-existing cultural vocabularies and the discursive arena of the nation-state, while simultaneously drawing upon transnational cultural flows from multiple sources. Some deviant-declared practices become reinvented within the MIB State's symbolic parameters, alongside the more universal languages of bureaucracy, cultural globalisation, nationalism, marketisation, 'scientisation' and 'statisticalisation', among other hybridised registers. This goes beyond what Herzfeld called 'the organic part played by symbols in creating the new order out of the old': the BoI, as social phenomenon, here also integrates a vertiginous mixture of other influences, such as Japanese water-crystal photography, the objectifying powers of PowerPoint, digital metaphors, future-oriented corporate governance and transnational trends in pedagogy, to name only a few. Such accommodative reconfigurations should not be surprising, as they reflect a wider global condition. What makes the Bruneian case special is how the MIB State, and state actors in an expanded sense, passionately seek to purify local culture, while the pathways towards realising this orthodoxy are hybrid and remarkably flexible. Such micro-level negotiations of state power and Sharia-framed normativity tell a different story from the meta-narratives of Islamisation that dominate portrayals of Brunei and often narrowly draw upon official policies, government declarations and legal provisions. In fact, the MIB State's 'firewall' of national-cultural protectionism is itself expressed through vocabularies of cultural globalisation and shaped by transnational forces that it cannot (entirely) control.

Bureaucratised thinking, speaking and planning, which accompanies translations of Islam into the language of bureaucracy, informs the quest for objectified evidence-making, as manifested in Darusysyifa's case and the MIB bureaucracy's statistical success rates, 'visions and missions' and five-year-plans, among other examples. The systematisation and reflection that Eickelman calls an 'objectification of Muslim consciousness' form a necessary condition. In objectified modes of being Muslim, earlier practices and social institutions, such as the *bomoh*, are systematically re-examined vis-à-vis their (un)Islamicness. Yet, subsequent 'abandonments' are themselves *culturally productive* and should be analysed as such, instead of reproducing their self-idealising logics by solely describing them in their own terms. The alternative would be what Bourdieu, Wacquant and Farage (1994: 1) calls 'the risk of taking over (or being taken over by) a thought of the state, i.e., of applying to the state categories of thought produced and guaranteed by the state'.

A possible 'conflict between domestic and foreign accounts of Brunei' (Brown 1988: 81) on such matters is unavoidable, but neither the Bruneian nor the external side should be essentialised. Bruneian perspectives on the MIB State's bureaucratisation of Islam (and by extension, the 'thought of the state' more broadly) are themselves diverse, albeit this is seldomly expressed publicly, let alone studied academically. Many Bruneians themselves personally hold much more nuanced and complex understandings of the social meanings that Islamisation policies in their country acquire, as opposed to what both domestic official and international media portrayals of Brunei would suggest – examining these diverse popular understandings remains a task hopefully taken up by social scientists in the future. As the first foreign anthropologist conducting long-term anthropological fieldwork in Brunei, Donald Brown's rich work compellingly demonstrated the necessity and benefits of *listening* to Bruneian voices and sources (oral and written), and to study and think through them in depth over long periods of time, before jumping to quick conclusions of any kind. It is precisely such listening, careful examining and epistemic exchange with Bruneian thinkers and decision-makers with whom he engaged that is missing from much of contemporary international knowledge-production about Brunei and its Islamisation policies.

Notes

* Research for this chapter was supported by the German Research Foundation's Emmy Noether Program, the Max Planck Institute for Social Anthropology and Harvard University's 'Islamic Legal Studies Program: Law and Social Change'. I would like to thank Michael Peletz and Lawrence Rosen for their comments. I am indebted to my interlocutors, and most grateful for the exceptional openness of the Ministry of Religious Affairs, the MIB Supreme Council's Secretariat, and Darusysyifa' Warrafahah, who helped me with my research, while tolerating that some of my 'outsider's' interpretations will inevitably differ from some of theirs. A different version of this chapter has been published by the *Journal of Current Southeast Asian Affairs*, 2018: 141–183. Most names are pseudonyms, and some circumstantial information has been changed to protect identities. I have slightly altered some of my interlocutors' wording for better readability.

1 Exceptions are possible where following the 'orthodox tenets' oppose 'public interest', and where His Majesty directs otherwise. Then, the 'less orthodox tenets' of Sunni Shafi'i Islam should be applied. If even those contradict public interest or the Sultan's orders, the Islamic Religious Council, headed by the Sultan, can refer to other Sunni legal schools (Religious Council and Kadis Courts Act 1984, henceforth RCKCA, Article 43).

2 The second phase is scheduled to begin 12 months after the Syariah Criminal Procedure Code has been gazetted. It was finalised in March 2018.

3 Darusysyifa' members narrated how the Sultan saw a possessed girl at a school in 2005, asking the *jin*: 'Why do you possess her? Get out of this girl!' He was successful,

'because he is the khailfah'. He has powers, not only over humans, over everything, over all makhluk (creations) in his country'. They added: Some loggers tell trees, themselves makhluk, creations of Allah; they have the Sultan's permission. This narration appears to reflect a long-standing popular perception, mentioned also by Brown (1988: 84), according to which the Sultans traditionally have 'magical powers', while the 'royal line' had long been 'credited with divine or semi-divine origin'.

4 Emoto held a PhD from a controversial distance-learning school in India.

References

Abdul Aziz Juned (1992) *Islam di Brunei*. Bandar Seri Begawan: Pusat Sejarah.

Abdul Aziz Juned (2017) *The King Who Shapes History: A Tribute in Conjunction with the Golden Jubilee of the King's Ascension to the Throne*. Bandar Seri Begawan: State Mufti's Office & Prime Minister's Office.

Abdul Latif Ibrahim (2003) *Issues in Brunei Studies*. Bandar Seri Begawan: Akademi Pengajian Brunei.

Amin Abdul Aziz (2015) *Governance in a Contemporary Islamic Negara*. Paper presented to the Inaugural Symposium on Islamic Governance: Functionality and Relevance in a Modern Negara, Institute of Policy Studies Universiti Brunei Darussalam, 21 November. Available at: www.islamic-governance.org/gal/pdf/governance-in-a-contemporary-islamic-negara.pdf.

Asiyah az-Zahra Ahmad Kumpoh (2011) Islamic Da'wah in Brunei: Past Developments, Challenges and Future Prospects. *Journal Darussalam* 11 (1): 38–60.

Borneo Bulletin (2010) Acting Minister Visits Schools, 18 May.

Bourdieu, Pierre (1991) The Production and Reproduction of Legitimate Language. In John B. Thompson (ed.), *Language and Symbolic Power*. Cambridge, MA: Harvard University Press, pp. 43–65.

Bourdieu, Pierre, Loic J. D. Wacquant and Samar Farage (1994) Rethinking the State: Genesis and Structure in the Bureaucratic Field. *Sociological Theory* 12 (1): 1–18.

Brown, Donald E. (1980) Hiranyagarbha: The Hindu Cosmic Egg – and Brunei's Royal Line. *The Brunei Museum Journal* 4 (4): 30–37.

Brown, Donald E. (1984) Brunei Through the Sha'er and the Silsilah. *Solidarity* 99: 10–15.

Brown, Donald E. (1988) *Hierarchy, History, and Human Nature: The Social Origins of Historical Consciousness*. Tucson: University of Arizona Press.

Brunei Times (2013) Brunei Raya Celebrations a Reflection of MIB Concept. *Brunei Times*, 26 August.

Chen, Nancy M. (1992) 'Speaking Nearby': A Conversation with Trinh T. Minh-ha. *Visual Anthropology Review* 8 (1): 82–91.

Dewan Majlis (2014) *Laporan Majlis Mesyuarat Negara*, 18 March.

Eickelman, Dale (2015) Transnational Religious Identities (Islam, Catholicism, Judaism): Cultural Concerns. In James Wright (ed.), *International Encyclopedia of the Social & Behavioral Sciences*. Oxford: Elsevier, pp. 602–606.

Hahn, Hans-Peter (2016) *Appropriation, Hybridisation, Bricolage: Improvisation as Aesthetic Practice*. Symposium 'Can the Universal Be Specific?', Heinrich-Böll-Stiftung, Berlin.

Herzfeld, Michael (1992) *The Social Production of Indifference: Exploring the Symbolic Roots of Western Bureaucracy*. New York: Berg.

Iik Arifin Mansurnoor (2002) Islam in Brunei Darussalam and Global Islam: An Analysis of Their Interaction. In Johan Meuleman (ed.), *Islam in the Era of Globalization: Muslim Attitudes towards Modernity and Identity*. London: Routledge, pp. 71–98.

Kementerian Hal Ehwal Ugama (n.d.) Pengenalan. Available at: www.kheu.gov.bn/Site Pages/Pengenalan.aspx (accessed 31 July 2019).

Kershaw, Roger (2001) Brunei Darussalam: Malay, Monarchical, Micro-State. In John Funston (ed.), *Government and Politics in Southeast Asia*. Singapore: ISEAS, pp. 1–35.

Mohd Taib Osman (1988) *Bunga Rampai: Aspects of Malay Culture*. Kuala Lumpur: Dewan Bahasa dan Pustaka.

Muhammad Hadi Muhammad Melayong (2016) Pelan Tindakan Strategik Pejabat Sekretariat Majlis Tertinggi Melayu Islam Beraja 2015–2020. *Pelita Brunei*, 9 August.

Müller, Dominik (2018) *The Bureaucratisation of Islam and Its Socio-Legal Dimensions in Southeast Asia*. Munich: Max Planck Institute for Social Anthropology Working Paper.

Norafan Zainal (2007) *Perkembangan Ajaran Sesat di Negara Brunei Darussalam*. Bandar Seri Begawan: Pusat Da'wah Islamiah.

Siti Norkhalbi Wahsalfelah (2005) Traditional Woven Textiles: Tradition and Identity Construction in the 'New State' of Brunei Darussalam. Unpublished PhD Thesis, University of Western Australia.

5 Inside or outside the mainstream? An ethnolinguistic study of the status of minority indigenous groups in Negara Brunei Darussalam

Noor Azam Haji-Othman and James McLellan

Introduction

This chapter begins by outlining what has been written by Donald Brown (1970: 3–10) about the status of minority ethnic groups 'of lesser significance' in Negara Brunei Darussalam. The initial focus is on the distinction between those designated in the 1959 Constitution as *puak jati* (indigenous groups), namely Brunei Malay, Kedayan, Tutong, Dusun, Bisaya, Belait and Lun Bawang, and those deemed non-indigenous, particularly the Iban and the Penan.

Following an analysis of how these groups and their languages have been described in official documents and in subsequent anthropological and sociolinguistic research studies, an analytical framework is developed: the languages of all these groups may be considered as dialects of Malay for political purposes, whilst linguistically they demonstrate varying degrees of difference and distinction from the core Brunei Malay, restyled 'Pan-Bruneian Malay' by Noor Azam (2012).

In our discussion we offer some evidence for a recent shift in the official position concerning ethnic groups other than the majority Brunei Malays: rather than promoting assimilation, there is now the acknowledgement of linguistic and cultural diversity, even though it is not actively celebrated.

Brunei society can be conceptualised and thus analysed using either a broader historical lens, or a narrower synchronic lens focusing only on Brunei within its present geopolitical boundaries. This can be summarised as 'big Brunei' and 'smaller Brunei'. King (1994, 2001) takes a broader, more inclusive 'big Brunei' view when defining 'Brunei society', seeing this as comprising not only the land-based Kedayan community (*Urang Darat*) but also other Borneo indigenous groups, including those who were part of the historical Brunei empire extending around Borneo and through parts of the Philippines.

Others, including Brown (1970: 4), view Brunei society in narrower terms ('smaller Brunei'), as comprising only the Brunei Malay ethnic group who are perceived to be the original inhabitants of Kampong Ayer, the Water Village. Even the *puak sakai* inhabitants of Kampong Saba in Kampong Ayer are considered to be of lower status (Brown 1970: 5). This may be because in the *Syair Awang Semaun*, a key document for the study of Brunei's early history, the *puak sakai* are said to have migrated to Borneo from the Minangkabau area of western Sumatra (Rajiee Hadi 2016).

The differing approaches to the issues of social stratification, hierarchies and ethnic labelling in north-western Borneo underscore this present enquiry into whether minority indigenous groups in Brunei should be considered as part of Brunei society, and in particular whether their languages should be viewed as part of Brunei's linguistic ecology.

Consequently, there are choices that we have to make in the geographical coverage in this chapter: whether to cover the formerly extensive thalassic empire extending around most of Borneo and into parts of the southern Philippines, or to remain within the current (disputed and divided) political boundaries of post-1984 Negara Brunei Darussalam. A historically valid account would require close analysis of the complex relations between the Brunei sultanate, other polities in and beyond Borneo, and interior groups such as the Kayan (Rousseau 1990: 298–299). For reasons of space, we choose to restrict our coverage to within the boundaries of present-day Brunei. Whilst historical investigations are a necessary element in any discussion of such a topic, our main focus is synchronic and contemporary. In line with our academic background and training, our approach is socio-linguistic rather than anthropological or political.

As Brown (1970: x) states in his foreword, 'Ethnic classification in northwest Borneo presents thorny problems for the investigator'. Using linguistic evidence (Nothofer 1991), the Kampong Ayer Malay dialect and Kedayan are sufficiently close in terms of their high percentage (94%; see Table 5.1) of shared cognates to be considered as varieties of Brunei Malay, whilst Tutong, Dusun, Bisaya, Belait and Lun Bawang (Murut) are distinct languages.

Brown refers to a decline in the number of 'ethnic groups of lesser significance' (1970: 4), both those recognised in the 1959 Constitution of the State of Brunei as *puak jati*, and others, including Iban, Penan and Melanau, who are Borneo-indigenous but not Brunei-indigenous. This he principally attributes to the continuing process of *masuk Melayu* (becoming Malay), whereby the Brunei Malay community expands through intermarriage with those of other ethnic origins and through conversion to the Islamic faith. With reference to St. John (1862, II: 268), Brown suggests that the Kedayan, like the *puak sakai*, are descended from the Murut, and he points out that both groups can hold only the lowest level of offices (*menteri darat*) in the Brunei stratified hierarchy (1970: 5).

We next review Brunei demography from government Annual Reports from 1906 onwards, highlighting changes in the nomenclature of ethnolinguistic groups, and from more recent sociolinguistic studies that focus mainly on language maintenance and shift among the minority ethnic groups of Brunei. This raises the question of whether the languages of all the *puak jati* are perceived as dialects of Malay, or as distinct and separate languages.

Official census data from 1906 onwards

Noor Azam (2005) argues that ethnic identity and nomenclature have been a long-standing problem in the anthropological literature on Borneo, and identifies the same issues in his study of indigenous groups in Brunei. Brown (1970: 3) cites Harrisson's observation that 'the identification and classification of Bornean ethnic groups is "a problem that plagues the social scientist and the census taker for a number of reasons"', one of which Brown describes as 'the contrasts between what people called themselves and what others called them'. The significance of ethnic identification in the study of language in Brunei is that the names of ethnic communities are also used as the names of their languages, which can be problematic at times. To put this into context, the Nationality Act of Brunei 1961 and its definition of the Malay race is quoted here:

> Subject of His Majesty by operation of law 4. (1) (a) any person born in Brunei Darussalam before, on or after the appointed day who is commonly accepted as belonging to one of the following indigenous groups of the Malay race, namely, Belait, Bisayah, Brunei, Dusun, Kedayan, Murut or Tutong.
>
> (Government of Brunei 1961)

This document has since been adopted as the hard-and-fast rule of citizenship in determining ethnic affiliation of Brunei citizens. The first proper records of ethnic classification, however, can be found in the Brunei Annual Reports (BAR) beginning in 1906:

Est. Population	25,000:
Malays	12,000
Kadayans	7,000
Bisayas	4,000
Muruts	1,000
Chinese	1,000
Other Nat.	500

(Government of Brunei 1906)

Note that 'Malays' in this earliest report refers to a distinct group, the Brunei Malays. Note also that in the 1906 BAR there is no inclusion of the Tutong and Dusun population, although there is mention of the Bisayas who 'are chiefly found on the headwaters of the Tutong and Belait Districts' (Government of Brunei 1906:19).

This highlights the problems with nomenclature and population statistics: Does 'Bisayas' include the Dusun, as well as the Tutong for that matter? The figure of 4,000 does seem unrealistically high in relation to the total population at that time, and does not match current proportions in the population chart. In 1910 the BAR did not supply a population figure, although the Tutong and Dusun are now recognised as separate communities.

The Population Census in Brunei taken on 24 April 1921 reported that the total population was 25,454. The 1921 BAR explained that:

> Malays and Bornean Races comprised 23,938. The constituent races of the 'Malay' population were approximately as follows:
>
> | | |
> |---|---|
> | Malays | 13,784 |
> | Kedayans | 4,641 |
> | Tutongs | 2,391 |
> | Dusuns | 1,115 |
> | Bukits | 580 |
> | Muruts | 556 |
> | Belaits | 449 |
> | Dyaks | 235 |
> | Javanese | 150 |
> | Banjarese | 38 |
> | Others | 54 |
>
> (Government of Brunei 1921)

While the term 'Malay' is still used here to refer specifically to the Brunei Malays, the other groups that were recognised as *jati* (indigenous) in the 1959 Constitution, are all listed, although in the 1921 document the Bisayas are referred to as the 'Bukits', an obvious reference to their traditional habitation (*bukit* meaning 'hill'). However, it was only in 1941 that the report began to use the term 'Bruneis' to specify the 'Malays':

> the principal indigenous races of the state are Bruneis (as the Malays proper are called), Kedayans, Tutongs, Dusuns, Murats [*sic*] and Dayaks.
>
> (Government of Brunei 1941)

Six years later, in 1947, after World War II and the occupation of Brunei by the Japanese, the term 'Brunei Malays' began to appear:

> the principal indigenous races of the State are Brunei Malays, Kedayans, Tutongs, Dusuns, Belaits, Murats, and Dyaks.
>
> (Government of Brunei 1947)

The 'Dyaks' (also spelt 'Dayaks') were later excluded from the definitive *puak jati* (indigenous ethnic group) list in the Brunei Constitution of 1959, while the Bisayas, who since the 1906 report had rather curiously been consistently left unmentioned, were now suddenly included in the 1959 document. This is the legal and constitutional definition of the 'Malay race' that remains in use today.

In Section 1 (Area, Population and Vital Statistics) of the preliminary findings report of the 2001 Census, the following footnote appears:

> (2) In 1971, 1981 and 1991 the definition of 'Malay' was changed to [the] indigenous population of the Malay race which consisted of 'Malay, Dusun, Murut, Kedayan and Bisaya' and the last four of which were included in the Other Indigenous in previous censuses.
>
> (Government of Brunei 2003)

In the preceding excerpt, the Belaits and Tutongs seem to have been either absorbed into the Malay group or (mistakenly?) omitted. However, if indeed the Belaits and Tutongs were included in the Malay group (perhaps on religious grounds), the 2003 document does not offer any explanation why the Kedayans (who are Muslims too, if religion was the basis of Malay definition in this particular document) are listed separately.

This attempt to clarify the definition of 'Malay', in addition to the examination of the Brunei Annual Report figures, demonstrates the complexities of group labelling and nomenclature. The 2001 census document also does not break down the population figure for 'Malays' into different constituent ethnic groups, or at least the breakdown is not made public, suggesting a de-emphasising of ethnic differences among the population.

In 2011, the Brunei population was reported to be 393,162 in total (Department of Economic planning and Development 2012). The next population census will be conducted in 2021 (once every 10 years) but for now, the 2017 updated figures put the total population at 421,300, with the breakdown as follows: Malays (277,300 or 65.8%), Chinese (43,100 or 10.2%) and Others (100,900 or 23.9%) (Department of Economic Planning and Development 2018).

It is evident that the government is continuing not to publish ethnic population statistics for the indigenous groups, except under the label 'Malays', although a note is provided as follows: 'Malays refer to Brunei Malays, comprising [*sic*] persons belonging to one of the following ethnic groups of the Malay race, namely Brunei, Tutong, Belait, Kedayan, Dusun, Bisaya and Murut.'

Alongside these changes in census labels, identity shift in Brunei was observed by earlier researchers. Leach discusses the problems of classification of Borneo ethnic populations because they have 'become Malay' (1950). A similar observation has also been made by Brown that very clearly describes the shifting identities in Brunei:

> With the changes brought about in this century, such as improvements in communication, travel and education, Westernization, the growth of political parties and so on, the number of ethnic groups appears to have declined. Two processes seem to have been at work: the recognition of socio-cultural affinities previously obscured by classifications based on locality, and the merging of lesser ethnic groups with the greater . . . In Brunei we can clearly see a process whereby ethnic groups of lesser significance decrease in numbers through the movement of their members to classification as Malays.
>
> (Brown 1970: 4)

> It is socially advantageous to identify with Brunei Malays, and there is a considerable 'passing' of indigenes into this category – at least so far as census data is a reliable guide.
>
> (Brown 1970: 9)

The factors that Brown identifies as the causes of shifts in identity are essentially similar to the ones that influence language shift. In addition to Brown's study, Maxwell discusses the shifts in semantic classification of indigenous Brunei ethnic groups (1980: 189–197). Maxwell's later study on Malay polysemy and political power unpacks five polysemous senses of Malayu/Malay in the Brunei context in a hyponymic tabulation (Maxwell 2001). Studies on identity in Brunei, such as those of Braighlinn (1992: 20), Gunn (1997) and R. Kershaw (1984, 2001: 124), have suggested that identity shifts occur more as a result of deliberate political pressures or even inventions to create a national identity, towards which the indigenous populations are shifting. Noor Azam's study investigated this and found no evidence to support or refute this contention, but he did find a close link between the emergence of a 'pan-Bruneian' identity that parallels the emergence of a 'pan-Brunei Malay' language variety (2005).

The importance of accurate identification and categorisation of the ethnic populations with the emergence of the modern state of Brunei, and the perceived need for a unified national identity in which minority ethnic groups may be downplayed and marginalised, are evident from this brief outline of Brunei Annual Reports and population census data.

Standard Malay or Bahasa Melayu?

This section distinguishes between two definitions of Brunei Malay:

- the first language or mother-tongue of the Brunei Malay community, and
- the contemporary lingua franca and principal default language of oral interaction among Bruneians of all ethnic backgrounds, termed 'Pan-Bruneian Malay' by Noor Azam (2007).

Both of these can be distinguished from the so-called Standard Malay, or Bahasa Melayu, which is the designated official language of Negara Brunei Darussalam according to the 1959 Constitution. We discuss language shift towards both Standard Malay and Brunei Malay by the minority groups.

According to Nothofer (1991), the Austronesian languages and dialects spoken in Brunei are Belait, Bisaya, Dusun, Brunei Malay, Kedayan, Murut, Tutong, Mukah, Iban and Penan. The standard form of Malay in Brunei is referred to as 'Standard Malay'. 'Bahasa Melayu' is used as a superordinate term to refer to the Malay language in its various forms, including Standard Malay, the vernacular Brunei Malay and Kampong Ayer Malay.

Nothofer (1991) argues that some indigenous languages of Brunei had been inaccurately labelled as dialects of 'Malay' when they were clearly different

Table 5.1 Cognates for languages and dialects of Brunei

	Ked.	Br.M	K.A	Iban	Tutong	Belait	Dusun	Bisaya	Penan	Murut	Mukah
St.M	80	84	82	65	33	29	40	38	29	24	35
Ked.	–	94	95	64	37	28	43	45	27	26	38
Br.M	–	–	94	64	37	28	41	43	26	25	36
K.A	–	–	–	65	39	30	42	43	26	24	35
Iban	–	–	–	–	34	24	38	36	27	28	34
Tutong	–	–	–	–	–	54	40	42	34	33	32
Belait	–	–	–	–	–	–	35	36	34	33	32
Dusun	–	–	–	–	–	–	–	82	31	29	33
Bisaya	–	–	–	–	–	–	–	–	31	30	33
Penan	–	–	–	–	–	–	–	–	–	30	37
Murut	–	–	–	–	–	–	–	–	–	–	30

Source: Adapted from Nothofer (1991: 158).

Key:

St.M	Standard Malay
Br.M	Brunei Malay
K.A.	Kampong Ayer
Ked.	Kedayan
	Dialects of the Malay language
	Dialect of the Dusun language

Note: Numbers are expressed in percentages. Shaded areas represent dialects of the same language rather than different languages if the only criterion for making the distinction is percentage of shared cognates. The cut-off point is 80% (adapted from Martin and Poedjosoedarmo 1996: 7).

languages. Noor Azam (2005: 19) suggests that this confusion can be traced to the inclusion under the constitutional label 'Malay' of two traditionally Malay-speaking groups, Bruneis and Kedayans, and five traditionally non-Malay-speaking ethnic groups: Belaits, Bisayas, Dusuns, Muruts and Tutongs. To this day, however, it is still generally assumed by Brunei government agencies such as the Dewan Bahasa dan Pustaka (2011) that the ethnic languages that these groups traditionally speak are indeed dialects of Malay, although in strict linguistic terms the latter groups are all less than 40% cognate with Bahasa Melayu (Nothofer 1991: 158). According to Nothofer's study, a cognate percentage of 80% is the determinant between a language and a dialect in Brunei.

Nothofer points out that the principal dialects of the Malay language in Brunei include only Brunei Malay, Kampong Ayer, Kedayan and Standard Malay, excluding the other five indigenous codes. Standard Malay is the standard supra-regional code, more similar to Standard Malaysian Malay in form and sound, that is used in formal situations such as in schools, public speeches or media broadcasts, and writing. The indigenous and mainly spoken Brunei Malay, Kampong Ayer and Kedayan are used in informal domains of daily communication (Poedjosoedarmo 1996).

Language shift in Brunei

Language shift is defined as a gradual or sudden move away from one language to another. This shift to a different code altogether whilst abandoning their own native language has been observed in Brunei by informants in Noor Azam's study (2005). Many of the informants can be considered as the final generation of speakers of their language ('terminal heirs', E. M. Kershaw 1994: 187). But just as many of Noor Azam's informants also expressed regret and concern over the loss of their ethnic languages (2005) – a sense of remorse that can be attributed to Martin's finding that Brunei's indigenous languages can both be a source of stigma and pride (1992b). Paradoxically, despite the gloomy outlook for ethnic languages in general, or perhaps even because of it, Noor Azam has also reported that acceptance and awareness of different ethnic languages among the general public have increased in recent years (2005). This highlights the impact of linguistic research that UBD has had on public awareness (and appreciation) of ethnic languages in changing their attitudes toward them, and reducing the stigma associated with them. The fact that more and more speakers of ethnic languages are now moving away from their native tongues and adopting Brunei Malay implies that the use of individual ethnic languages is diminishing, hence suggesting a diminishing linguistic diversity.

This reduction in linguistic diversity can be linked to two concurrent processes of language shift which can be discerned from Noor Azam's informants' observations: A shift from non-Malay ethnic languages to Malay; and a shift from Kedayan and Kampong Ayer (alias Balandih) to Brunei Malay at the dialectal level (2005). In fact, there is evidence to suggest a movement of all the ethnolinguistic groups towards a 'pan-Brunei Malay', and this is presented in the next two sections. The following discussions will show that as much as there is a shift from ethnic languages to (Brunei) Malay, there is also a shift from dialects of Malay to Brunei Malay. The latter is discussed first.

Shift at dialectal level

A number of ethnic Brunei Malay informants have reported differences between the Malay that they speak and the code spoken by the younger generation of Bruneis, suggesting a dialect-to-dialect convergence. Further observations have been made which highlight the influence of the standard variety, which is the variety taught in the schools and used in most formal settings, as well as in the traditional and new (social) media (from Brunei, Malaysia, Singapore and Indonesia). The shift is characterised by the substitution of phonetic, prosodic and lexical features of Kampong Ayer Malay with those of the more 'modern-sounding' variety of Malay, some examples of which are as follows:

1 Phonetic changes

'karang'	(lit. 'later')	/kʌjʌŋ/	→	/kʌrʌŋ/
'karita'	(lit. 'car')	/kʌrɪtʌ/	→	/kərɪtʌ/
'maliat'	(lit. 'to see')	/mʌlɪʌt/	→	/məlɪʌt/

2 Lexical changes

'salt' (n.)	'sira'	→	'garam'
'dog' (n.)	'kuyuk'	→	'anjing'
'foot' (n.)	'batis'	→	'kaki'
'(to) call' (v.)	'lagau'	→	'panggil'

Similar findings have been reported by Sumijah Alias and Poedjosoedarmo, who additionally comment on the prosodic changes they analysed using the SIL Speech Analysis System and the CECIL computer programme:

> Balandih (Kampung Ayer Malay) speed of delivery was slower than Brunei Malay . . . the pitch for the Balandih sentence was higher than for the Brunei Malay sentence . . . With regard to stress, Balandih exhibited greater differentiation between stressed and unstressed syllables in terms of both length and loudness than occurred in Brunei Malay (1996: 108).

Sumijah Alias and Poedjosoedarmo also found that

> those 30 years old and under tended to speak Brunei Malay exclusively while those in the 31 to 55 age range tended to codeswitch between Brunei Malay and Balandih as indicated by their choice of lexical items (1996: 112).

In addition, a number of informants in the present study reported that typical Kedayan characteristics such as the r-dropping and the lengthening of the preceding vowel in some cases have now also been replaced with realisations of the phoneme /r/, and shortening or change of vowel. For instance:

3

'mosquitoes' (n.)	'(r)angit'	/ʌngɪt/	→	/rʌŋɪt/
'clear' (adj.)	'ta(r)ang'	/ta:ŋ/	→	/tʌrʌŋ/
'running' (v.)	'balusi(r)'	/bʌlusi:/	→	/bəlusɪr/

In relation to this, one of the outcomes of language contact was identified by Rosenberg as language convergence at dialect-to-dialect level (2001). It can be argued, therefore, that the Malay dialects of Kampong Ayer and Kedayan are possibly converging toward Brunei Malay. Brunei Malay now is seen as a 'Pan-Bruneian' language that every Bruneian irrespective of ethnic background could claim to be their own, but distinct from Standard Malay. Whereas ownership of the Kampong Ayer dialect, commonly identified by laypersons as 'the real Brunei Malay', could only be claimed by and identified with the Brunei Malays, just as the Kedayan variety can only be claimed by the Kedayan people.

Shift at language level

Previous researchers have suggested that shift has occurred in the form of adult speakers of indigenous languages abandoning their language and adopting the Malay language instead. According to Noor Azam, an increasing percentage of the younger generation of the ethnic communities have been brought up in Brunei Malay since birth (2005).

The younger generation is seen as the final line of defence of their ethnic language, yet at the same time they are the ones who are abandoning it. But through mixed marriages and intergenerational language transfer, the older generation too plays a critical role in language shift processes. Shifts from Brunei ethnic languages to Malay have been well documented by Martin (1992a, 1992b, 1995) and by E. M. Kershaw (1994). It may be argued that, based on observations on intergenerational language transfer, and supported by the findings of Martin and Kershaw, adults who transmit ethnic languages to their children and younger siblings are becoming fewer in number, influenced by the unfavourable conditions for minority language maintenance discussed in the preceding sections. Malay, on the other hand, has derived its strength and high status from the greater number of speakers it has, both locally and internationally. With no institutional support for ethnic languages provided by the government or created by the ethnic groups themselves, and negative attitudes toward them, the odds are stacked against ethnic languages. Noor Azam argues that sympathetic attitudes and calls for support, however, never materialise into concrete action (2005). Intra-group support, such as the ethnic family unit, has been shown to be weakening, suggesting an indifferent attitude to ethnic language loss, and a sense of impotence on the part of ethnic language speakers.

A 'national language', according to Noor Azam, although never officially proclaimed, in fact exists in the form of Brunei Malay, which, so informants say, best expresses 'Bruneianness' – Brunei Malay being thc language that everyone who claims to be Bruneian shares (2005: 236). The ethnic languages, on the other hand, express individual ethnic identities, but many younger Bruneians cannot speak their parents' traditional languages. Noor Azam found that there is an ongoing shift in language among Bruneians, particularly among the minority ethnic population, and that while there is much verbal support for these ethnic languages and for linguistic diversity in Brunei, institutional support for ethnic languages is lacking (2005: 267). As discussed here, there are already signs among the Malay-speaking communities, the Brunei Malays and the Kedayans, that their languages are moving away from their traditional characteristics. But at the same time, so are the languages of the non-Malay-speaking communities.

Figure 5.1 depicts the two processes of language shift occurring at the same time: dialect shift and language shift. The most significant outcome of the ongoing language shift processes is the convergence toward a Malay variety that is used throughout the country. The term 'Pan-Brunei Malay' was suggested by Noor Azam to highlight its 'supra-ethnic' qualities in terms of its dissociation from any particular ethnic group, including the Brunei Malays (2005: 264). 'Pan-Brunei Malay' refers to the form of Malay that most Bruneian youths now are making their own and which they speak as their first language all over the country. It may be described as a variant of Brunei Malay that contains elements of Standard Malay (adopted through exposure via the education system and the media), and perhaps even elements of English (obtained through their facility in English as an additional language through the Dwibahasa (bilingual) education policy and the media), with minor variations in terms of lexis depending on the speakers' location.

This finding supports those of a study that deals specifically with language convergence in Brunei, by E. M. Kershaw (1994), in which she critically analyses the process of language convergence using concrete linguistic evidence of language change in the Dusun language. This finding also appears to be consistent with Sercombe's observation of an apparent general levelling process in the coastal areas,

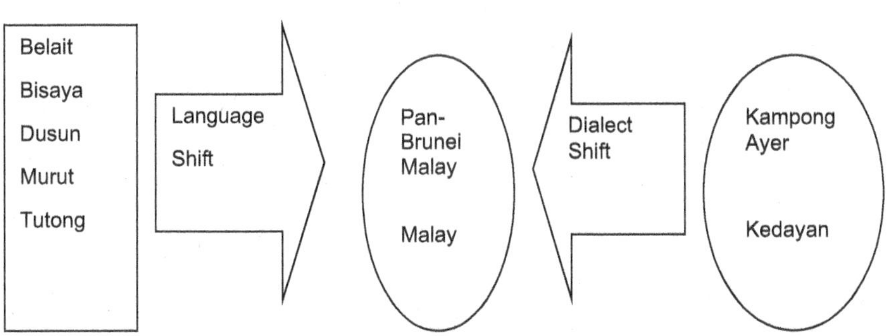

Figure 5.1 Language and dialect shift in Brunei

mostly toward Malay, in his review of the literature on language shift and maintenance in Borneo (2002). The implication in terms of indigenous languages is that the younger Bruneians, regardless of their ethnicity, are becoming monolingual speakers of Brunei Malay, hence suggesting a reduction of linguistic diversity. In fact, Noor Azam's study has reported that some ethnic language speakers have abandoned their languages altogether and that the younger generations of all of these communities, it seems, are being brought up speaking Malay as a first language (2005). The maintenance of these languages, it seems, is not an important priority.

What emerges from these discussions is a linguistic hierarchy in which the Malay language supersedes the other ethnic languages in Brunei. This ranking is attributed to various factors such as positive and negative images of languages, the available number of speakers, and the support the language receives. All of the languages have significant symbolic value in expressing ethnic identity, but because of negative stereotypical notions associated with ethnic languages, their status is perceived to be low. On the other hand, Malay enjoys association with the elite and powerful. Malay is also seen to have wider national and international currency than the ethnic languages, perpetuated by its academic value, and its historical value as a regional lingua franca. Noor Azam reports that the working policies of government institutions too do not generally reflect the diverse linguistic make-up of Brunei, nor do they see the need for it (2005). Based on all these factors, Noor Azam and Siti Ajeerah (2016) updated Martin's (1995) assessment of the effect of the culmination of all the factors described and each of the languages' vitality rating.

Martin's vitality rating takes into account the inter-generational rate of transmission of each language/dialect, the media and institutional support the language enjoys, and the geographical concentration of speakers, although Martin admits that these ratings are impressionistic. These vitality rates remained the same when compared with ratings given by Coluzzi (2010), Sercombe (1997) and Rabinah (1994). A more realistic and current EV rating of these languages is presented in Table 5.2 in the prediction column based on Noor Azam and Siti Ajeerah's reassessment of all the factors (2016).

Table 5.2 Ethnolinguistic vitality rating of languages of Brunei (on a scale of 0–6: higher figures indicate greater vitality)

Language/ Dialect	*Martin (1995) EV Rating*	*Noor Azam and Siti Ajeerah (2016)*
Brunei Malay	6.0	6.0
Kedayan	3.0	2.0
Tutong	2.5	2.5
Belait	0.5	0.1
Dusun	2.0	2.0
Bisaya	3.0	1.0
Murut	3.5	2.0

Source: Adapted from Martin (1995); updated by Noor Azam and Siti Ajeerah (2016).

Institutional support for minority languages

The third type of ethnolinguistic vitality variable referred to by Martin (1995), Noor Azam (2005) and Noor Azam and Siti Ajeerah (2016), is the institutional support variable. This is the formal or informal representation that a language receives in various institutions in the community. It is clear that the Malay language, as befits its official language status, receives institutional support from both government and non-government agencies. In this section, the working policies of the education system at different levels, the Language and Literature Bureau (LLB) and the media with regard to Malay and ethnic languages are outlined.

Language and the education system

There is no doubt that in Brunei, the most important and most effective government agent in upholding the official language status of Malay is the Ministry of Education through the school system. In a written response to interview questions, the Director of the Department of Curriculum Development (DCD) states that the National Education Policy of Brunei prioritises the Malay language as the official language over the ethnic languages as one of the media of instruction. Noor Azam reports that in a statement issued by the Director of DCD it becomes clear that the MOE perceives the ethnic languages of Brunei as 'dialects' of the Malay language (2005):

> **[Director of curriculum development, MOE]**
>
> This is evident in the interpretation of the Malay race as outlined in the Brunei Constitution (1959), which states that all ethnicities that are Belait, Bisaya, Brunei, Dusun, Kedayan, Murut and Tutong are categorised [in their use of the] Malay language.
>
> (Trans.)

This contention is, of course, linguistically inaccurate according to Nothofer (1991), as noted earlier. Although it is understood that Brunei Malay and Kedayan are Malay language variants, there is in fact nothing in the Constitution that states that the ethnic languages are Malay dialects. This is a clear illustration of the confusion resulting from the inclusion in the Constitutional label 'Malay' of two Malay-speaking groups, Bruneis and Kedayans, and five non-Malay-speaking ethnic groups: Belaits, Bisayas, Dusuns, Muruts and Tutongs. Yet, politically, it serves the purposes of the educational authorities to refer to the ethnic languages as Malay dialects. The crux of the statement on the teaching of 'dialects', because they have been so categorised, is very clear: 'dialects do not need to be taught as they do not have the status of a language' (Noor Azam 2005). The dialect status therefore nullifies a code's worthiness to be taught in the Bruneian classroom, translating it into a subordinate position in the hierarchy of languages. This situation is by no means unique to Brunei, but it highlights the lack of attention to ethnic languages within the education system.

This policy is translated into the national curriculum in which Malay is a compulsory core language subject for which a credit (Grade C6) is a prerequisite for transition from secondary- to tertiary-level education. The following reasons have been offered for the exclusion of the indigenous languages of Brunei from the curriculum:

> **[Director of curriculum development, MOE]**
>
> The other languages in this country are not taught in schools because:
>
> i) Those languages cannot perform the formal and official function as a language of education, compared to Malay and English which have a complete corpus in terms of lexis, phonology, morphology and syntax.
> ii) The area of spread of these languages are [is] limited and do[es] not transcend the speakers' geographical boundaries. They are spoken in informal situations. Malay is used as a main regional language in MABBIM* member countries. English on the other hand is an international language.
> iii) The number of speakers of those languages is small and limited to each ethnic group. In the ASEAN region, Malay is spoken by roughly 250 million people while English is used by the global population.
>
> (Trans.)
>
> * "Majlis Bahasa Brunei Indonesia Malaysia", Language Council of Brunei-Indonesia-Malaysia

Implied in the first point is that the absence of a proper writing system for the ethnic languages, as suggested in the earlier discussion of language status, has made these languages virtually impossible to teach. However, even if these languages were codified and standardised, it is highly doubtful that they would ever be taught in the schools given the marginal status they are ascribed. The second and third points in the official statement also confirm the contention of the widespread usage of Malay and the relatively limited number of ethnic language speakers.

The implications of the National Education Policy on linguistic diversity are significant. When asked whether the education system reflects Brunei's wealth of indigenous languages, the Director of Curriculum Development admits that it does not:

> **[Director of Curriculum Development, MOE]**
>
> The working policy of the Department of Curriculum Development and the Ministry of Education in general . . . neither reflects the multiethnicity nor the multilinguality of the population.
>
> (Trans.)

Seen in relation to the discussion of the academic value of ethnic languages, it may be inferred from this extract that there is no perceived need for linguistic diversity to be reflected in the education system.

Another form of institutional support is from the ethnic communities themselves. When asked if ethnic languages should be taught or included in the schools, the response from the sample, who had appeared supportive of linguistic diversity and fiercely proud of ethnic languages, was very surprising; a majority of the informants in Noor Azam's (2005) study was in fact opposed to the idea. Some informants, while averse to formal teaching, were more agreeable to voluntary learning of the languages or for it to be done as optional extra-curricular activity in the schools, as opposed to their being made compulsory and examinable subjects.

While some of the minority ethnic languages may not currently be fully developed orthographically, it would not take much to develop them. What seems to be missing is the will to develop them. In this respect, why this has not yet been done may have little to do with practical considerations and could be linked to the earlier suggestion of implicit policies.

It may be concluded from the evidence presented here that, at least in one respect, some congruence may be found between what the sample thinks and what the official language education policy purports, that these 'dialects' have low academic significance and hence need not be taught in schools. The grounds on which the informants and the officials base their judgements are different, however. The informants perceive the low academic value of ethnic languages based on a pragmatic response to their uncodified quality, as well as their perceived low social status. On the other hand, it suits the authorities to consider ethnic languages as 'dialects' of Malay, which therefore does not warrant them a place in the national curriculum.

The Language and Literature Bureau (LLB)

The Language and Literature Bureau (LLB), a government agency under the Information Department (Prime Minister's Office) is directly involved in linguistic matters and acts as the State's regulator of the use of Malay language in publications. The LLB itself is responsible for various publications, including academic studies in languages, although its priority lies in the Malay language. The original aim of the creation of the LLB was to develop the Malay language. This suggests that the LLB cannot be accused of neglect of the ethnic languages because they were not the responsibility of the LLB in the first place. Nevertheless, the LLB published a Tutong-Malay dictionary in 1991 and other academic works relating to ethnic languages in Brunei. The LLB also works very closely with academics at Universiti Brunei Darussalam (UBD) in producing and publishing such research. It is one of the aims of the university to conduct research, including linguistic research. But research into minority ethnic languages remains much smaller in proportion to the work on and publications in the Malay language by the LLB or by UBD. Ethnic languages do not receive the same level of institutional or official backing as Malay.

National university: UBD language centre's Borneo languages programme

In 2012, the Language Centre of Universiti Brunei Darussalam became the first educational institution in Brunei to offer formal classes in Tutong, Dusun and Iban languages (Noor Azam 2014). As of November 2018, only Dusun is taught (by a permanently appointed lecturer), whilst Tutong and Iban modules, which were offered, are now in abeyance because there are no suitably qualified staff available to teach these languages. But, according to Muhammad Najib and McLellan (2018: 228), the students taking the Dusun modules have expressed positive reactions, even though the majority of them are of Brunei Malay rather than Dusun ethnicity. A Brunei Malay student who took one Dusun module explained his motivation for choosing to study Dusun:

> *Ya, kerana tidak semua orang tahu akan berbahasa Dusun dan kita mestilah bangga kerana kita tahu berbahasa Dusun yang merupakan salah satu puak yang berada di Brunei.*
>
> (Yes, because not everyone knows how to speak the Dusun language, and we ought to be proud because we know how to speak Dusun as one of the indigenous languages in Brunei.)
>
> (Muhammad Najib and McLellan 2018: 226)

Broadcast media: Radio Televisyen Brunei

One government body which indirectly deals with languages is Radio Televisyen Brunei (RTB), which is also under the Department of Information, Prime Minister's Office. RTB plays an essential role in the spread of the Malay language through its TV and radio broadcasts, conveying official information and news using Bahasa Melayu primarily. Prior to the arrival of satellite TV transmitted from overseas, RTB was the only broadcaster in Brunei (apart from Malaysia's RTM, which Bruneians could receive as well). Despite the strong competition from satellite TV, RTB remains the main source of local news and official information. The official guideline for RTB transmission issued by the Prime Minister's Office outlines the following regulation as regards language use in broadcasting:

> **[RTB broadcasting guideline 1998]**
>
> ***15. Language***
>
> a) The language to be used in news programmes, current affairs and local documentaries is the official Standard Malay or English (whichever is appropriate).
> b) With the exemption of specific programmes aimed at elevating Brunei Darussalam's culture and traditions, interviewers, hosts, and others, should peruse Standard Malay or the English language (whichever is appropriate) even if the interviewee speaks in Brunei Malay.
>
> (Trans.)

There is no mention of ethnic languages in the document.

Most of RTB's programmes are in Malay, either produced locally or imported from neighbouring Malay-speaking countries. A popular programme that began in the late 1990s that invited a representative from each ethnic community to a forum that discussed cultural matters such as customs, beliefs and language in general broadcast, on both radio and television, continues to be produced and broadcast on radio on a weekly basis, *Bahasa Mengenali Bangsa* (Language Identifies Race/Ethnicity). The discussion in this programme was conducted mainly in Brunei Malay, interspersed with the other languages and dialects. A popular comedy series, *Darah Kedayan* (Kedayan Blood) was fully in Kedayan. In the early 1980s RTB also broadcasted the news fully in the Dusun language on Radio Brunei, but this was short-lived. According to the Director of RTB (2003), the Dusun news broadcast ceased following a clear directive from the Prime Minister's Office. Although the Director did not provide any reason for the halting of the Dusun news production, he did mention the administrative consideration of 'cost-effectiveness' of Dusun programmes in relation to number of users. Understandably with a small and fragmented market to cater for, productions in minority ethnic languages, for which expertise is not readily available, would be an uphill struggle, both practically and financially. The Director of RTB reminded the researcher that RTB's responsibility is to transmit information to the masses, but not to educate them on language issues, a clear signal that language in general is not RTB's main priority.

The previous discussion suggests that the currency or the 'market value' of a language is a very significant consideration in RTB's policy on language, rather than its social status or the perceived academic value. But the ultimate decision on the production of programmes in any particular language lies in the hands of RTB's higher authority, the Prime Minister's Office. A salient theme that can be seen in the RTB guidelines cited earlier is that the use of Brunei Malay (and Kedayan) on radio and television is not seen to be out of line with the 'official language' definition, and they are therefore readily used in television and radio programmes and advertisements. What is also clear is the fact that linguistic diversity is not necessarily reflected in RTB's working policy. Government policies on language have not been favourable in the sense that they have only provisions for the use of Malay in official business. Implicit in this choice is perhaps the need to uphold the official language of the country i.e., Malay. While there have been no overt coercive policies to reduce linguistic diversity, the obvious absence of ethnic languages from the education system, official administration and the media does also contribute to a sense of inevitability in the dominance of Malay. This in turn could be perceived as implicit strategies on the part of the government to reinforce the ideological dominance of Malay. One such move is the labelling of non-Malay languages as 'Malay dialects' (as demonstrated in the case of the Language and Literature Bureau's stance outlined earlier). Certainly, there is little resistance at all to the forces of language shift, but then there have never been explicit bans or dismissal of ethnic languages, hence removing all possibilities of overt resistance and protestation: there is nothing to protest against.

Noor Azam states that the main force behind the shift to Malay language and identity is the pressure on the ethnic communities to conform to a more modern and homogeneous Bruneian lifestyle, where the population is highly mobile and more socially integrated than it used to be, and in which it is more important to be 'Bruneian' than to express membership of any particular ethnic community (2005: 242). It can be argued that this trend in Brunei is a reflection of a 'local globalization' (cf. Mufwene 1998, 2001), in which Malay identity and language assume greater prominence and bring greater benefits than any of the others. Globalisation in the international sense, on the other hand, is manifest in the growing significance of English alongside Malay in Brunei daily life. The adoption of Malay identity and language (and the adoption of Malay identity *through* language), is therefore a reflection of the reality of present-day Brunei. This process of adoption of Malay language and identity is reinforced by, and reinforces, the dominance of the Malay epicentre.

Discussion: recent developments

There is some evidence for a recent change of official attitude towards the languages of the minority groups. Rather than allowing them to die out through a *laissez-faire* approach to ongoing language shift, there is some evidence of moves towards making the minority groups and their languages part of the 'Malay centre' (Martin 2002: 189). We suggest that there are three possible reasons for this:

1 Acceptance by the Brunei government of the argument that the languages are dialects of Malay and are therefore to be preserved and supported as part of the 'Melayu' aspect of MIB.
2 Initiatives to introduce courses and a minor programme in Borneo languages (Tutong, Dusun, Iban) at the UBD Language Centre, which have resulted in students viewing these languages as part of Brunei's heritage, rather than as peripheral and moribund languages.
3 What might be termed ethnic and linguistic tourism: using the diversity of Brunei's ethnic groups, their languages and aspects of their cultures, such as dances and folktales, for purposes of tourism promotion.

If the official view of the minority indigenous languages as dialects of Malay is accepted, then it follows that the government has an obligation to maintain and preserve them, just as it is obliged to do for Malay, being one of the three core elements in the nation's *Melayu Islam Beraja* (Malay Islamic Monarchy) philosophy. By acknowledging the unifying role of 'Pan-Brunei Malay' as *de facto* national language, policy-makers are also showing recognition for Malay as a pluri-centric language comprising a number of varieties, some of which have undergone processes of standardisation: Bahasa Malaysia and Bahasa Indonesia are examples. For users of Kedayan, Tutong, Belait, Dusun, Bisaya and Lun Bawang, there is a trade-off: accepting the status as dialects of Malay may help ensure that these are maintained and supported. As with minority languages worldwide, it is necessary for the community of speakers to be proactive in maintenance and revitalisation efforts. The effectiveness of top-down initiatives from central government, even in an absolute monarchy, is limited (McLellan and Jones 2015).

This shift in attitude is also found in the feedback from students who have enrolled in the modules in Tutong and Dusun offered at the UBD Language Centre (Noor Azam 2014; Muhammad Najib and McLellan 2018). From initially feeling that Brunei's minority languages were on the way to extinction, students who took these modules have come to appreciate that they are also part of Brunei's national heritage and thus are worthy of preservation. Focusing particularly on the teaching and learning of Dusun, Muhammad Najib and McLellan (2018) conclude, as does Noor Azam (2014), that the introduction of courses in minority indigenous languages at tertiary level may play some role in maintaining these languages, even if that was not the prime motivation for their introduction.

The third reason for a shift in attitude derives from a perceived economic imperative: it has long been felt that the national economy needs to diversify and reduce its dependence on oil and natural gas exports. Tourism, a major income earner for Brunei's ASEAN neighbours, is seen as one strategy for achieving this diversification. The Brunei Tourism Development Department was established in 2005 under the Ministry of Primary Industries and Resources (www.tourism.gov.bn/SitePages/Introduction.aspx). Since mass tourism is not deemed appropriate for this small nation, the focus is on niche tourism, especially ecotourism (King 2016). Aspects of the 'ethnic *adat* (custom)' and cultural practices which do not contravene the MIB philosophy are now being promoted as tourist attractions (Asiyah az'Zahra 2014: 168). These include material culture, traditional dances, songs, festivals and folktales, as well as places of historical significance and natural attractions such as jungle treks and waterfalls. One such example is the ASEAN Heritage site of Tasek Merimbun which lies in the Dusun area of Tutong District. Performances and events such as the Dusun Adau Gayoh harvest festival attract local and international tourists and may also contribute to language maintenance. Another example is the *Festival Kebudayaan Perkahwinan Etnik Melayu di Brunei Darussalam* (Cultural Festival of Ethnic Malay Weddings in Brunei Darussalam) held in 2013. This illustrates both a tourism promotion initiative, showcasing wedding customs and costumes across Brunei, and the tendency to subsume minority ethnic groups under the Malay umbrella. A feature report in the print media quotes the then Director of the LLB: 'Preserving the language is important because it is our identity . . . we must maintain our ethnic dialects to prove that we are the people of Brunei' (Piri 2015).

Conclusion

We began this chapter by summarising Brown's (1970) statement about Brunei's indigenous minority ethnic groups, before reviewing what changes have taken place in the subsequent 50 years. We are obliged to conclude that little has changed in terms of the status of Brunei's minority ethnolinguistic communities, not least because the nation still adheres to the provisions set out in the 1959 Constitution. Brown's stated aim was to describe the inner core elements of the structure of Brunei society, and for this he adopted a narrow ('smaller Brunei') perspective, viewing the minority groups as being 'of relatively little political significance' (1970: 6). Hence the endangered status of the minority languages is not of central concern to those in positions of power and influence, who are members of the Brunei Malay core nobility. Elders and leaders of the minority communities can only aspire to the office of *menteri darat* (land chief), as noted in the introduction to this chapter.

We remain uncertain as to whether the three recent developments, outlined in the Discussion section earlier, will develop into significant factors which may help slow down or reverse the ongoing processes of language shift and endangerment. Those communities in Brunei which also have substantial populations in neighbouring Sarawak, namely the Iban, Lun Bawang, Bisaya, Mukah Melanau and Penan are perhaps better placed in terms of prospects for the maintenance of their languages. Those found exclusively within the current borders of Brunei, the Tutong and Dusun, are more threatened, along with the Belait community whose language is already close to extinction.

References

Asiyah az'Zahra Haji Ahmad Kumpoh (2014) Some Insights into the Impacts of the Islamic Education on the Non-Muslims in Brunei Darussalam. *TAWARIKH: International Journal for Historical Studies* 5 (2): 161–176. Available at: http://fass.ubd.edu.bn/staff/docs/AK/asiyah-2014.pdf (accessed 19 August 2019).

Braighlinn, G. (pseud.) (1992) *Ideological Innovation under Monarchy: Aspects of Legitimation Activity in Contemporary Brunei*. Amsterdam: VU Press.

Brown, Donald E. (1970) Brunei: The Structure and History of a Bornean Malay Sultanate. *Bandar Seri Begawan: Brunei Museum* 2 (2).

Coluzzi, Paolo. (2010) Endangered Languages in Brunei: A Survey among the Iban and Murut (Lun Bawang) in Temburong, Brunei. *Oceanic Linguistics* 49 (1): 119–143.

Department of Economic Planning and Development, Negara Brunei Darussalam (2012) *Population and Housing Census 2011: A Preliminary Report*. Bandar Seri Begawan: Department of Economic Planning and Development.

Department of Economic Planning and Development, Negara Brunei Darussalam (2018) Population and Housing Census 2017. Accessed 10 November 2018. Available at: www.depd.gov.bn/SitePages/Population.aspx (accessed 19 August 2019).

Dewan Bahasa dan Pustaka, Negara Brunei Darussalam (2011) *Daftar Leksikal 7 Dialek Brunei Darussalam*. Bandar Seri Begawan: Dewan Bahasa dan Pustaka.

Government of Brunei (1906) *Annual Report on the State of Brunei* (by M. S. H. McArthur). Singapore: Government of Brunei.

Government of Brunei (1921) *Annual Report on the State of Brunei for 1921* (by L. A. Allen). Kuala Lumpur: Government of Brunei.

Government of Brunei (1941) *Annual Report on the State of Brunei for 1941* (by Ibrahim Jaafar). Singapore: Government of Brunei.

Government of Brunei (1947) *Annual Report on the State of Brunei for 1947* (by L. H. N. Davis). Singapore: Government of Brunei.

Government of Brunei (1961) Undang2 Taraf Kebangsaan Brunei. Undang2 No. 4. In *Surat2 Perlembagaan Negeri Brunei*. Kuala Belait: Government Printer, Brunei Nationality Act, No. 4, in Constitutional Letters of the State of Brunei, pp. 115–135.

Government of Brunei (1965) *State of Brunei Annual Report 1963*. Kuala Belait: Brunei Press.

Government of Brunei (2003) *Population Census of 2001*. Bandar Seri Begawan: Government of Brunei (Economic Planning Unit).

Gunn, Geoffrey C. (1997) *Language, Power, and Ideology in Brunei Darussalam*. Athens, OH: Ohio University Center for International Studies.

Kershaw, Eva M. (1994) Final Shifts: Some Why's and How's of Brunei Dusun Convergence on Malay. In Peter W. Martin (ed.), *Shifting Patterns of Language Use in Borneo*. Williamsburg, VA: Borneo Research Council, pp. 179–194.

Kershaw, Roger (1984) Illuminating the Path to Independence: Political Themes in *Pelita Brunei* in 1983. *Southeast Asian Affairs*: 67–85.

Kershaw, Roger (2001) *Monarchy in Southeast Asia: The Faces of Tradition in Transition*. London: Routledge.

King, Victor T. (1994) What Is Brunei Society? Reflections on a Conceptual and Ethnographic Issue. *South-East Asia Research* 2 (2): 176–198.

King, Victor T. (2001) A Question of Identity: Names, Societies and Ethnic Groups in Interior Kalimantan and Brunei Darussalam. *Sojourn: Journal of Social Issues in Southeast Asia* 16 (1): 1–36.

King, Victor T. (2016) Brunei Darussalam: 'A Kingdom of Unexpected Treasures'. In Ploysri Porananond and Victor T. King (eds.), *Tourism and Monarchy in Southeast Asia*. Newcastle upon Tyne: Cambridge Scholars Publishing, pp. 20–38.

Leach, Edmund R. (1950) *Social Science Research in Sarawak*. London: His Majesty's Stationery Office.

Martin, Peter W. (1990) The Pattern of Language Communication in Brunei Darussalam and Its Pedagogic Implications. In Verner Bickley (ed.), *Language Use and Language Teaching and the Curriculum*. Hong Kong: Institute of Language in Education, pp. 175–185.

Martin, Peter W. (1992a) A Review of Linguistic Research in Brunei Darussalam. In Dato' Haji Abu Bakar (ed.), *Sumbangsih UBD: Essays on Negara Brunei Darussalam*. Bandar Seri Begawan: Akademi Pengajian Brunei, pp. 106–117.

Martin, Peter W. (1992b) Shifts in Language Allegiance in Borneo: The Belait Community of Brunei. *Borneo Research Bulletin* 24: 6–23.

Martin, Peter W. (1995) Whither the Indigenous Languages of Brunei Darussalam? *Oceanic Linguistics* 34: 44–60.

Martin, Peter W. (2002) One Language, One Race, One Nation? The Changing Language Ecology of Brunei Darussalam. In Maya K. David (ed.), *Methodological and Analytical Issues in Language Maintenance and Language Shift Studies*. Frankfurt-am-Main, Germany: Peter Lang, pp. 175–193.

Martin, Peter W. and Gloria R. Poedjosoedarmo (1996) An Overview of the Language Situation in Brunei Darussalam. In Peter W. Martin, Conrad Ożóg and Gloria Poedjosoedarmo (eds.), *Language Use and Language Change in Brunei Darussalam*. Athens, OH: Ohio University Press, pp. 1–23.

Maxwell, Allen R. (1980) Urang Darat: An Ethnographic Study of the Kadayan of Labu Valley, Brunei. Unpublished PhD thesis, Yale University.

Maxwell, Allen R. (2001) Malay Polysemy and Political Power: Census Categories, Ethnicity and Citizenship in Brunei Darussalam. *South East Asia Research* 9 (2): 173–212.

McLellan, James and Gary M. Jones (2015) Maintaining and Revitalising the |Indigenous Endangered Languages of Borneo: Comparing 'Top-Down' and Community-Based Policy Initiatives and Strategies. In Mari C. Jones (ed.), *Policy and Planning for Endangered Languages*. Cambridge: Cambridge University Press, pp. 18–30.

Mufwene, Salikoko (1998) *The Ecology of Language: New Imperatives in Linguistics Curricula*. Paper presented at the symposium on The Linguistic Sciences in a Changing Context, University of Illinois, Urbana-Champaign, 30–31 October.

Mufwene, Salikoko (2001) *The Ecology of Language Evolution*. Cambridge: Cambridge University Press.

Muhammad Najib Noorashid and James McLellan (2018) Teaching and Learning an Ethnic Minority Language at University Level: The Case of Dusun in Brunei. *GEMA Online Journal of Language Studies* 18 (1): 217–233.

Noor Azam Haji-Othman (2005) The Changing Definitions of the Malay Person: Problems of Nomenclature. Unpublished PhD thesis, Leicester University.

Noor Azam Haji-Othman (2007) English and the Bilingual Bruneian. In Katie Dunworth (ed.), *English in South East Asia: Challenges and Changes*. Perth, Western Australia: Curtin University of Technology, pp. 59–70.

Noor Azam Haji-Othman (2012) Is It Always English? 'Duelling Aunties' in Brunei Darussalam. In Vaughan Rapatanaha and Pauline Bunce (eds.), *English Language as Hydra: Its Impact on non-English Language Cultures*. Clevedon: Multilingual Matters, pp. 175–190.

Noor Azam Haji-Othman (2014) Teaching an Unwritten Language: Tutong Language. In Peter Sercombe, Michael Boutin and Adrian Clynes (eds.), *Advances in Linguistic and Cultural Research in Borneo: Studies in Memory of Peter W. Martin*. Phillips, ME: Borneo Research Council, pp. 15–32.

Noor Azam Haji-Othman and Siti Ajeerah Najib (2016) The State of Indigenous Languages in Brunei. In Noor Azam Haji-Othman, James McLellan and David Deterding (eds.), *The Use and Status of Language in Brunei Darussalam: A Kingdom of Unexpected Language Diversity*. Singapore: Springer, pp. 17–28.

Nothofer, B. (1991) The Languages of Brunei Darussalam. In H. Steinhauer (ed.), *Papers in Pacific Linguistics: Pacific Linguistics*. A-81 Canberra: Australian National University, pp. 151–176.

Piri, Sally (2015) Losing More Than Just Words. *The Brunei Times*, 6 April, p. A10.

Poedjosoedarmo, Soepomo (1996) An Overview of Brunei Malay Morphology. In Peter W. Martin, Conrad Ożóg and Gloria Poedjosoedarmo (eds.), *Language Use and Language Change in Brunei Darussalam*. Athens, OH: Ohio University Press, pp. 43–59.

Rabinah Uja (1994) Language Maintenance and Shift in the Iban Community in the Seria-Belait Area. Unpublished BA (Education) Project Paper. Bandar Seri Begawan: Universiti Brunei Darussalam.

Rajiee Hadi (2016) Orang Brunei Berasal dari Minangkabau? Available at: http://drrajiee hadi.blogspot.com/2016/10/orang-brunei-berasal-dari-minangkabau.html (accessed 12 February 2019).

Rosenberg, Peter (2001) *Comparative Speech Island Research: Some Results from Studies in Russia and Brazil*. Paper presented at 'Deutsche Sprachinseln' Conference, March, Lawrence, Kansas. Available at: www.kuwi.euv-frankfurt-o.de/~swlwww/doc/kansas2.doc (accessed 26 August 2019).

Rousseau, Jérôme (1990) *Central Borneo: Ethnic Identity and Social Life in a Stratified Society*. Oxford: Oxford University Press.

Sercombe, Peter G. (1997) Emic and Etic Perceptions of Linguistic and Cultural Change among the Penan of Brunei. Paper presented at 7th meeting of Southeast Asian Linguistics Society, University of Illinois, Urbana-Champaign, Illinois, May.

Sercombe, Peter G. (2002) Language Maintenance and Shift: A Review of Theoretical and Regional Issues with Special Reference to Borneo. In M. K. David (ed.), *Methodological and Analytical Issues in Language Maintenance and Shift Studies*. Berlin: Peter Lang, pp. 1–19.

St. John, Spenser (1862 [1974]) *Life in the Forests of the Far East: Travels in Sabah and Sarawak in the 1860s*. Oxford: Oxford University Press.

Sumijah Alias and Gloria R. Poedjosoedarmo (1996) Language Shift in Kampong Ayer. In Peter W. Martin, Conrad Ożóg and Gloria R. Poedjosoedarmo (eds.), *Language Use and Language Change in Brunei Darussalam*. Athens, OH: Ohio University Press, pp. 105–118.

6 *Menteri darat* and incorporation

Integration of Dusun society into the organisational structure of the Brunei sultanate

Pudarno Binchin

Introduction

The name 'Dusun' is an ethnic label given by the coastal Malays to encompass a collection of cultural groups that are largely found in Sabah, though these are culturally and linguistically distinct from the Brunei Dusuns (see Appell 1966, 1976a, 1976b; Evans 1923, 1953, 1990 [1922]; Pudarno (1992); Williams 1966). In Brunei Darussalam, the Dusun population is estimated to be between 5,000 and 15,000 people (see Bantong 1993a, 1993b; Kershaw 1992). This excludes those Dusun living in the coastal areas of Belait-Tutong who have converted to Islam.[1] The Dusun share many cultural similarities with the Bisaya people in Kampong Bebuloh, Brunei Darussalam, and those Bisaya living in the Limbang District of Sarawak (Sandin 1972).[2] Most important of all, these two ethnic groups share a religious tradition called *tamarok* and a collection of sung oral tales called *siram* (*ditaan*).[3] Before the turn of the 21st century, like the Bisaya, the Dusun people were characterised by their rice culture and shifting cultivation. However, this agricultural practice has now been totally abandoned.

In Brown's study of 19th-century Brunei's ranked society, he touched only briefly on the Dusun people, except in generalised passages related to the institutions of *menteri darat* (land chiefs) and *ketua kampong* (village headmen) (see Brown 1969, 1970a, 1970b, 1973a, 1973b, 1973c, 1976a, 1976b). He provided broad descriptions of Brunei minority groups among which the Dusun people are included.[4]

Hence, before the British took over Brunei public administration in 1906, the sultanate's links with the Dusun people were conducted through the appointment of *menteri darat*, the 'inland' chiefs – as opposed to the 'sea' chiefs (*menteri laut*) of the Brunei 'water villages' (see Brown 1970a: 30). These *menteri darat* were conferred with honorific titles such as *dato* and *orang kaya* (Brown 1973c: 100). In Limbang, the Bisaya people were granted four common titles: *janang*, *panglima*, *penghulu* and *orang kaya* (see Peranio 1977: 48; see also King 1996: 156).

Historically, some Dusun elders had been appointed as *menteri darat*, as recognised 'leaders' of their people in relation to the sultanate; but these positions were controlled by the traditional Brunei sultanate's officials called *kepala menteri darat*, head of the *menteri darat* (or *penyuru*, tax gatherers).[5] These Dusun *menteri darat* became 'leaders' in their respective villages as representatives of the Sultan for tax-collection 'and to be responsible for preparing items which are needed in rural areas and which are found in rural areas' (Brown 1973c: 100–101).[6] However, there was some degree of 'exclusion' in the series of ranked positions within the Brunei sultanate, which excluded other ethnic groups from occupying the higher offices above the *menteri darat*. Brown uses the term 'non-Bruneis' (in contrast to 'Bruneis') to demarcate this exclusiveness, i.e., being 'Islamised Brunei' (i.e., the ethnic Brunei Malays) on the one hand, and 'non-ethnic Bruneis' (i.e., other ethnic groups) on the other. Nonetheless, the extent of Brunei influence over the Dusun people is not well-documented. Some of the research materials presented in this chapter are obtained through oral sources. However, the conversion of the coastal Dusun population to the Islamic faith, with the exception of a small enclave of non-Islamised Dusun in Sungai Liang and Lumut, provides evidence of the direct influences of the Brunei sultanate on those living in the coastal regions.[7] Those who live in the lowland and upland areas of the Tutong and Belait rivers, and where animistic and rice-cult beliefs and traditions were still practised, remained relatively untouched until the late 20th century.

The most significant paper written by Brown on the subject of the Brunei superordinated position in relation to other ethnic groups is entitled 'Inter-Hierarchical Commissions in a Bornean Plural Society' (Brown 1973c). In this paper, Brown explains the interactions between the Bruneis and other ethnic groups through the administrative link of 'inter-hierarchical' offices (Brown 1973c: 98) as 'the points of interpenetration of socio-political systems' of the Brunei sultanate in relation to non-Brunei communities. There were two types of inter-hierarchical offices: (a) inter-hierarchical positions occupied by ethnic Bruneis and (b) inter-hierarchical positions occupied by subjects who were not ethnic Bruneis but who held positions in the Brunei sultanate's administrative hierarchy (Brown 1973c: 99). I am concerned only with the second type, which refers to the role of Dusun *menteri darat*.

A detailed description of the role of this 'inter-hierarchical' office is supplemented by Peter Leys's work on the royal customs of visiting the countryside by Brunei officials and the types of taxes imposed on the inhabitants by these officials.[8] Apart from Leys's description, nothing deeper has been mentioned regarding the mechanism which the administration of the Brunei sultanate operated over the people living in their domains. Brown's basic argument is that the Brunei sultanate of the 19th century was a collection of corporate forms of certain kinds. The corporate configuration can be outlined through identifying features such as identity, presumptive perpetuity, closure, membership, exclusive common affairs, autonomy, procedures and organisation (Brown 1976b: 20, 199–200). The incorporation of non-Brunei populations, including the Dusun, into the Brunei administrative apparatus was made possible through 'voluntary association', i.e., 'as an act of joining, a wilful or voluntary affiliation of individuals to social units' (Brown 1976b: 26). Although this was not created by the Dusun people, it then became a part of the formal Brunei nation-state.

In this chapter, I attempt to reconstruct the political relationship of the Dusun people to the traditional Brunei sultanate by examining evidence found in some

Dusun organisational practices, oral traditions and epic tales. To a certain extent, Dusun social organisation could have been modified by the Brunei sultanate through the institutionalisation of the office of *menteri darat*. But to demonstrate this contention is not easy. We do not know how much the traditional Brunei sultanate asserted its administrative machinery deep into the Dusun social fabric in the past and changed the society in any significant way. Brown asked, 'Is it possible to predict, or retrodict, the historically recorded order in which the elements of a status system emerged, just from observation of the structure of the system?' (Brown 1977: 201). In the case of the Dusun people, this is almost impossible. Lacking written records, Dusun epic tales (*siram ditaan*) and some oral histories are the only reference sources that can provide useful information on Dusun history (Kershaw 1994). From here we can try to 're-construct' what the preceding organisational structure of Dusun society looked like, especially at the time when Islamic and Malay cultures began to penetrate Dusun social affairs in the last century and a half.

General background: Apical ancestor, *alai gayo* and *tetuwo* as social indicators of Dusun social identity

The Dusun people are categorised as an acephalous society. Although they possessed traditional governing bodies, they did not have centralised institutional mechanisms to regulate their collective affairs as an ethnic group (for example, in the form of a chiefdom). Their social organisation was generally seen as egalitarian, comprising small social groups, each group remaining autonomous, isolated and separated from one another across far-flung distances.[9] Each autonomous group had a council of elders called *tetuwo* that administered their social and religious affairs within each *alai gayo*, the 'big' house, the Dusun communal dwelling. Each *alai gayo* became the focus of social identity for each respective Dusun social group.[10] Before going further, I will introduce two analytical approaches developed by Shamsul Amri Baharuddin to understand the issues of identity-making. Shamsul explains that,

> identity formation takes place within what I would call a 'two social reality' context: first, the 'authority-defined' social reality, one which is authoritatively defined by people who are part of the dominant power structure; and, second, the 'everyday-defined' social reality, one which is experienced by the people in the course of their everyday life.
>
> (1998: 18)

For me, Brown has addressed what Shamsul calls the 'authority-defined social reality' provided by the Bruneis, and this perspective becomes the underlying basis for Brown's description of Brunei society. However, I propose an alternative viewpoint to Brown using Shamsul's second social reality that he calls the 'everyday-defined social reality', which was articulated by the Dusun people themselves. This can be seen through three major aspects of Dusun social character: (a) the establishment of *alai gayo* to form a collective group, (b) reference to apical ancestors and (c) the institution of *tetuwo*, an advisory body that administered the internal affairs of each Dusun social group. The Dusun concept of the communal dwelling, the *alai gayo*, has strong links to many previous *menteri darat*.

Site as identity: alai gayo, *the communal 'big house'*

Generally speaking, Dusun people inhabited the middle reaches of the Tutong and Belait Rivers, the two important communication links to the coastal trade networks. Peranio describes a similar settlement pattern of the Bisaya of Limbang composed of riverine sites called *pangkalan* that were distributed along the Limbang River (1977). Bisaya settlements were clustered in compact residential sites rather than scattered across a wide area. In Brunei, some Dusun ancestral sites are linked to rice fields and similar trading networks throughout the length of the Belait and Tutong Rivers. In this regard, Lingenfelter observes that,

> Territory and residence appear to be a widespread factor which people utilize for social identity and structure. A primary interest of each social group is the land and land rights that impact their subsistence and survival. . . . The river-based systems provide the avenue for communication as the people travel up and down them. Language groups tend to cluster along rivers, as travel produces frequent contacts, links, friendships, and a common cultural heritage. . . . The longhouse appears to be associated with the headhunting past and strategies for defence against this aggression. In spite of the demise of longhouses in Sabah, people continue to live in village clusters, associated with permanently settled society, organized for social control.
>
> (1990: 3)

Kampong ('village') is a rather new territorial concept, which includes a much larger area than the Dusun notion of *alai gayo* (big house) or *pulau* (hamlet). In the past, Dusun families lived collectively in an *alai gayo* to form a social group. Each *alai gayo* became part of Dusun social identity that later became the ancestral site for each group of families. Staying in an *alai gayo* was a common practice in the past, and this pattern provided defence (to ward off attacks from rival peoples) and labour deployment (a large workforce to cultivate rice farmlands). The residential pattern was reinforced when marriages occurred between close relatives to strengthen kin ties. Though most of the *alai gayo* were shaped like a longhouse, comprising a series of 'family' rooms called *lubok*, the Dusun people never refer to their *alai gayo* as an *alai awad* (longhouse). Most *alai gayo* were not long enough to resemble Iban longhouses, for example. The Dusun *alai gayo* were hardly built to house a population that covered up to twenty doors or apartments (*bilek*) like those of the Iban (cf. Freeman 1958, 1961, 1976).[11] Some former locations of *alai gayo* are still remembered in Kampong Ukong to this day.

Waris*: Dusun social group*

The Dusun concept of a collective residential house and associated farmlands constitutes one of the major foundations of Dusun social organisation. This concept refers basically to a residential site identified as belonging to a certain group of families which lived and continued to live there as descendants of former inhabitants who had founded the site. This group was identified as a *waris*. Peranio explains that *waris* 'is not a kin term; it refers collectively to all of one's kinsmen (consanguineal and affinal)' (Peranio 1977: 248).[12] Among Dusun people, the term *waris* basically means 'offspring', but it also provides two contextual meanings: (a) *waris* referring to a descent group or descendants and (b) *waris* referring to a social group consisting of blood-related and marriage-related individuals in relation to an influential person. The first meaning includes descendants within three or four generations of surviving members who form an autonomous social group at a residential location. The second meaning is a comprehensive term that includes both living descendants and dead ancestors. Hence a group of individuals, who have family and blood ties, living at a residential location, are considered as one *waris*, an autonomous social group. Through this *waris* group, residential rights and inheritance, birth rights and marriages and death, including the practice of *tamarok*, the application of *adat* laws and rice-cultivation, are systematically administered and organised.

Waris autonomy was nurtured and developed by the founder of such a group. In other words, each *waris* group was started by a person of influence, who was locally identified as *tetuwo suguton*, 'elder person(s) to follow' or, *alan suguton*, 'a benefactor to follow (i.e., to rely on)'. This brings me to address the important role of Dusun founding individuals to form a corporate unit and maintain the kinship relations that radiate from such an apical ancestor (Pudarno 2017: 91–166).

Apical ancestor and influential 'big man'

Similar to origin traditions found in many Austronesian-speaking societies, generally speaking, each *waris* group had its own founder who became the genealogical reference for the group (see Druce 2021). I call such founders 'influential individuals' as they are referred to as *jilama gayo* ('big men') by the Dusun and Bisaya; they seem to share some similarities with Sahlins's (1966) 'big man' concept, particularly those conferred with the honorific titles of *dato* and *orang kaya*. Such individuals developed an entourage of their kin groups and acquired strong support from their immediate family members. Wolters (1982: 9), based on some Hindu inscriptions, suggests that there were small territorial units in Southeast Asia, possibly a cluster of blood-related families as in the Dusun case, of which a 'man of prowess' could bring support and develop alliance under his personal influence. Such groups or entourages united to create a collective identity and common goals, particularly in the economic field (cf. Earle 1994: 951), and lived together in a particular location to guarantee a sustainable living on the basis of the available resources from the surrounding area. In Melanesia, according to

Sahlins (1966: 162), an ecological and residential area administered by a big-man normally

> consists of many autonomous kinship-residential groups. Amounting on the ground to a small village or a local cluster of hamlets, each of these is a copy of the others in organization, each tends to be economically self-governing, and each is the equal of the others in political status. The tribal plan is one of politically unintegrated segments – segmental.

Among the Dusun and Bisaya, these influential founders (either dead or alive) become a genealogical reference – according to Peranio (1977), a 'genealogical anchor' – to determine membership in a *waris* group or *alai gayo*. Here the term *waris* is used to refer to members that are related to such well-known individuals that constitute the apical origin of the group. For example, Dato Pemancha Saging bin Ebaah was one such apical ancestor for Kampong Ukong because he was the first person to established the village with his eight brothers.[13] Often building an *alai gayo* (at least one *alai gayo* for each *menteri darat* throughout his lifetime) became the hallmark of an influential individual in leading a *waris* group under his care by acting as 'leader', genealogical anchor or apical ancestor.[14] When an influential elder achieved extraordinary accomplishments, especially titles and a collection of prestige artefacts, and wealth, a celebration, called *panakod*, would be organised with bountiful supplies of rice and meats from hunting.[15] Members of his *waris* and other related *waris* groups were invited and gathered to enjoy the shared celebration. A person who had gained the status of 'big man' (as in Sahlins's usage of the term) would be selected by the Brunei officials to become the *menteri darat* to represent their respective *waris* group. In a highly patriarchal Malay society, the *menteri darat* were selected from the group's male members (see Brown 1973c: 113).

Dusun council of elders, the tetuwo

In each *alai gayo* or *waris* group, there was a council of elders called *tetuwo* (lit., 'old people'). *Tetuwo* was a group of influential and respected individuals that provided consultation, management and protection for members of the *waris* group (see Pudarno 2004: 171–172).[16] They occupied the top echelon of the *waris* group's organisational structure, as 'administrators', but they were not leaders (or headmen) like the *tuai rumah* of the Iban longhouse (cf. Freeman 1958, 1961, 1976). To relate this to Brown's notion of corporation and Brunei traditional offices, I quote Smith (1974: 178) who explains that,

> Within corporate groups, we often find collegial units constituted as presumptively perpetual decision-making bodies in which only a minority of the group membership participates. Such *colleges* or councils are governmentally specialized corporations that should be distinguished from the corporate groups they regulate on various grounds. To organize and administer their

> collective affairs routinely, all but the smallest and most intimate corporate groups require specialized regulatory structures of corporate character, which must thus be determinate, unique, and presumptively perpetual. *Colleges* provide one possible agency of such public regulation, *offices* provide another. (Emphasis in original)

Conversely, the Dusun *tetuwo* functioned as an advisory council in their respective *waris* groups at the local level only. Smith further points out that there is a wide range of corporate groups which lack stable leaders. They may have some senior members whose authority is at best advisory and representative; yet others have a definite council or an official head, or both. Furthermore, the senior members of a corporate group 'may form a collegial body to administer the common affairs of the public, with variable powers' (Smith 1974: 95). In the Dusun case, *tetuwo* members comprised men and women, who served the *waris* members by providing expertise in traditional medicine (as *dukun*), dealing with the *adat* (customary laws) and religious affairs, and various roles and duties related to *waris* administration. The *tetuwo* members were regularly consulted, for example, like the female *tetuwo* members, called *balian pengiaw* (the chief priestesses), who were consulted on matters related to *tamarok*.

In addition, *tetuwo* members also acted as intermediaries between *waris* groups. When the Dusun community was in contact with outsiders, the male members (not the female *tetuwo*) were required to handle these encounters as intermediaries. These interactions usually involved negotiation with representatives from other ethnic groups or government officials. The elected individuals for such purposes were usually those appointed *menteri darat*. For this role, *menteri darat* were often assumed as the 'leaders' to represent the *waris* group (or the *alai gayo* where they resided). But these individuals were simply acting as intermediaries with the outside world.

Tetuwo council, public authority and personal 'power'

Generally speaking, decision-making in Dusun social affairs involve matters associated with kinship and marriage (related to *adat* laws), rituals and prohibitions, labour and other related economic activities. These activities involved the distribution of resources and opportunities towards ensuring a harmonious social life and steady sources of livelihood for members of the *waris* group. These activities generally involved interactions that were directed towards execution of social exchanges between *waris* members and their *tetuwo* council, namely: (a) reciprocity between the *waris* members and *derato* entities in the form of a *tamarok* ceremony (i.e., in the category of offerings and sacrifices), (b) exchange between *waris* members and influential individuals in the form of *panakod* celebrations (i.e., as an act of 'wealth-sharing') and (c) exchange of protection and loyalty between *tetuwo* council and *waris* members (i.e., in the safeguarding of 'security' and 'well-being'). The roles of certain *tetuwo* members, such as *menteri darat* and *balian pengiaw*, in particular, were to perform certain duties and social functions to ensure harmonious relationships among *waris* members. In order to make these transactions work, the authority and power that came with these roles were organised through ritualised and formal channels. However, these channels were basically operated by cultural experts and influential individuals who carried authority. In reality, these channels could be undertaken through some form of negotiation and consensus based on common interests. Roger Keesing (1987: 161–162) explains that,

> views of culture as collective phenomena, of symbols and meanings as public and shared, need to be qualified by a view of knowledge as *distributed* and *controlled*. . . . Culture as texts . . . are differently read, differently construed, by men and women, young and old, experts and nonexperts, even in the least complex societies. . . . We need to ask who *creates* and *defines* cultural meanings, and to what ends. . . . Cultures . . . must be *situated*, placed in a context – historically, economically, politically.

The question here is that the driving forces in any social activity of a Dusun *waris* group are not vested in an individual person for decision-making purposes. Actions and decisions are managed through collective consensus. Collective interests come first where opportunities and individual rights were protected for the benefit of all members of the *alai gayo* and *waris* group. The ceremonies of *tamarok*, for instance, are not only seen as ritual events, but they also become a symbol in which *derato* entities are essential in embodying collective 'authority'. This move rendered both Dusun public offices (i.e., *menteri darat* and *balian pengiaw*) as lacking the personal authority to make decisions. This was not about prioritising the interests of certain individuals over the others. Hence, King (2013a: 18) correctly points out that,

> culture is not homogeneous, integrated, and agreed rather it is contested and is part of systems of power and privileges, as well as generated, sustained and transformed in strategies, discourses and practices; these contests and struggles operate at different levels and in different arenas.

Hence, to achieve collective consensus, the power and responsibility of the *tetuwo* council was not solely allocated to any one person or a powerful individual with a privileged position. Any decision taken by a congregation must, at least, be guided in accordance with the agreed wishes of the group. Each Dusun *waris* group would determine the distribution of power and authority through collective leadership. Thus, as King noted, every decision was subject to 'contests and struggles' among members of the influential *tetuwo* council. In the management of the *waris* group, therefore, power and authority were not readily accessible by a single influential person. There was a separation of *authority* and *power* in Dusun administrative mechanisms. In this regard, Smith (1974: 29) explains,

> Authority is the right to order certain actions, power is the ability to secure their performance. Authority is an allocated and defined right. Power is a condition

> with varying degrees of latency, legitimacy, and legality. . . . Power . . . is relativistic in nature and expression, and cannot be centralized. The 'centralization' of power proceeds by its transformation into authority, with a specific administrative hierarchy of its own. In contrast, authority is always by definition to some extent centralized, since it consists in an allocated right, and this is true even in such small groups as the family.

The primary purpose of managing the social affairs of members was to regulate 'opportunities' over accessibility to food supplies, partners for marriages, justice (due to social transgression) and many more. These measures ensure equal opportunities for every member by encouraging and stimulating collective sharing (see Pudarno 1993: 46). Thus, in a typical Dusun social setting, authority and power were not centralised. Putting Smith's ideas into a Dusun social framework, those individuals who administered *waris* social affairs could only access public authority and power through two channels: one religious and the other secular. The execution of power and authority in this dual process required the council of *tetuwo* to separate the sources of power into two separate channels. In this process the notions of *leadership* and *authority* were separated but also closely intertwined in the symbolic and public representation of 'centralised' authority, i.e., in the form of the *derato* entities. Through these two channels, *tetuwo* members made decisions accordingly (see Pudarno 2004).[17] In the religious sphere, for example, the power to decide was elevated into the personification of *derato* and the executive authority rested with the *balian pengiaw*. The religious 'power' was centred on the divine being of *derato* but, in reality, the resulting decision was generally reached through consensus among *tetuwo* members. In this way, power through the actions of *balian pengiaw* is seen to be an endorsement of the wishes of the *derato*, making the administration of 'authority' symbolically embodied in the divinity of the *derato*. Accessibility among *tetuwo* members to administering 'power' became strictly controlled. Hence, 'power' became sacred and all-truthful without giving room for manipulation by influential individuals, especially the *balian pengiaw*.[18]

As noted earlier, the executive power in Dusun secular affairs (i.e., customs and *adat* laws) was invested in the authority of the male *tetuwo* members (such as *menteri darat*, *penghulu* or *ketua kampong* as the leading members of the council); while, on the other hand, the executive power for Dusun religious affairs (i.e., ritual beliefs and religious ceremonies) was invested in the authority of the female *tetuwo* members (especially, the *balian pengiaw*). In a slightly different context, however, the separation of authority and power for administrative purposes was also crucial in any *waris* group. The separation of the Dusun secular domain from the religious domain, I speculate, was also an attempt by Dusun *tetuwo* to prevent *derato* authority from being impaired (*masamar*, 'polluted', i.e., corrupted) by outside influences. Such a separation of administrative processes served to protect the position and status of the *derato*. In certain situations, *menteri darat* did have the absolute power to act as leaders of the *waris* group through the authority vested in them by the Malay sultans. Perhaps because of such possibility, 'power', 'office' and 'leadership' were deliberately carried out through different application and separate individuals among the Dusun to prevent corruption and manipulation.

There were incidents in which manipulation of power had occurred in the mid-20th century when a certain person of influence abused his power by imposing erroneous fines on violations of *adat* laws.[19] To prevent such a situation, 'leadership' and 'authority' were separated and could not be invested in a single person who held a position of power. Rather, such a privileged position was encapsulated in an independent instrument, i.e., through *derato* and the *tetuwo* council, to fulfil the collective will of the *waris* group. Hence, complementary roles between the two categories of *tetuwo* members comprised two ways of managing power in the *waris* group: the division of administrative authority into secular authority (held by the male *tetuwo*) and religious authority (entrusted to the female *tetuwo*). Different positions held by members of the *tetuwo* provided channels for separate control of authority and power and hence prevented power from being centralised and subject to abuse.

The *waris* group as a corporate unit

In his book *Principles of Social Structure*, Brown provides further explanation of the use of corporate analysis for understanding social structure and social morphology as an alternative approach to the structuralism of Claude Lévi-Strauss and the functionalism of Bronislaw Malinowski (1976b: 11–17). In examining the Brunei case, Brown argues that the Brunei data can be suitably analysed by conceptualising Brunei political organisation in terms of corporations. Brown (1976b: 20) explains,

> The characteristics of fully corporate forms are identity, presumptive perpetuity, closure, membership, exclusive common affairs, autonomy, procedures and organization ([see] Smith 1966: 116, 1968: 194). The fully corporate forms are the corporate group, the college and the office; quasi-corporate forms include the corporate category and various kinds of commissions ([see] Smith 1966: 116–17, 123–5, 1968: 195–6). The principles which inform corporations include sex, age, ethnicity, locality, descent, common property interests, ritual or belief, occupation, rank, and voluntary association ([see] Smith 1966: 126, 1968: 195).

Applying this framework to the Dusun social context, each *waris* group can be considered as a corporate entity and, traditionally, it demonstrated some degree of autonomy, exclusive identity, restricted common affairs, real socio-cultural and ecological boundaries, selected membership and independent organisation. Thus, living on the basis of a subsistence economy, the *waris* group organised its social activities and public administration to function as a 'collective' and independent unit. Peranio, however, describes the Bisaya, unlike the Brunei Dusun, as having corporate groups based on the *lobok* organisation: 'The house as such is not a corporate group, but does enter into important transactions as an aggregate or collectivity' (Peranio 1977: 147). In other words, each Bisayan family operated as an autonomous unit, though living under one roof in a single house with other families. In contrast, each Brunei Dusun *waris* group organised its members into a coalition of individuals to exploit resources by cooperative labour and to unite members of the *alai gayo* as a socio-political unit (see also Harrison 1976: 978). Smith (1974: 98, 99) explains that,

> Corporations are linked individually to one another in a complex series of alliances and associations, with overlapping margins in such a way that they all are related, directly or indirectly, in the same network. . . . However they are articulated in societies which lack central institutions, it is the extensive replication of these corporate forms which defines the unit as a separate system. Institutional uniformities, which include similarities of organization, ideology, and procedure, are quite sufficient to give these acephalous societies systematic unity, even where . . . competing institutional forms divide the allegiance of their members. . . . This is so because corporate organization provides the framework, content, and procedures for the regulation of public affairs.

Normally, the establishment of a corporation based on a *waris* group is closely related to survival strategies. Keesing rightly states that, 'Being in this corporation is the cornerstone of a person's property rights, group participation, and religious life' (1975: 20). From the most complex social structure of the Brunei sultanate to the most simplified social entity of a rice-cultivating society like the Dusun *waris* groups, the corporate nature of Brunei society was a visibly common feature. According to Brown,

> Since by definition all corporate groups regulate their own affairs, all of them are governments, differing only in the kinds of affairs they regulate, the spatial and demographic range of their regulation, and the procedures and organization employed. To repeat, the corporate group is characterized by sufficient autonomy, procedures, and organization to regulate its exclusive body of common affairs.
>
> (1976b: 37)

In this connection and in sociological terms, Weber (1947: 360) points out that,

> The corporate group, which is subject to charismatic authority, is based on an emotional form of communal relationship. The administrative staff of a charismatic leader does not consist of 'officials'; at least its members are not technically trained. It is not chosen on the basis of social privilege nor from the point of view of domestic or personal dependency. It is rather chosen in terms of the charismatic qualities of its members. . . . There is no such thing as 'appointment' or 'dismissal', no career, no promotion. . . . There is no hierarchy; the

> leader merely intervenes in general or in individual cases when he considers the members of his staff inadequate to a task with which they have been entrusted. There is no such thing as a definite sphere of authority and of competence, and no appropriation of official powers on the basis of social privileges.

Evaluating the *waris* group as a corporate entity, the study no longer focuses on certain individuals as the sole actors, as noted by Weber (1947). In this sense, social institutions are created as distinct entities that continue to exist beyond an individual's lifetime as Brown described: corporations 'endure beyond the life spans of the individuals who inhabit them. . . . That is, they are *intended* to endure, by replacing lost members' (1976b: 13). Autonomy was a necessity for survival for each *waris* group. Hence, the corporate management that was run by the *tetuwo* council was the best option for the Dusun people to guarantee an appropriate survival strategy. This is implied by Smith (1974: 44): '[the] notion of corporateness . . . includes group unity, authority, exclusiveness, co-ordinated or common action, continuity, and internal organization', and these are necessary features in the Dusun case for each *waris* group to maintain sustainability in relation to the carrying capacity of the surrounding environment.

Menteri darat and the outside world: the administrative mechanism

The extent of penetration of Brunei administration into the Dusun social fabric is impossible to gauge. This is specifically related to the key role of those appointed *menteri darat* in asserting the sultanate's authority and power into Dusun social life.[20] King says that there are no detailed studies of the mechanics of the historical assimilation processes of the Dusun, Tutong, Belait and others into Malay culture as they operated in Brunei society (King 1996: 159). For this purpose, my proposed mechanism of integration of Dusun *waris* groups into Brunei society is highly speculative based on the limited available evidence. To a certain extent, this can be relevant only for the Dusun case and not for the other ethnic groups who were also part of Brunei society. From the perspective of the *waris* group, *menteri darat* were the proper agents that linked the *waris* group (or the *alai gayo*) to the outside world.

King further points out that the non-Brunei leaders were not granted hereditary titles because it was not in Brunei's interest to establish a stable and secure rural leadership (King 1996: 156). Although the position of *menteri darat* appeared to be an office, it was not a perpetual or even hereditary post (Brown 1973c: 11–112; see King 1994: 183–184). Thus, the office of *menteri darat* was seen as a non-permanent position, and instituted by the Bruneis in the form of an 'office-like' commission or a commission 'disguised' as an office (Brown 1973c: 115). Truly, the role of *menteri darat*, as appointed personnel of the Brunei sultanate, was not based on their role of governing, but simply to administer the collection of taxes and other forms of payment for their sponsors – the titleholders, or landlords, of the territory in which they resided.

For trading purposes and controlling the networks, the Bruneis adopted a practical mechanism without actually colonising the people that lived in any of the river tributaries that they controlled. However, without being able to observe how this mechanism really worked on the ground, I can only speculate that this was done through 'voluntary association' (see Brown 1973c: 173–176, 217–219). Again, adopting Smith's concept, Brown points towards two types (or methods) for incorporating the non-Bruneis into the sultanate, namely: to institute the *corporation sole* form or the *corporation aggregate* form upon the interior population to bring them into the riverine trade networks. Referring to Sir Henry Maine (1960 [1861]), Brown (1976b: 12) distinguishes between 'corporation aggregate' and 'corporation sole' as follows:

> Each [type of corporation] was ascribed a unitary personality for certain legal purposes; and yet each – unlike real individuals, who are mortal – 'lived forever'. The corporation aggregate was a plurality enduring through time; the corporation sole – or office – was at any given time but a single person who was, however, only one in a series of incumbents stretching before him and after him in time.

Maine's and Smith's thinking on these two types of corporation is useful if adopted from the economic point of view. However, lacking real data on the ground and failing to observe those trading activities in action, this notion of incorporation is still speculative. Among the Dusun population (if this idea is really applicable), *corporation sole* existed in the form of a single *menteri darat* controlling an independent, simple-structured *waris* group through charismatic authority.[21] This could be what was actually seen from the Bruneis' point of view, the 'authority-defined social reality' adopted by the Bruneis in their construction of the Dusun people. However, the Dusun looked upon this economic role very differently. Personal power bestowed by the Brunei sultanate focused on *menteri darat*, the most influential *tetuwo*, like Dato Pemancha Saging bin Ebaah, was based on his charismatic influence. In this case, the 'power' and 'authority' that such a *menteri darat* could command was borne out of personal ability and reputation, occasionally nurtured by holding a *panakod* celebration.[22] Dato Pemancha Saging established *alai gayo* in Kampong Sungai Damit Pemadang and, later in Kampong Ukong, in which his *waris* group functioned as a *corporation sole* under his personal leadership and supported by a number of his brothers.

Some other researchers claimed that this was made possible by directing the non-Bruneis towards the adoption of the Malay lifestyle and embracing the Islamic religion, *masuk Melayu* (see Bernstein 1997; Kershaw 1992, 2000). But, in my view, this was not the most likely case as compared to the 'voluntary' form of incorporation. The notion of 'corporate group' embodying the Dusun *waris* groups for administrative practicality is still valid to a certain extent. As Smith points out, 'the external relations of a lineage are primarily political relations, while its manifold internal relations are primarily administrative' (1974: 31), and this was true of Dusun *waris* groups. Consequently, the 'corporation aggregate' type may also be found among the later Dusun *waris* groups that had established separate autonomy from Dato Pemancha Saging and were administered by councils of *tetuwo*. Having strengthened the stability of the *waris* groups, such as by ensuring the adequate availability of food supplies (rice fields, domestic farms, hunting and jungle collecting), only then did the management of the *waris* group expand to become a corporate aggregate entity. However, each corporate group, the *waris* of a single influential person, would still need a capable agency, a highly influential person, who had the charisma, the skill, and the knowledge to negotiate and manoeuvre the complex demands of the outside world. Unlike the offices of *ketua kampong* and *penghulu* which were introduced by the British in the first decades of the 20th century, these incorporated Dusun social groups constituted, according to Metcalf,

> [the] periphery, or series of peripheries, to the Islamic centre, personified by the Sultan and his nobles. In this sense, Islam functioned in much the same way as Hinduism had before it, providing charismatic resources that were by definition limited. Consequently, Islam was not an actively proselytizing force in Brunei.
>
> (2010: 134)

Therefore, King rightly says that, 'If Brown had studied some of the lower social orders, or the non-Brunei groups, he would have received rather different views of the characteristics and distinctions of the stratification system' (1994: 186).

Dusun people and the outside world: *siram ditaan* and other Dusun oral history

Brown also argues for the need to address the historical processes of incorporation of non-Bruneis into the Brunei administrative structure. Such processes are not easily discernible from the available data in Dusun oral sources. But these scant sources might still help to understand the role of certain historical incidents that were important catalysts behind particular Dusun economic and political events. Firstly, the Dusun people of Brunei, like their Bisaya counterparts in Limbang, began their origin tale with the event of a *labur gayo* (big catastrophe), i.e., the Great Deluge, which led the Dusun people to discover the *derato* country.[23] The tale of *labuh gayo* spawned a repertoire of tales called *siram ditaan*.[24] In *siram ditaan* tales, *derato* communities are portrayed as rice cultivators. Several *derato* characters portray the roles of 'sultans', 'raja', *tuan* (master, i.e., prince) and *tuan puti* (princess). Some *derato* are also described as living with *amba rayat* (citizens, populace).[25] Conversely, however, the 'governing' concept does not exist in *siram ditaan* texts. These characters are supposedly modelled from the old Brunei kingdom of possibly Hindu and also Islamic origins, which allows *derato* protagonists to take the role of benefactors. Nevertheless, although 'Malayised' *derato* are incorporated into the narratives that are supposed to portray the stratified nature of ranked Brunei society but which demonstrate that the egalitarian nature of Dusun society is still strongly preserved in *siram ditaan* tales, status or rank was literally supressed.[26] Therefore, the *siram ditaan* texts do not portray the lives of rajas and sultans as in the traditional Malay sultanate by living in palaces, with entourages of retainers and warriors, like those normally depicted in traditional Malay *hikayats*. This is consistent with Brown's argument that 'deep elements', i.e., those fundamental elements in a society will be the most resistant to change (Brown 1973a: 446; see also Brown 1976b: 226). Perhaps, in order to protect traditional Dusun ideology and beliefs, *siram* singers constructed things this way to restrict cultural intrusion from outside, especially, in their efforts to reduce and mitigate the impacts of the Brunei sultanate on Dusun society. Brown (1973b: 116) speculates that,

> If, however, Brunei represents a case of *internal* conquest combined with differential borrowing of high culture (such that the dominant upper strata absorb and utilize it, while the subjects retain their primitive features), then it is an almost inescapable conclusion that Brunei's peoples possess an erroneous conception of their *ethnic* makeup. . . . Bruneis perceive their society, traditionally, as a collection of *bangsa* (people, race, stock, kind, etc.), each with distinctive origins.

Siram singers have offered their opinion that can bring a different conclusion: they see those *derato* that carry the title Yawang Kabincuan and Dạyang Buncu as the highest ranked *derato* in *siram ditaan* tales.[27] I suggest that these 'historical' evidences from *siram ditaan* on past Dusun social organisation indicate *derato* titles as remnants of old Dusun administrative traditions which, I suggest, might have come from an Indian origin that disappeared when the influence of Brunei administration began to take firm roots in Dusun society. Although the old ideological ideas still have strong resonance in contemporary Dusun society, that society is still powerfully connected to its animist past and very little to the present Brunei society (see Pudarno 2016: 77–87). This is what Shamsul calls the 'everyday-defined social reality', which is the everyday viewpoint of the Dusun people about themselves. In contrast, Brown's description of Brunei society, as far as the non-Bruneis were concerned, is an interpretation by the Bruneis about their economic relations with the non-Bruneis. Shamsul (1998: 18) further clarifies that,

> Although intricately linked and constantly influencing and shaping each other, [the two social realities] may or may not be identical . . . because the 'everyday-defined' social reality is experienced [whereas] the 'authority-defined' is only observed and interpreted. Both, then, are mediated through the social class position of those who observe and interpret social reality and those who experience it.

Dusun identity has changed so much, but not due to the influence of Islam and to Dusun individuals converting to Islam (*masuk Melayu*). It is the economic changes that have driven the society towards modernisation and individualism. *Tamarok* was a ritualised religious activity for collective sharing, which has now been greatly eroded in that rice is no longer cultivated and it can easily be bought from supermarkets at a lower cost. However, the two types of 'social realities' that Shamsul proposes can also be considered in a geographical context, especially regarding settlement patterns and group and population distribution. King notes that 'the non-Brunei groups can be fully understood only in the context of their location traditionally, and for some of them currently, in a Brunei-dominated socio-political system' (1994: 187).

Traditionally, the Brunei sultanate identified its political jurisdictions based on three major categories of territorial control: *kerajaan*, *kuripan* and *tulin* (or *pesaka*) (see Leys 1968).[28] The Tutong River valley was under the control of one of the Sultan's brothers, a person who carried one of the highest ranked titles, *Pengiran Di-Gadong*. It was *kuripan* land, which was under the jurisdiction of the *Pengiran Di-Gadong*, Head of the Army (for further details, see Leys 1968: 120–122, 124; cf. Peranio 1977: 48–56). Each river system was controlled by a *kepala menteri darat* who acted on behalf of the owner(s) stationed at each river mouth. Under these various types of territorial management and ownership, the Dusun were controlled and administered by Brunei officials for tax purposes and trade. The sultanate's political powers, though exercised in loosely defined territorial areas, were based on control of river mouths and the inhabitants living along the rivers. The administrative concerns were judicial, fiscal and commercial, specifically judging criminal offences, levying taxes and controlling trade (see Pringle's notes in Leys 1968: 118; see also Leys 1968: 126–128 for details on types of taxes; and see also Horton 1986: 360). Outside the immediate vicinity of the Brunei water villages, however, 'the exercise of the sultanate's power was periodic' (King 1994: 191).

In Kampong Ukong, the introduction of *menteri darat* began with the appointment of Dato Pemancha Saging bin Ebaah, the founder of the village, who died in 1905. Towards the early part of the 20th century, Kampong Ukong had two *menteri darat*, Orang Kaya Laksamana Arir and his son-in-law, Orang Kaya Andar Amou bin Yuan, who each owned separate *alai gayo* (see Pudarno 2001: 95n1). They were supervised by a *kepala menteri darat* stationed downriver at Kampong Tanjung Maya and sometimes Tutong Town, known only by his honorific title *Dato di-Gadong*.[29] Using a similar historical setting, Brown later characterises the 'non-Brunei' population as 'heterocephalous' by demonstrating the nature of their link to the Brunei sultanate, as noted earlier, through 'inter-hierarchical' connections or 'commissions' (1973c: 98). These connections were invariably established through the aforementioned *menteri darat*.[30]

However, this categorically 'authority-defined' social reality, sponsored by the Bruneis, is misleading in providing the 'official' characteristics of the interior populations of Borneo, like the Dusun and Bisaya who were given different ethnic labels even though they are two closely related ethnic groups. In this case, these people were identified and defined according to their economic and trading activities. Generally speaking, the Brunei political system was unified by various economic relationships. Brown notes that the subjugated societies were dominated by the Bruneis in a way 'like a caste system, with different strata, local units, and ethnic groups having different occupational or economic specialization, yet each providing complementary functions for the other' (1970a: 4; see also King 1994: 186). This is only partially true for the Dusun people because as far as Brown's data can allow, this claim referred only to the inhabitants of the Brunei water village itself (see Pudarno 1998a). The Dusun people did not provide any specialised role (as craftsmen, warriors, traders, fishermen, etc.) other than offering payment of taxes to the Brunei sultans.[31] Similarly, Peranio says that the Bisaya 'recognize an affinity with the Malays and yet they feel themselves to be alien' (1977: 47).

This situation can also be explained on the basis of historical events that occurred around the middle of the 19th century. In his book *The Life of the Longhouse*, Metcalf describes how interior Borneo people were protected under Brunei rule. They were categorised as those who lived 'inside the Sultan's fence' and those others who were outside the 'fence' (Metcalf 2010: 123–137). His description of Kayan excursions to plunder coastal areas and the mid-reaches of Brunei-controlled major rivers is interesting, particularly in the case of the Baram and Limbang Rivers. Apart from engaging in the coastal-interior trade networks, the Kayan were also trying to obtain greater access to the trade goods through raiding and plunder (Metcalf 2010: 127–188). Those who were under the protection of Brunei sovereignty had better chances of remaining untouched and bypassed by Kayan marauding expeditions. In Kampong Ukong, the Kayan expeditions came twice when Dato Pemancha Saging was still alive. The Sultan's army did not come to protect them. The Kayan were defeated in the second excursion.[32] Consequently, some terrified populations moved towards the coast seeking protection from the Brunei government that was better equipped with powerful cannons and superior military skills (Metcalf 2010: 131–132; cf., Pudarno 2014a: 194–177). By moving to the coastal areas and becoming Malay, these refugee populations adopted Malay identity to discourage Kayan aggression (Metcalf 2010: 131). This might also have been the case for those Dusun populations that migrated to coastal settlements such as Kampong Danau, Kampong Telisai, Kampong Sungai Liang and Kampong Lumut.[33] However, the Kayan actions did not have similar effects on those Dusun populations along the middle and upper reaches of the Tutong and Belait Rivers, and also among the Bisaya of the Limbang River.

A major issue is as follows: the Dusun were not traders. They were regularly taxed by the Brunei sultanate. They only traded their jungle products for certain luxury goods like gongs, clothes, brass cannons, swords, knives and other metal products through the *pengalus*, the boat-rowing traders. The *pengalus*' trade items were mainly produced by skilled craftsmen from the Brunei water villages on the Brunei River. Being subsistence farmers, the Dusun collected only jungle products and fruits from their gardens for trading purposes, hence the given name 'Dusun' (orchard) by the Brunei Malays. It was not their real ethnic identity but a description of their economic commodities, because the 'authority-defined social reality' was readily made and imposed upon them by the dominant Bruneis and, finally, adopted by the British colonial administration at the turn of the 20th century.

Conclusion

Referring to the other ethnic groups as 'non-Bruneis', the Brunei Malays were not using the term as in the modern concept of statehood. Conversely, the Dusun people also called the Brunei *abai* and the water village as *pagun abai*, the 'country' of the *abai*. *Abai* is a term used by the Belait, Bisaya, Dusun and Tutong to identify the Bruneis who lived at the Brunei River. Informants have no specific knowledge of what the term means. They demonstrated a sense of 'foreignness' when they used the term *abai*. In contrast, all four groups, Belait, Bisaya, Dusun and Tutong, have close affinity to the rice-cultivating Kedayan (whom they called *punyit* or *pungit* people) which is now ethnologically considered as a sub-ethnic group of the Bruneis.

The Dusun never considered themselves as part of the Brunei sultanate. The real relationship between Dusun and Brunei was not based on political dominion but was initially facilitated through trade. Trade was carried out by Malay and Chinese traders, called *pengalu*, who navigated the major rivers in their large boats laden with supplies of goods for trade and barter. The appointment of *menteri darat* was one peaceful way of coercing the local population into submission and facilitating trade flows, which otherwise could have been implemented through military means, called *ayau* (i.e., in the form of armed 'bullying' as the Kayan did), to extract taxes from the general population (cf. McArthur 1987 [1904]). Historically, the Dusun people had always been outside of 'the sultan's fence' (in Metcalf's term) regarding protection, welfare and survival, except on matters related to taxes.

It is still valid to see the Brunei sultanate as having a large collection of indigenous peoples governed by a small group of Brunei Malays. The autonomous and egalitarian Dusun *waris* groups were always at a disadvantage against the highly stratified, specialised and militarised Bruneis. However, this is also a superficial argument that lacks detailed research on the actual social, cultural and political relationships on the ground. Against this reality, Brown concludes that, 'Superficially, this looks much like a typical conquest state, in which a conquering high-culture immigrant minority rules a collection of "primitive" indigenes' (Brown 1973b: 115). This was made possible due to the strategic geographical location of the Brunei Malays living along the coast. The control of coastal trade led the Bruneis to gain superior and strategic positions to create a robust government that thrived on trade. With the Bruneis securing advantage over the other ethnic groups, it, thus, involved the other ethnic groups occupying the lower positions in the ranked hierarchy of the Brunei sultanate (see also Brown 1973c: 114). It was in such a situation that *menteri darat* functioned, but their role was merely as mediators, instead of administrators, over small groups of people, such as those local Dusun *waris* groups that were scattered along river tributaries. The *menteri darat* were not governors over an entire ethnic group or society. Furthermore, the office of *menteri darat* did not emerge from the traditional needs of the local people. Being a non-traditional office, *menteri darat* evidently could not provide the linking roles and functions to govern and organise an effective centralised administrative apparatus that could mediate on behalf of the different autonomous Dusun *waris* groups. Thus, it did not constitute a deep penetration of Brunei authority and power into the daily world of Dusun social affairs and political organisation.

'What is Brunei society?' King asks. This has to be studied in detail on the ground and by using historical evidence wherever available. What Brown describes as Brunei society is written from the Brunei Malay point of view, the 'authority-defined social reality'. It is the 'official' way in which the Brunei Malays want their social organisation to be seen and portrayed. Thus, other ethnic groups are seen as contingent in which the Dusun people are included as a category and as people of the 'orchards', and producers of wild jungle products). Brown uses Pengiran Mohd. Yusof's book *Adat Istiadat Brunei* (Yusof 1958) as a main reference. Thus, he regards the ranked and stratified offices of the Brunei political structure of the 19th century correctly and subscribes to this exclusive Brunei Malay view. Alternatively, the second point of view that Shamsul provides demonstrates a rather different context and understanding of what is called traditional Dusun society: the 'everyday-defined social reality' which I have attempted to capture in this chapter.

Notes

1 The Brunei government provides no official figures on the country's population based on ethnicity. The Dusun people are categorised as *rakyat jati* (*jati*, 'original', which means one of the indigenous peoples of Brunei). They are labelled as 'non-Bruneis' in Brown's papers (Brown 1970a: 31, 1973a: 437n2). They live in the middle reaches of the Tutong and Belait Rivers and also along the coastal stretches of the Tutong and Belait districts. Those Dusun populations living along the Belait River were labeled as 'Bisaya' in the Brunei Annual Report 1906 (McArthur 1907: 18–19). This label was later changed to 'Dusun' (Harvey 1912: 6). Besides these terms, they were labelled as 'Bukit' in 1958 (see Harrisson 1958: 319–320).

2 The similarities are compared, especially, in terms of language, religious beliefs and social practices. McArthur described the Dusun and Bisaya people of 1904, but he did not provide any information on how the Brunei sultanate administered these rice-cultivating communities at the turn of the 20th century (McArthur 1987 [1904]). My research area generally focuses on Kampong Ukong in the Tutong District. This also includes the neighbouring villages, namely, Kampong Sungai Damit Pemadang to the north, Kampong Rambai to the south and Kampong Bukit to the west.

3 Without a writing system, this is the only source of 'historical' evidence on Dusun (and also Bisaya) social history, which, to a certain extent, reveals Dusun's past social life. Some social elements found in the oral texts can be used to compare them with present Dusun social forms (see Pudarno 2007, 2009, 2014a for more detail; see also Maxwell 1989). The narrative form of sung *siram* traditions is called *siram ditaan* in Brunei (known as *siram anak raja* in Limbang), a corpus of tales about deities called *derato* or *duwato*. These epic tales provide the foundation of Dusun and Bisaya religious beliefs, which centre on a series of ritual ceremonies called *tamarok* (see Peranio 1977; Pudarno 2014a, 2016, 2017).

4 They are collectively known as *orang darat*, 'land people' (or inland inhabitants), which include the other five Brunei minority ethnic groups (Brown 1973c: 100). Brown states that, to define the non-Bruneis, those 'beneath [the Bruneis] are both more complex and less clear' (Brown 1970a: 28). He states that, at the time of his research, 'the

non-Brunei subjects – Kedayans, Tutongs, Belaits, Dusuns, Muruts . . . are essentially unstudied, and I do not know their attitudes at present with relation to social stratification' (Brown 1970a: 36).

5 There are four *kepala menteri darat*, each representing the four respective districts, but only one was filled during Brown's research period, and the one *kepala menteri darat* supervised several *menteri darat* under him in the 1960s (Brown 1970a: 101). Basically, Brown points out that the number of *menteri darat* was not fixed. The number of offices was considered to be slightly higher than that of *ketua kampong*, the village headmen (Brown 1970a: 30, 33). Furthermore, the post of *ketua kampong* was not a traditional part of the Brunei sultanate (Brown 1973c: 100) because it was introduced by the British colonial administration, a position adopted from the Federated Malay States in Peninsular Malaysia.

6 When Brown conducted his research, *menteri darat* no longer functioned as tax collectors for the Brunei government.

7 There is lack of documentation on the coastal Dusun, especially those Muslim Dusun living in the coastal areas of Tutong-Belait such as in Kampong Telisai, Kampong Danau, Kampong Sungai Liang and Kampong Lumut. Asiyah az-Zahra's study focuses mainly on the recently converted Dusun community of Kampong Kiudang-Mungkom in the Lamunin area. She also does not include a comparative study between the Islamised Dusun of Kiudang-Mungkom and the Islamised coastal Dusun. Coastal Dusun had no strong relation to rice cultivation and were essentially fishermen. Living along the coast, it was easier for the Bruneis to convert them to Islam. Asiyah az-Zahra (2011), Bernstein (1997) and Kershaw (1992, 2000) indicate that Islam is the determining factor in changing and de-culturalising Dusun social institutions. But I think this is not really the case. In recent decades, major economic change has been the most significant factor undermining Dusun social institutions and cultural practices. The development of the Brunei oil and gas industry and its significant contribution to the state's national income have had a tremendous impact on the Brunei population as a whole.

8 Pringle raises the question of to what extent the system described by Leys was a continuation of the system, which operated in happier times, and to what extent it represented degeneration and decay (Pringle in Leys 1968: 118–119). Brown also points out that 'not . . . everyone in northwest Borneo was satisfied with Brunei dominance in the last century', but it was not 'a measure of radical rejection of the Brunei socio-political hierarchy. Rather, it was a measure of opposition to high-handed or unjust Brunei rule' (see Brown 1970a: 36).

9 Dusun social organisation was not based on a highly stratified social complex like those of the Bruneis (cf. Brown 1970b; Sellato 2002). They never had a centralised social organisation to form an ethnic-based political body, not to mention establishing a chiefdom or 'kingdom' with a ruler to lead and unify the different Dusun social groups.

10 Some of these locations of *alai gayo* have remained as important historical and ancestral sites for some Dusun social groups until today. Some of these locations of *alai gayo* have remained as important historical and ancestral sites for some Dusun social groups until today.

11 Among the various *alai gayo* I visited, there were seven families living in one at Pangkalan Lampaku in Kampong Ukong. Another at Kampong Sungai Damit Pemadang contained 31 residents at the turn of the 20th century, which consisted of a group of families from eight siblings. These were the *waris* group of Orang Kaya Panglima Tingang, which originally consisted of 15 siblings: 10 males and 5 females. Each *lubok* could accommodate family members of 5 to 10, and sometimes more than 20, but this was quite rare. The word 'village' is a term introduced by the British colonial government in the early 20th century. Perhaps because of this, many of Borneo's cultural researchers found that the 'identity' of some inland societies has been constantly changing because of the change in the pattern of their settlements and house architectures during the British colonial era (cf. Alexander 1989). When compared to typical hamlets

in Kampong Ranau, Sabah, Harrison found that the average number of residents was roughly 147 persons for each residential cluster (Harrison 1976: 92). Such a residential group maintained a certain group size, and membership was limited to individuals who were eligible to live together at a residential location. Their social status was assessed based on the degree of kinship ties to the apical ancestor.

12 The concept of *waris* is a common Bisaya-Dusun term adapted from the Malay words *warith* and *waris*. The meaning of the term in the Malay language refers to each individual's right to inheritance through blood and marriage ties (see Teuku 1970: 1304, 1343). When the Malay term is converted into a Dusun cultural context, the word *waris* is used to mean 'descent group'. In another section, Peranio adds that, '[a] person's *waris* consists largely of an undifferentiated body of kin; both cognate and affinal, to whom some kind of genealogical connection is assumed, but not necessarily demonstrable. . . . In brief, the word *waris* is only used when referring to kin in the most general terms; it is in fact the term with the broadest meaning, referring to a category of relatives of any kind' (Peranio 1977: 306). According to Brown, '[membership of a social group] refers to the unit's having an empirical existence, i.e., it has members and is not just an imagined or remembered institution,' (see Brown 1976b: 22).

13 In Melanesia, according to Sahlins, 'the rising big-man necessarily depends initially on a small core of followers, principally his own household and his closest relatives. Upon these people he can prevail economically: he can capitalize in the first instance on kinship dues and by finessing the relation of reciprocity appropriate among close kinsmen' (1966: 167). An influential individual needs his kindred circles to become 'his followers' or, at least, to be willing to provide assistance in any way. When Dato Pemancha Saging built his first *alai gayo* in Penjuma at Kampong Sungai Damit Pemadang, he relied heavily on support from his siblings. When his siblings started to have their own families, the layer of the generations thickened to two, three or four *tiris* (genealogical layers). Based on these circumstances, an influential individual rarely stood alone to administer his own *waris* group single-handedly.

14 Dato Pemancha Saging had successively built five *alai gayo* throughout his lifetime.

15 An influential individual sometimes held a ceremony called *panakod*, a celebration of his wealth and influence, which required the provision of a multi-level structure called *mpuun*, a structure of multi-layered food trays. This ceremony was usually sponsored by *menteri darat, ketua kampong* or *penghulu*. In Limbang, it was called *dulang pagar* (see Sandin 1971) or *tumuakar* (Peranio 1977: 75). The *panakod* ceremony (lit. 'uplifting' the status, or, according to Woodward and Russell [1989], 'feast of merit') was a ceremony of communal gathering. Its purpose was to state to *waris* members that the sponsoring individual had the ability to acquire prestige, wealth, strong followers and abundant foods, and, through this celebration, he displayed (*tadangah*) his ability and superior influence in the public arena.

16 Spenser St. John once described the administration system of the Ida'an Dusun in Northern Borneo by saying, 'each village is a separate government, and almost every house independent. They have no established chiefs, but follow the councils of the old men to whom they are related' (1862: 375).

17 The social 'power' (in the secular domain) and the divine 'power' (in the religious domain) are completely separated. The separation between the two 'powers' implies an opportunity to avoid 'pollution' (or power corruption); thus, religious administration needs to be separated from the secular social administration.

18 If viewed from this perspective, the execution of prescribed actions was not decided and implemented by certain individuals, such as *balian pengiaw*, to oversee religious obligation and dispense religious authority. In such a situation, *balian pengiaw* were merely treated as intermediaries in the execution of authority, mostly 'wishes' instructed or desired by the *derato* which then would be endorsed by members of the *tetuwo* council through consensus. In this manner, a *balian pengiaw*'s duty was not to lead. *Balian*

pengiaw worked as mediators to channel to the Dusun audience advice from the *derato* during the performances of *tamarok* ceremonies.

19 These actions led to accusations against certain *penghulu* and *ketua kampong* in that they abused their position and power in gaining wealth by levying offenders with heavy fines. One case is noted by informants whereby a *penghulu* practised such abuse and ended in having his *alai gayo* and prestige property inside the building burnt to the ground due to arson.

20 However, this delineation is based on a theoretical construct as an ideal social situation – according to Max Weber, as part of the 'discrepancy between normal human interest and expectations in any situation' (see Parsons 1969: 59) – whereby any social scheme needs to be assessed with the reality of what actually happened in the daily experience of a Dusun community. Brown points out that 'there is a certain gap between the ideals and the actual, but the [Brunei] Government's enunciation of and commitment to the ideals are clear' (1970a: 37).

21 Dato Pemancha Saging had such a charismatic authority, and he was appointed as a *menteri darat* by one of the Brunei sultans (probably by Sultan Hashim Jalilul Alam Aqamaddin).

22 As described earlier, *panakod* ceremonies were held to raise the self-esteem and expand the influence of a *tetuwo*. Among the Bisaya community, Peranio states similar efforts are also held through several types of feasts such as *babulang* (cock-fighting), holding a *tumuakar* or *dulang pagar* (or multi-tiered trays of foods), erecting *ulong*, and the like (see Peranio 1977: 75–76; Sandin 1971: 8).

23 The Deluge occurred a long time ago and is comparable to the biblical flood of Noah's time or the last Ice Age that occurred about 10,500 years ago. The event of *labur gayo* inadvertently provided a Dusun family, the only survivors, the opportunity to obtain the first grains of rice from a *derato* family in *pagun sawat*, which then became the central foundation of Dusun religious beliefs and economic practices. This was the time when Dusun people discovered rice cultivation as a secure foundation for their cultural and ethnic survival.

24 Theoretically, I presume that most of these *siram ditaan* tales reflect the social and political scenario of Dusun social life in the last 500 years, between the 15th and 19th centuries.

25 Some of these *derato* are given Malay ranked titles such as 'sultan' (Surutan Haji Nayan, Surutan Palambang), 'raja' (Raja Jawa Pumpungan, Raja Sabala, Raja Siyakung), 'tuan' ('master' means the king's son, for example, Tuan Pemagat) and 'tuan puti' ('princess', for example, Tuan Puti Yamas Nyuramin, Tuan Puti Bukid Dandang Pangayuh, Tuan Puti Sari Kumala Si Laut Sabila Adaw) (see Sileh 1989: 152–159, 296). Raja Siyakung and Raja Jawa Pumpungan are considered as *raja gayo* (the 'great' kings).

26 Each male *derato* character is portrayed as living alone in his own dwelling and only having a wife (*yuning*) or younger sibling (*ruput*) with him. According to Sileh, status difference among the *derato* characters in *siram ditaan* tales has been suppressed and almost non-existent; the *derato* all live like most ordinary Dusun. They are equally involved in rice-planting activities (see Sileh 1989: 56–57). Similarly, the character of Yawang Kabincuan in the *siram* tale of Dayang Buncu Bersarung Nkukom is portrayed as living at a fruit farm (Sileh 1989: 57, 260–261).

27 Most *derato* characters who have these two titles remain the main characters in most *siram ditaan* tales, such as Yawang Kabincuan Si Bukid Parai Amas, Yawang Kabincuan Ambun Tanirai, Yawang Kabincuan Ropoh Tanidong, Yawang Kabincuan Kuta Basi, and Yawang Kabincuan Si Bukid Kabon Kulung for the male *derato*, and Dayang Buncu Bakirai Amas, Dayang Buncu Laut Karimpadan, and Dayang Buncu Tanjung Parai Amas for the female *derato*. In my opinion, these are original titles bestowed on actual *derato* characters but after the Dusun people were colonised by the Brunei sultans. Additional Malay characters were also incorporated into the

siram narratives such as sultans, rajas, *tuan puti* and so on. The incorporation of new characters and changes of narrative content may also reflect a revamp of Dusun social organisation in the early stages of the longstanding Brunei rule over the Dusun people.

28 *Kerajaan* lands were owned personally by the reigning Sultan; *kuripan* lands were controlled by the administering offices of the sultanate, and *tulin* (or *pesaka*) lands were privately owned by individuals, irrespective of office and rank. The idea of territorial control and people were tailored to such administrative categories to enable the Bruneis to regulate flows of trade at river mouths.

29 My informants never knew his real name; nor is it provided by Horton (1987) or McArthur (1987 [1904]). It is not clear whether the title for the *kepala menteri darat* followed from the title given to the owner of the *tulin* land, i.e., Pengiran di-Gadong. At that time Kampong Ukong was represented by Orang Kaya Laksamana Arir. While Dato di-Gadong became *kepala menteri darat* of the Tutong River, two neighbouring villages located to the south and north of Kampong Ukong also had separate *menteri darat*, namely Orang Kaya Temanggong Ari of Kampong Rambai and Orang Kaya Panglima Tingang of Kampong Sungai Damit Pemadang. The *kepala menteri darat* was murdered by a group of Dusun from Kampong Ukong under the order of Sultan Hashim Jalilul Alam Aqamaddin (1885–1906) or Sultan Muhammad Jamalul Alam (1906–1924). He was murdered for two related but different reasons: for the people of Kampong Ukong, Dato Di-Gadong had over-taxed the village erroneously for his personal gain (see Pudarno 2001, 2016); for the reigning Sultan, Dato Di-Gadong had protested over the extorting of taxes, and he led a revolt in Limbang in 1898 against the Sultan (see Horton 1987). Besides that, there was also the practice of 'forced trade' (*dagang serah*), a kind of dunning (see Peranio 1977: 50; Leys 1968: 126), which could have led to such an outcome.

30 When the British colonial administration introduced the first *penghulu* in Kampong Ukong in the 1930s, Kambar bin Mandi, who was not a *menteri darat*, was chosen. The *penghulu* office was established as a break-off strategy to discontinue the old Brunei administrative traditions. It was said that Orang Kaya Andar Amou inherited his position as *menteri darat* from Orang Kaya Laksamana Arir, his father-in-law. Other informants claimed that Orang Kaya Andar Amou acquired his position as a reward from Sultan Hashim Jalilul Alam Aqamaddin for killing Dato di-Gadong. Kambar bin Mandi was connected to Dato Pemancha Saging by his marriage to Dato Pemancha Saging's grand-daughter, Yasun binti Yaba. This appointment created conflict of jurisdiction between Orang Kaya Andar Amou bin Yuan, who was still a *menteri darat* at the time in Kampong Ukong, and the newly appointed *penghulu*, Kambar bin Mandi, by the District Officer (see Pudarno 2001, 2016).

31 The Dusun never asked for protection from the Sultan's army. So, what were the tax payments for? These are the issues for which I have not secured answers from my current informants. Those forebears of current Dusun elders had mentioned that the taxes were too demanding and beyond the limit of their capacity to pay.

32 The head of the Kayan expedition was killed by a poisoned dart that came from a Dusun blowpipe.

33 Metcalf points out that some parts of these dramas were played out by the Brooke Raj, to characterise Brunei misrule over the Baram territory and, hence, the imposition of heavy taxes on certain populations of the Limbang area (Metcalf 2010: 124–125).

References

Alexander, J. (1989) Culture and Ethnic Identity: The Case of the Lahanan of Ulu Belaga. *Sarawak Museum Journal* 40 (61) (NS). Special Issue No. 4, Part I: 51–99.

Appell, G. N. (1966) Residence and Ties of Kinship in a Cognatic Society: The Rungus Dusun of Sabah, Malaysia. *Southwestern Journal of Anthropology* 22 (2): 280–301.

Appell, G. N. (1974) Comment [on D. E. Brown's Corporations and Social Classification]. *Current Anthropology* 15 (1): 41.

Appell, G. N. (1976a) Introduction. In G. N. Appell (ed.), *The Societies of Borneo: Explorations in the Theory of Cognatic Social Structure*. Washington: American Anthropological Association, pp. 1–15.

Appell, G. N. (1976b) The Rungus: Social Structure in a Cognatic Society and Its Ritual Symbolization. In G. N. Appell (ed.), *The Societies of Borneo: Explorations in the Theory of Cognatic Social Structure*. Washington: American Anthropological Association, pp. 66–86.

Asiyah az-Zahra Ahmad Kumpoh (2011) Conversion to Islam: The Case of the Dusun Ethnic Group in Brunei Darussalam. Unpublished PhD thesis, University of Leicester.

Bantong Antaran (1993a) The Brunei Dusun: An Ethnographic Study. Unpublished MPhil thesis, University of Hull.

Bantong Antaran (1993b) Brunei Dusuns. *The Brunei Museum Journal* 8: 1–16.

Bernstein, J. H. (1997) The Deculturation of the Brunei Dusun. In Robert L. Winzeler (ed.), *Indigenous Peoples and the State: Politics, Land, and Ethnicity in the Malayan Peninsula and Borneo*. New Haven, CT: Yale University Southeast Asian Studies Monograph 46, pp. 159–179.

Brown, D. E. (1968) Two Colonial Office Memoranda on the History of Brunei. *Journal of the Malaysian Branch, Royal Asiatic Society* 41: 83–116.

Brown, D. E. (1969) The Social Structure of Nineteenth Century Brunei. *Brunei Museum Journal* 1 (1): 166–179.

Brown, D. E. (1970a) Social Stratification in Brunei. *South-East Asian Journal of Sociology* 3: 27–38.

Brown, D. E. (1970b) Brunei: The Structure and History of a Bornean Malay Sultanate. *Special Monograph of the Brunei Museum* 2 (2).

Brown, D. E. (1971) Four Brief Notes on the History of Brunei. *Brunei Museum Journal* 2 (3): 173–176.

Brown, D. E. (1973a) Social Classification and History. *Comparative Studies in Society and History* 15 (4): 437–447.

Brown, D. E. (1973b) Hereditary Rank and Ethnic History: An Analysis of Brunei Historiography. *Journal of Anthropological Research* 29 (2): 113–122.

Brown, D. E. (1973c) Inter-Hierarchical Commissions in a Bornean Plural Society. *Southeast Asian Journal of Social Science* 1 (1): 97–116.

Brown, D. E. (1976a) Social Structure, History, and Historiography. In G. N. Appell (ed.), *Studies in Borneo Societies Social Process and Anthropological Explanation*. DeKalb: Northern Illinois University/Center for Southeast Asian Studies, pp. 44–50.

Brown, D. E. (1976b) *Principles of Social Structure: Southeast Asia*. London/Duckworth/ Boulder, CO: Westview Press.

Brown, D. E. (1977) Social Classification and History: India and Burma. Essays in Anthropology in Honor of Morris Edward Opler. *Papers in Anthropology* 18 (2): 201–216.

Brown, D. E. (1984) Patterns in Brunei History and Culture. *Borneo Research Bulletin* 16: 28–33.

Brown, D. E. (1995) Mechanisms for the Maintenance of Traditional Elites in Brunei, to the Eve of Independence. In Victor T. King and A. V. M. Horton (eds.), *From Buckfast to Borneo: Essays Presented to Father Robert Nicholl on the 85th Anniversary of*

His Birth 27 March 1995. Hull: Hull University/Centre for South-East Asian Studies, pp. 408–419.

Brown, D. E. (1998) Issues in the Nature of Brunei Society and Polity. *Janang* 7: 85–90.

Druce, Stephen C. (2021) A Comparative Analysis of the Brunei Origin Tradition with the Wider Austronesian World. In Victor T. King and Stephen C. Druce (eds.), *Origins, History and Social Structure in Brunei Darussalam*. London: Routledge, pp. 42–56.

Earle, T. (1994) Political Domination and Social Evolution. In T. Ingold (ed.), *Companion Encyclopaedia of Anthropology: Humanity, Culture and Social Life*. London: Routledge, pp. 940–961.

Evans, I. H. N. (1923) *Studies in Religion, Folklore and Customs in British North Borneo and the Malay Peninsula*. London: Cambridge University Press.

Evans, I. H. N. (1953) *The Religion of the Tempasuk Dusun of North Borneo*. London: Cambridge University Press.

Evans, I. H. N. (1990 [1922]) *Among Primitive Peoples in Borneo*. London: Seeley.

Freeman, J. Derek. (1958) The Family System of the Iban of Borneo. In J. Goody (ed.), *The Developmental Cycle in Domestic Groups*. London: Cambridge University Press, pp. 15–52.

Freeman, J. Derek. (1961) On the Concept of the Kindred. *Journal of the Royal Anthropological Institute of Great Britain and Ireland* 91: 192–220.

Freeman, J. Derek (1976) *Report on the Iban of Sarawak*. London: Oxford University Press.

Harrison, Robert (1976) Hamlet Organization and Its Relationship to Productivity in the Swidden-Rice Communities of Ranau, Sabah, Malaysia. In G. N. Appell (ed.), *The Societies of Borneo: Explorations in the Theory of Cognatic Social Structure*. Washington: American Anthropological Association, pp. 87–109.

Harrisson, Tom (1958) Origins and Attitudes of Brunei Tutong-Belait-Bukit-Dusun, North Borneo 'Dusun' and Sarawak 'Bisayan', Meting and other Peoples. *Sarawak Museum Journal* 8 (11): 293–321.

Horton, A. V. M. (1986) British Administration in Brunei 1906–1959. *Modern Asian Studies* 20 (2): 353–374.

Horton, A. V. M. (1987) The Disturbances in the Tutong and Belait Districts of Brunei (1899–1901). *Journal of Southeast Asian Studies* 18 (1): 93–107.

Keesing, Roger (1975) *Kin Groups and Social Structure*. New York: Holt, Rinehart and Winston.

Keesing, Roger (1987) Anthropology as Interpretive Quest. *Current Anthropology* 2 (28): 161–176.

Kershaw, Eva M. (1992) Final Shifts: Some Why's and How's of Brunei-Dusun Convergence on Malay. In Peter W. Martin (ed.), *Shifting Patterns of Language Use in Borneo*. Vol. 3. Williamsburg, VA: Borneo Research Council Proceedings Series, pp. 179–193.

Kershaw, Eva M. (ed.) (1994) *Dusun Folktales: Eighty-Eight Folktales in the Dusun Language of Brunei*. Honolulu: University of Hawaii at Manoa Centre for Southeast Asian Studies, Southeast Asia Paper No. 39.

Kershaw, Eva M. (2000) *A Study of Brunei Dusun Religion: Ethnic Priesthood on a Frontier of Islam*. Monograph Series No. 4. Williamsburg, VA: Borneo Research Council.

King, Victor T. (1994) What Is Brunei Society? Reflections on a Conceptual and Ethnographic Issue. *South East Asia Research* 2: 176–198.

King, Victor T. (1996) Reflections on the Nature of Brunei Society. *Janang* 6: 65–84.

King, Victor T. (2013a) *Culture and Identity: Some Borneo Comparisons*. Institute of Asian Studies, Universiti Brunei Darussalam, Working Paper Series No. 1.

Leys, Peter (1968) Observations on the Brunei Political System, 1883–1885. *Journal of the Malaysian Branch of the Royal Asiatic Society* 41 (Part 2): 117–303.

Lingenfelter, S. G. (ed.) (1990) *Social Organization of Sabah Societies*. Kota Kinabalu: Sabah Museum and State Archives Department.

Maine, Sir Henry (1960 [1861]) *Ancient Law*. London: Dent.

Maxwell, Allen R. (1989) A Survey of the Oral Traditions of Sarawak. *Sarawak Museum Journal* 15 (61): 167–208.

Maxwell, Allen R. (1996) Headtaking and the Consolidation of Political Power in the Early Brunei State. In Janet Hoskins (ed.), *Headhunting and the Social Imagination in Southeast Asia*. Stanford, CA: Stanford University Press, pp. 90–125.

McArthur, M. S. H. (1907) *Report on the State of Brunei for the Year 1906*. Brunei: British Resident's Office.

McArthur, M. S. H. (1987 [1904]) *Report on Brunei in 1904*. Introduced and Annotated by A. V. M. Horton. Athens, OH: Ohio University Monographs and International Studies/Southeast Asia Series, No. 74.

Metcalf, Peter (2010) *The Life of the Longhouse: An Archaeology of Ethnicity*. Cambridge: Cambridge University Press.

Parsons, Talcott (1969) Religion and the Problem of Meaning. In R. Robertson (ed.), *Sociology of Religion*. New York: Penguin, pp. 55–60.

Peranio, Roger D. (1977) The Structure of Bisaya Society: A Ranked Cognatic Social System. Unpublished PhD thesis, Columbia University.

Pudarno Binchin (1992) Masalah Pengkajian Etnik di Borneo dan Pengajarannya bagi Negara Brunei Darussalam. *Brunei Museum Journal* 7 (4): 49–56.

Pudarno Binchin (1993) Pembentukan Struktur Sosial Masyarakat Dusun melalui Perlaksanaan Kepercayaan Temarok. *Jurnal Beriga* 41, Oktober–Disember: 31–48.

Pudarno Binchin (1998a) Upacara Temarok sebagai Saluran Pengukuhan dan Penyatuan Pengalaman dalam Konteks Kekeluargaan Masyarakat Kampong Ukong. In Matassim Haji Jibah (ed.), *Warisan Budaya Brunei*. Bandar Seri Begawan: Ministry of Culture, Youth and Sports, pp. 200–247.

Pudarno Binchin (1998b) The Role of the Brunei Arts and Handicrafts Training Centre in Preserving Traditional Crafts. In Edwin Thumboo (ed.), *Cultures in ASEAN and the 21st Century*. Singapore: University of Singapore Press, pp. 26–39.

Pudarno Binchin (2001) Peristiwa Pembunuhan Datu Di-Gadong di Tutong: Satu Catatan Awal. *Jurnal Darussalam* 4: 93–102.

Pudarno Binchin (2004) Local Leadership among Brunei's Dusun. *Contributions to Southeast Asian Ethnography* 12, July: 159–185.

Pudarno Binchin (2007) Pengaruh Kerajaan Kesultanan Brunei Lama terhadap Masyarakat Dusun di Masa Lampau: Gambaran Melalui Teks-Teks *Siram Ditaan*. In Anon. (ed.), *Pemuliharaan: Sejarah dan Tamadun Borneo – Ke arah Pengukuhan Negara Bangsa*. Bandar Seri Begawan: History Centre, pp. 557–576.

Pudarno Binchin (2009) *Siram Ditaan* sebagai Sebuah Genre Sastera Tradisi bagi 'Pembekuan' Informasi mengenai Amalan Budaya Masyarakat Dusun di Masa Lampau. *Jurnal Pangsura* 27 (14), Julai–Disember: 60–93.

Pudarno Binchin (2014a) *Singing Siram Ditaan: Composition, Performance and Transmission of Epic Tales of* Derato *in Brunei Dusun Society*. Phillips, USA: Borneo Research Council, Inc, Borneo Research Council Monograph Series 14.

Pudarno Binchin (2016) *Budaya Masyarakat Dusun: Imbasan Kembali*. Bandar Seri Begawan: Brunei Museums Department.

Pudarno Binchin (2017) *Masyarakat Dusun dan Tamarok: Amalan Tradisi dan Masalah Interpretasi*. Bandar Seri Begawan: Brunei Museums Department.

Sahlins, Marshall D. (1966) Poor Man, Rich Man, Big Man, Chief: Political Types in Melanesia and Polynesia. In Ian Hogbin and L. R. Hiatt (eds.), *Readings in Australian and Pacific Anthropology*. Melbourne: Melbourne University Press, pp. 159–179.

Sandin, Benedict (1971) The Bisayah of Limbang. *Sarawak Museum Journal* 19 (38–39): 1–20.

Sandin, Benedict (1972) The Bisayah and Indigenous Peoples of Limbang. *Sarawak Museum Journal* 20 (40–41): 41–52.

Sellato, Bernard (2002) *Innermost Borneo: Studies in Dayak Cultures*. Paris: SevenOrients and Singapore: Singapore University Press.

Shamsul, A. B. (1998) Debating about Identity in Malaysia: A Discourse Analysis. In Zawawi Ibrahim (ed.), *Cultural Contestations: Mediating Identities in a Changing Malaysian Society*. London: ASEAN Academic Press, pp. 17–50.

Sileh Yutong (1989) Cerita Anak Duwato Penglipur Lara Dusun: Satu Pengenalan. Unpublished BA thesis, Universiti Brunei Darussalam.

Smith, M. G. (1966) A Structural Approach to Comparative Politics. In David Easton (ed.), *Varieties of Political Theory*. Englewood Cliffs, NJ: Prentice-Hall, pp. 113–128.

Smith, M. G. (1968) Political Organization. *International Encyclopedia of the Social Sciences*. New York: Macmillan and Free Press.

Smith, M. G. (1974) *Corporations and Society: The Social Anthropology of Collective Action*. New Brunswick, USA/London: Aldine Transaction.

St. John, Spenser (1862) *Life in the Forests of the Far East*. Vol. 1. London: Smith, Elder and Co.

Teuku Iskandar (1970) *Kamus Dewan*. Kuala Lumpur: Dewan Bahasa dan Pustaka.

Weber, Max (1947) *The Theory of Social and Economic Organization*. A. M. Henderson and T. Parsons (trans.). New York: Free Press.

Williams, Thomas Rhys (1966) *The Dusun: A North Borneo Society*. New York: Holt, Rinehart and Winston.

Woodward, Mark and Russell, Susan (1989) Introduction: Transformation in Ritual and Economy in Upland and Lowland Contrasts in Mainland Southeast Asia. In Susan Russell (ed), *Ritual, Power and Economy: Upland, Lowland Contrasts in Mainland Southeast Asia*. DeKalb, IL: Northern Illinois University, pp. 1–25.

Wolters, O. W. (1982) *History, Culture, and Region in Southeast Asian Perspectives*. Singapore: Institute of Southeast Asian Studies.

Yusof, Pengiran Haji Mohd. [Yusof] bin Pengiran Abdul Rahim (1958) *Adat Istiadat Diraja Brunei (Darussalam)*. Brunei: Jabatan Percetakan Kerajaan.

7 The place of the Kadayan in traditional Brunei society

Allen R. Maxwell

Introduction

The Kadayan have long occupied a pivotal role in Brunei, but the position of this native Malay-speaking population in the overall society has remained obscure for a number of reasons. The radical economic and social changes of the twentieth century have masked much of the character of traditional Brunei society. Until recently, studies of Brunei have suffered from inadequate attention being given to the nature of Brunei society, insufficient differentiation between the two native Malay-speaking demographic components of the ethnic category 'Malay' – the Kadayan and the Barunay – and underutilization of nineteenth-century observational reports, which began to appear with frequency only after the arrival of James Brooke on the Borneo scene, in 1839. Combining information drawn from these sources with the results of ethnographic study with the Kadayan allows the emergence of a much clearer picture of the economic and political importance of this group in traditional Brunei. Local publications present Barunay historical traditions concerning the Kadayan and underscore the significance of this group in the larger society. The Kadayan have also occupied an important ritual position in the country. Integrating these diverse sources of information with data on Kadayan settlement patterns yields a synthesis showing how this group has been a crucial component in the life of Brunei Darussalam.

The problem

What was the traditional position of the Kadayan Malay rice farmers in the overall social structure of the Brunei Sultanate? The answer to this question has never been clear (Brown 1969b: 166–167, 1970: 16, 1976: 184–185, 1978: 141; cf. Harrisson 1963: 8, 11, 20–22, 1970: 155) and has been raised again recently (King 1994: 177–178, 188–189, 195–196).[1] A major reason why a satisfactory answer to this question has remained elusive is to be found in the nature of the Brunei social system, namely that it is a plural society (Brown 1976). A plural society has '. . . a social structure characterized by fundamental discontinuities and cleavages and [simultaneously] a cultural complex based on systematic institutional diversity' (Smith 1971a: 27). It is thus a society with sharp differences between ethnic groups which are nevertheless brought together within the same political unit (Kuper and Smith 1971: 3). The characteristics of a plural society – and especially the friction between groups which is channelled along the fault lines of ethnic differences – often mask the extent to which the different groups are integrated into a single social system.[2]

There are three main factors which have prevented observers from understanding the role of the Kadayan in traditional Brunei society. First, there is a paucity of detailed, high-quality descriptions of Brunei dating from earlier centuries (Brown 1970: vii–ix; Ranjit Singh 1984: 12–13; Saunders 1994: 3, 35–44). Second, the period of the most extensive reportage in European languages, primarily English, was the second half of the nineteenth century, following the arrival of James Brooke in Sarawak. However, this was a time of severe social and political disruption, caused in large measure by a deeply-rooted dispute over succession to the throne within branches of the Brunei royal family which lasted for decades (Brown 1970: 146–155; Ranjit Singh 1984: 32–33, 49–50; Saunders 1994: 71–73).

Finally, a number of the earlier reporters failed to distinguish between the two Malay ethnic groups in Brunei, the Barunay and the Kadayan (for example, Jesse 1775; Forrest 1780; Roorda van Eysinga 1832; Forbes 1848: 308–309; Guillemard 1886: 11, 123–130; Clutterbuck 1891: 207–223; and while Low 1848: 98 'lists' the Kadayan, he does not distinguish them in his own discussion of Brunei 1848: 105–110). These three factors have acted in concert to obscure a clear understanding of the plural nature of the Brunei social system and the place of the Kadayan within it.

Despite the turmoil of the nineteenth century, the Kadayan remained a part of the plural society of Brunei, but until recently little attention has been paid to how the Kadayan have been integrated into the larger society. As will be seen, the Kadayan have played important economic, political, and social roles in the traditional Brunei society of the past. The nature of their relations to the larger society has shifted in the twentieth century, due in large part to the radical economic changes made possible by Brunei's vast oil and gas reserves, and its, presumably, financially astute investment policies (see, for example, Low 1987: 253; Brunei 1988: 55–56; Anon. 1994: 92).

Nineteenth-century Brunei

The bulk of our first hand documentary material on Brunei derives from the latter half of the nineteenth century. The Sultanate experienced two disquieting developments having major consequences for its future: a severe dynastic dispute and the arrival of permanent European influence. The disagreements over succession to the throne began in the late eighteenth century and were not really settled until a century later (see Mundy 1848: I, 183–184). James Brooke, an English adventurer who was to become the founder of his own century-long dynasty in Sarawak, arrived on the Borneo scene amidst the strife in 1839 and quickly became an important force in the dispute. Brooke also represented a kind of final link between Brunei and the outside world, permanently binding the Sultanate to the larger forces of world-wide economic, social, and political change which affect the Sultanate to the present day.[3]

The stage was set for the long and sometimes bloody dispute over succession toward the end of the eighteenth century when the reigning monarch, Sultan Omar Ali Saifuddin I, abdicated in favour of his son, Sultan Muhammad Taijuddin, in 1780 (Brown 1969a: 148). The difficulties which were to develop all stemmed from disagreements over which of Sultan Omar Ali Saifuddin I's later descendants should succeed to the throne. He ruled for about two decades before he abdicated and he did not die until 1794 (Brown 1969a: 148). Sultan Muhammad Taijuddin ruled until 1793, abdicating in favour of his son, Sultan Muhammad Jamalul Alam I, when he reached his age of majority. Unfortunately, however, Sultan Muhammad Jamalul Alam I died quite unexpectedly after reigning for only a few months. Because Sultan Muhammad Jamalul Alam's own son, Pangiran Muda Omar Ali Saifuddin, was still a small child, his father, Sultan Muhammad Taijuddin, then reassumed the throne, ruling until he died in 1806. Realising that his own grandson was still too young to reign, Sultan Muhammad Taijuddin had directed that he be succeeded by his younger half-brother, the Pangiran DiGadung Muhammad Kanzul Alam (Roorda van Eysinga 1832: 14), who was also a son of Sultan Omar Ali Saifuddin I. Sultan Muhammad Kanzul Alam ruled until his death, and past the age at which Pangiran Muda Omar Ali Saifuddin had reached his majority.

Some elements of the royal family, especially the Pangiran Muda's mother, Raja Nur Alam, a daughter of Sultan Muhammad Kanzul Alam by his first wife, Pangiran Saleha (Mohd. Jamil 1963), believed the young son of Sultan Muhammad Taijuddin should have taken over the throne when he came of age. However her younger half-brother, Pangiran Muda Muhammad Alam – also known by the epithet Raja Api (lit. Fire King/Prince), because of his fiery disposition (Mundy 1848: I, 185–187; II, 21) – had gained such authority and influence in the affairs of Brunei that his father, Sultan Muhammad Kanzul Alam, was virtually powerless to oppose him (Roorda van Eysinga 1832: 14). While he is usually so listed by Brunei sources (for example, Sweeney 1968: 69), it is unclear whether Raja Api ever succeeded to the throne, and if he did, whether his father, Sultan Muhammad Kanzul Alam, reassumed the throne until his death. Raja Api was put to death sometime in the third decade of the nineteenth century as a result of his cruel and capricious actions. Finally, Pangiran Muda Omar Ali Saifuddin succeeded to the throne and ruled until his death in 1852. Thus, Sultan Omar Ali Saifuddin II was the reigning monarch when James Brooke paid his first visit to the capital of Brunei in 1842.[4]

While he was certainly the most important, James Brooke was not the only European attracted to Brunei in the nineteenth century. A succession of American, Austrian, and British entrepreneurs and adventurers – as well as Italian, Dutch, and German – also expressed interest in acquiring Brunei's territories lying to the north of Brunei Bay (Tarling 1978: 95–179). The history of the three Brooke regimes in Sarawak – during which most of Brunei's territories south of the modern capital were consumed in a series of territorial acquisitions – commencing with James Brooke's appointment as Governor of Sarawak in 1842, and ending with Charles Vyner Brooke's relinquishment of Sarawak to the British Crown in 1946, is too well-known to need restatement here (see, for example, St. John 1879, 1899; Baring-Gould and Bampfylde 1909; Runciman 1960; Brown 1970; Pringle 1970; Tarling 1971, 1982; Reece 1982; Ranjit Singh 1984; Saunders 1994). Brunei's loss of territory in the northern parts of Borneo was more intricate and complex. It involved transfers and sales of territorial rights to a number of Austrian, British, and American concessionaires. Finally, the British North Borneo (Chartered) Company was formed in 1881. The Company ceased to exist in 1946 and, like Sarawak, the territory became a crown colony (see, for example, Tregonning 1960, 1965; Tarling 1971, 1978).[5]

The history of Brunei over the last century and a half is not without its ironies. From the vantage point of the twentieth century, we see that Brunei had suffered the loss of more than 90 per cent of all her Borneo territories. We read the death knell of the Sultanate in the most egregious and self-righteous language of Sir Hugh Clifford in 1902 (Clifford 1902). We note that in 1941 Brunei had agreed to a Sarawak plan financially to redress the Limbang problem,[6] only to have it cancelled by the High Commissioner of the Straits Settlements (Tregonning 1958: 88). It is as if events were taking Brunei to its own demise. However, the cataclysm of the Second World War changed all this forever. Sarawak and British North Borneo ceased to exist as autonomous and independent territories, eventually becoming states in the Malaysian Federation in 1963. Brunei's economy began to grow after the war, and under astute management, slowly entered the modern world. She proceeded very carefully in the transition from the status of protected state to independent nation, achieved in 1984. Now Brunei has emerged as one of the wealthiest societies in the world.[7]

The Kadayan and the Barunay

The Kadayan and the Barunay are the two native Malay-speaking and Muslim ethnic groups which made up the Malay population of Brunei.[8] The Kadayan have long been associated with the Sultanate of Brunei. They traditionally lived in agricultural communities of dispersed houses widely scattered through areas of secondary tropical rain forest and scrub. The socially and politically dominant Barunay traditionally settled in very densely packed pile-dwelling communities, located on tidal, estuarine mud flats.[9] In earlier times Kadayan communities were concentrated in a zone circumscribing the modem capital of Brunei, Bandar Seri Begawan. Kadayan began migrating out of this core area at least as early as the 1860s, moving to the island of Labuan, north to the Kota Kinabalu area of Sabah, and down into Sarawak as far as Balangian (St. John 1863: II, 294–295; Treacher 1890: 43; Hose and McDougall 1912: 21; Rutter 1922: 79–80; McArthur 1987: 113).[10] One Barunay tradition indicates that a son of Sultan Hasan, Raja Tangah, left Brunei near the beginning of the seventeenth century to take up rule as the Sultan of Sarawak, with the name of Sultan Ibrahim Ali Omar Shah, and that he took 1,000 retainers with him, including Kadayan (Yura Halim and Jamil Umar 1958: 68; Mohd. Jamil 1991: 38).

The Kadayan have long been one of the least known peoples of Borneo, despite being one of the most easily accessible groups on the island (Harrisson 1959: 76, 1963: 21). While their historical origins are unclear (see Maxwell 1983, 1996, 1982), they have traditionally been followers and supporters of the Sultans of Brunei (Baring-Gould and Bampfylde 1909: 361n.; Rutter 1922: 80; McArthur 1987: 132, 238n.). The strength of the Sultanate's attraction for Kadayan now living in Malaysian territory, however, may well have diminished recently (Sather and Hatta 1974: 249). This issue has been clouded by the Brunei Rebellion of December 1962 with which the Kadayan have been closely linked (Harrisson 1963: 21; Leigh 1974: 44). This rebellion was the first salvo in Konfrontasi, the Malaysian-Indonesian Confrontation of 1964 to 1966 (see Brackman 1966: 133–165, 175–176, 211; Walker 1969: 9, 17–18; Nihal Singh 1971: 67–69, 99, 131–134; Saunders 1994: 147–153).

Demographically the Kadayan comprise a substantial portion of the 'Malay' component (89,268 in 1971; 125,717 in 1981) of Brunei's total population (136,256 in 1971: Brunei 1976: 6; 192,832 in 1981: see [Table 7.1]).[11] While ever changing definitions of the census categories in the twentieth century make it difficult to be precise (see [Table 7.1]; Maxwell 1980), very conservatively the Kadayan probably constitute between a third and a half of all the Malays in Brunei.[12]

The Kadayan and the Brunei Sultanate

Even though the reasons for their involvement in the Brunei Rebellion of 1962 are less than clear,[13] it would be a mistake to conclude that the Kadayan were not historically an integral part of the fabric of Brunei society. This claim is supported by several types of evidence, including: accounts of nineteenth-century visitors to Brunei, local historical and ethno-historical traditions, and the continuity of traditional Malay settlement patterns from earlier to present times. The importance of the role that the Kadayan played within traditional Brunei society becomes more obvious once some of the many ways in which the two Malay ethnic groups, the Kadayan and the Barunay, were interlinked are more clearly delineated.

Economic relationships

A number of nineteenth-century visitors to Brunei observed that the Barunay, a traditionally non-agricultural people (see Maxwell 1980), did not produce their own agricultural staples (for example, Anon. 1878: 413; Dickenson 1838: 139; Roorda van Eysinga 1832: 21). The Barunay engaged in various types of fishing in Brunei Bay, and offshore in the South China Sea. They also specialised in the manufacture of wooden, iron, palm leaf, and brass goods, as well as a number of other economic activities such as trading, rice cleaning, oil making (from illipe nuts), and gold- and silver-smithery (cf. St. John 1863: 11, 278–281, 298; Owen 1910b; Brown 1970: 41–48, 57–59; Abdul Latif 1971: 58–67).[14] At least two nineteenth-century observers were puzzled over where the thousands of Barunay inhabitants of the capital obtained their food supplies (Dickenson 1838: 189; Anon. 1878: 413). However a number of early sources specifically state that it was the Kadayan who supplied the capital with 'all its vegetables' (Anon. 1878: 413), 'rice and sago' (Arthur Adams, in Belcher 1848: I, 180),[15] products of cultivation (Keppel 1846: II, 172), 'large amounts of rice, and nearly all the fruits and vegetables' (St. John 1863: II, 294). Early in the twentieth century, McArthur reinforces these views: 'It is obvious that in a town like Brunei [i.e., the capital, now Bandar Seri Begawan], with a large native population dependent on outside sources for all the necessaries of life, except a certain amount of rice supplied by Kadayan and Bisaya labour, the import trade must always be considerable' (1987: 126). It is not likely that the Kadayan were the exclusive provisioners of the capital in the nineteenth century. There were probably trade networks connecting the capital with the sago-rich valleys of Tutong and Belait to the south-west, as is suggested in some of the early annual reports on Brunei (for example, Owen 1910a: 5; Chevallier 1912: 6). In addition, there are indications that food was shipped in from areas located further away in modern-day Sabah and Sarawak (Sweeney 1968: 25–27; Parnell 1911). In any case it is clear that, while probably not their sole suppliers, the Kadayan were important provisioners of foodstuffs to the Barunay, concentrated in the capital.[16]

The location of the Kadayan homeland areas encircling the capital, the present-day distribution of Kadayan villages in northern Brunei and the Limbang District of Sarawak (see Maps 1–2), and the long-noted skills of the Kadayan as cultivators (for example, St. John 1863: 11, 294; Harrisson 1963: 21), all point to the Kadayan being the most significant sources of food for the Barunay before the present century. Just how important the Kadayan were as food producers for the Barunay is clearly illustrated by an incident recorded by Spenser St. John, one of the most sensitive and insightful observers of nineteenth-century Borneo.

> As a rule, these hill-men [i.e., the Kadayan] are never oppressed; a few, however, who seem to have had a claim over them, originating in debts due by their ancestors, were seized in April, 1861, by the widow of the late Sultan[17] and put in irons until some demands of hers should be satisfied. The whole city was thrown into confusion by this proceeding; all the Kadayans assembled under their chiefs, stopped the supplies of food, and threatened an attack from the neighbouring hills; deputations of nobles waited on the lady, and begged her to let go the men, but she sturdily refused. For three days every man was prepared to defend his portion of the town, business was suspended, and fears and panics prevailed, till at last her relations giving way to the anger of the rest of the inhabitants, insisted upon her letting her prisoners go.
>
> (St. John 1863: II, 294)

Whatever the relationship may have been in earlier times, St. John makes it clear that by the middle of the nineteenth century the capital of Brunei was dependent on Kadayan nearby for the bulk of their food supply.

Political relationships

The Kadayan occupied a position of special political significance in the Brunei Sultanate. Writing just three years after the appointment of a British Resident to Brunei in 1906, two historians sympathetic to the Brooke regime in Sarawak, Sabine Baring-Gould and C. A. Bampfylde, state that the Kadayan had traditionally been 'faithful followers of the Sultans and their main support' (1909: 361n.). Just two years later, the British Resident makes the same point, but even more emphatically, saying of the Kadayan, 'in past times their influence was sufficient to make and unmake Sultans' (Chevallier 1911: 13).

In Brunei today one gets little sense of the nature of this earlier balance of power, but this is not surprising. The traditional economic relationships between the Kadayan and the Barunay have undergone radical changes since the introduction of British administration in 1906. This influence and the development of Brunei's enormous wealth following the end of the Second World War have contributed to major alterations in the life-styles of both the Kadayan and the Barunay. The Barunay have become much less dependent upon the Kadayan as their economy has moved away from traditional patterns of subsistence and food production, and toward an increasingly important service economy, in the form of the large state bureaucracy which has grown steadily in recent decades. Some Kadayan have also been absorbed into government service, but a high proportion of them have continued in altered, but still traditional life-styles centred around the cultivation of rice.

Brunei in the nineteenth century bore only a faint resemblance to its earlier days of splendour and glory in the sixteenth century (Pigafetta 1969: 88–100; see also Nicholl 1975), as nineteenth-century sources make clear (for example, Keppel 1853: II, 118–124). Why did this decline occur? The major reason is probably the gradual erosion in the vibrancy and resilience of the traditional Malay maritime economy of Southeast Asia which had been in process for several centuries. The seventeenth- and eighteenth-century intrusions of the Europeans into the intricate and complex tributary trading system of the Malay world had far-reaching effects on all the indigenous commercial centres of the archipelago (Wolters 1970: 4, 178–179).

As early as the tenth century, Brunei had been trading with China (Wolters 1967: 175–176). In the fourteenth century Brunei was a vassal of Majapahit and sent annual tribute (Sweeney 1968: 51–52; Yura Halim and Jamil Umar 1958: 14; Low 1880c: 1–2). In the sixteenth century, sources indicate that Brunei traded and had political relationships with Manila, Cebu, the Calamines, Cavite, Patani, Jolo, Mindanao, Malacca, Ligor, Pahang, Ayuthia, Sumatra, Champa, Pegu, China, and possibly the Moluccas (see Nicholl 1975). Local genealogical traditions indicate that members of the Brunei royal family married women from Java in the fifteenth, sixteenth, and seventeenth centuries (Yura Halim and Jamil Umar 1958: 33, 47; Low 1880a: 9, 18, 21, 1880b: 27; Sweeney 1968: 69). While in Brunei I was once told by a very old high-ranking noble that he had sailed to Palembang and Java on trading expeditions in his youth.

This rich and complex web of economic, political, and social relationships spanning the archipelago was only a memory by the time the British began to visit Brunei regularly in the second half of the nineteenth century. By then, these reporters could see only piracy, treachery, and deception (for example, Keppel 1846: I, 259–260, 243–46; Belcher 1848: II, 159–162; Low 1848: 105–110; Marryat 1848: 101–102, 104–106; Mundy 1848: I, 188–190, II, 10–12, 87–90, 233–234; Keppel 1853: I, 277–301, II, 116–119, 123–124; Templer 1853: I, 146–148, II, 64–67, 132–146, 166, III, 57–62, 180–193; Brooke 1866: II, 98–99; Jacob 1876: I, 255, 299, 320–321; Rutter 1935: 51, 118–121). This discussion, of the political relationships between the Kadayan and the Barunay, thus refers primarily to the nineteenth century. One can project these inter-relationships backward in time, but there is no independent evidence available to justify doing so. The nineteenth-century accounts depict what appear to be the characteristics of a patron-client relationship between individual Barunay nobles and particular groups of Kadayan.

The reports of such men as Admiral Sir Henry Keppel, Captain Rodney Mundy, Sir James Brooke, and Spenser St. John contain brief, but unmistakably clear accounts indicating that the Kadayan, in supporting Sultan Omar Ali Saifuddin II and other nobles in their differences with the British, were underscoring a long-standing relationship with Barunay. Two incidents in particular stand out.

The first occurred in August 1845, probably during the middle of the month, when Pangiran Yusuf (or Usup), a son of Sultan Muhammad Taijuddin, attacked the capital with a force of 300 Kadayan supporters (Keppel 1846: II, 156–157). The attack seems to have resulted from the decision of Rear-Admiral Sir Thomas Cochrane, the Commander-in-Chief of the Far East Fleet, to punish Pangiran Yusuf on the grounds that he had detained two British subjects after he had entered into an agreement with Sir Edward Belcher, Captain of HMS Samarang. The agreement evidently did not countenance the taking of British subjects (Mundy 1848: II, 34). When Pangiran Yusuf did not appear after a British summons was served, the RearAdmiral fired one shot through the roof of his house, which his batteries returned immediately. The British then opened up a barrage and the occupants of the house fled (Jacob 1876: I, 294). Pangiran Yusuf's attack on the capital with the Kadayan force was repulsed by a force of about 300 men of Pangiran Badarudin a son of Sultan Muhammad Kanzul Alam (who was himself a half-brother of Sultan Muhammad Taijuddin). The attackers regrouped, attacked again, and were again repulsed (Keppel 1846: 11, 157).

After this skirmish, Pangiran Yusuf and his Kadayan followers fled the capital for his residence at Berakas (Mundy 1848: II, 37–38),[18] an area of Kadayan settlements. He was pursued by Pangiran Badarudin with about a thousand men-at-arms. This force encountered Kadayan supporters falling away all along the track to Berakas, until Pangiran Yusuf had been completely deserted (Keppel 1846: II, 157). The significance of this sequence of events is that Pangiran Yusuf, a Barunay noble, chose at a time of great danger to flee to his residence at Berakas, both then and now a Kadayan stronghold.

The second incident occurred in July 1846, following a British attack in substantial force on the eighth of the month. This attack appears to have been the culmination of a series of Brunei irritations, as perceived by the British; including, among others, a Brunei decision to prevent future British communication with the capital (Mundy 1848: II, 130), a British understanding that HMS Hazard, and Egerton, its captain, were to be lured into the capital and taken captive (Mundy 1848: II, 129–30, 140, 142), and the killing of members of the Brunei royal family believed to be sympathetic to the plans and aspirations of James Brooke (Mundy 1848: II, 130–137). The British took the city.

After the attack, the Sultan, Omar Ali Saifuddin II, fled the capital with a 500-man bodyguard to the village of Damuan, a Kadayan settlement upstream and west of the city. Despite a lively pursuit through the upper reaches of the Damuan River and the Kadayan villages of Kabiran Batu, Pilong, Mulaut, and Tanjung, with about half the Kadayan supporters of the Sultan falling away en route, the British party of James Brooke was never able to catch up with the Sultan (Mundy 1848: II, 162–166).[19] It is unclear whether the British party ever reached the village of Damuan itself. These events also indicate that when high-ranking Barunay – in this case including the Sultan himself – found themselves in times of great difficulty, they turned to their traditional allies, the Kadayan.

Barunay historical traditions and the Kadayan

Barunay traditional history also represents the Kadayan as playing important roles in the events of the Sultanate at the end of the seventeenth century. The fact that these events are part of Barunay historical traditions underscores the argument that the Kadayan were part of Brunei society, not external to it. The importance of these traditions lies not in the question of their veracity, but rather that they have become part of a general Barunay cognitive pattern about the past. These events exemplify Barunay attitudes, beliefs, and expectations about the Kadayan which are not hostile, but intimate and amicable. Both of the examples to be discussed show that Barunay viewed the Kadayan as their friends, comrades, and, sometimes, relatives.

The first series of events highlights the complex interplay found in Brunei between ethnicity and genealogical filiation. This case spans the period from the reign of Sultan Saiful Rijal in the late sixteenth century to that of Sultan Muhyiddin in the late seventeenth century. In a subtle way it symbolically both vindicates and validates the relationships of kinship between the Kadayan and the Barunay Malay ethnic groups down to the present day. The central figure in this drama is the Kadayan, Rajid bin Orang Kaya Kasim.[20]

During the time of Spanish attacks on Brunei around 1578 (see Nicholl 1975: 35–48), Sultan Saiful Rijal left the capital and took up residence in Jerudong, an area of Kadayan settlements just north of the Damuan area. Here he lived with a Kadayan *gundik* (concubine), who gave birth to a son, Pangiran Anak Kasim.[21] After the Spanish threat had subsided and his father, the Sultan, had returned to the capital, Pangiran Anak Kasim remained with his mother in Jerudong (Mohd. Jamil 1971: 79–80).

Sometime later in the seventeenth century, during the reign of his halfbrother, Sultan Hasan, Pangiran Anak Kasim was called to the capital. When he overheard the news being given to the Sultan that a Kadayan had come to pay homage, Pangiran Anak Kasim became angry. He was undoubtedly reacting as many Kadayan will do today when they are publicly referred to as 'Kadayan'. A pejorative connotation can be conveyed by the tone of voice or intonation with which the term Kadayan is uttered.[22] Pangiran Anak Kasim refused to remain in the capital as Sultan Hasan wished. Further, he indicated that he no longer wished to be called Pangiran Anak Kasim.[23] He wished to be referred to only as Si-Kasim, with the person-prefix 'Si-' indicating that he was a person of non-noble and non-aristocratic ancestry, in other words he wished to be known simply as a Kadayan.[24] Because he was the son of a Sultan, this wish was not only his right to assert but had to be respected.

Subsequently Sultan Hasan wished to confer one of the noble *citiria*[25] titles on Pangiran Anak Kasim – or Si-Kasim, as he preferred to be called. Being a *citiria* would have marked him as a person of very high noble rank in Brunei, but he refused to accept the title. Kasim wished instead to receive one of the much lower ranking Land Minister (*Mantri Darat*) titles, appropriate to his cultural status as a Kadayan. He thus became 'Orang Kaya Kasim' and later had two sons, Si-Imas and Si-Rajid. Si-Rajid became famous throughout Brunei for his extraordinary strength, obtained from a preternatural experience with a spirit (*jin*) in a cave in Jerudong, during the reign of Sultan Muhyiddin, during the late seventeenth century.[26] At this time the fourth vizier of Brunei, Pangiran Tumanggung Raja Digayuh, was believed to be a practitioner of sorcery (*ilmu sihir*) and wished to become Sultan himself. This vizier was a son of Sultan Abdul Jalilul Akbar by his third wife, a Bajau princess (Yura Halim and Jamil Umar 1958: 72), and thus a half-brother of Sultan Muhyiddin, who was himself a son of Sultan Abdul Jalilul Akbar by his second wife, the daughter of the Tumanggung of Grisik, in Java. Sultan Muhyiddin was convinced that this situation threatened the general peace of the country and called for the aid of Si-Rajid. Because of his immense strength, Si-Rajid was able to defeat the sorcerer and would-be usurper, Pangiran Tumanggung Raja Digayuh. As a reward for his loyal service, Sultan Muhyiddin declared Si-Rajid the new fourth vizier, Pangiran Tumanggung Rajid (Mohd. Jamil 1971: 81–85). When he died he was buried in the royal cemetery at Kianggih, on the eastern edge of the modem capital of Brunei (Mohd. Jamil reproduces a photograph of Pangiran Tumanggung Rajid's tombstone: 1971: 84).

The second case, involving the other son of Orang Kaya Kasim, Si-Imas, also reflects the complex symbolic linkage between ethnic identification, political power, and genealogy in Brunei. It also further illustrates the supportive role which the Kadayan have played historically to the Sultans of Brunei. Imas had already received his own Land Minister title, and was known as Orang Kaya Basar Imas. He is well-known in Barunay tradition for his support of Pangiran Bandahara Muhyiddin (later to become Sultan Muhyiddin, as indicated earlier) in regaining the throne of Brunei from a usurper, late in the seventeenth century (cf. Brown 1970: 144). The usurper, Pangiran Bandahara Abdul Mubin, had seized the throne after he had killed the Sultan, Muhammad Ali, in a fit of rage. Abdul Mubin's own son had been killed by the Sultan's son (Pangiran Digadung Omar in Low's account [1880a: 11n]; Pangiran Muda Alam in Yura Halim's fictionalized account [1951]), after the former had defeated him in a cockfight.

Orang Kaya Basar Imas of Subok was the leader of the Kadayan at the time and threw his support behind Pangiran Bandahara Muhyiddin to avenge the death of Sultan Muhammad Ali, who was both father's brother and father-in-law to Pangiran Bandahara Muhyiddin. According to tradition, the Kadayan executed a reign of intimidation and terror by dark. Each night bands of Kadayan roamed throughout the capital, banging on the undersides of the houses of the usurper and all his royal officials, by sharply thrusting their spears upward (cf. Sweeney 1968: 59–60).[27] In order to avoid the unknown foe, Abdul Mubin moved his residence to Carmin Island, located in the mouth of the Brunei River (see Map 10.2). Pangiran Bandahara Muhyiddin then had the usurper effectively isolated and prosecuted a twelveyear war which culminated in the death of Abdul Mubin and his own rightful succession to the throne, as Sultan Muhyiddin. This affair is one of the best-known events in Brunei history (Yura Halim and Jamil Umar 1958: 75–81). Individuals at all levels of modern Brunei society are acquainted with its outlines, no doubt due at least in part to the popular novel, with the subtitle of 'The bloody crown' (Mahkota yang berdarah, Yura Halim 1951) which gives a fictionalised account of the episode.

These examples illustrate how close personal ties between individual Barunay and Kadayan leaders operated to bind these two Malay ethnic groups together in previous centuries. Orang Kaya Basar Imas indeed had the power to make and unmake sultans, as is clearly recorded in Barunay tradition. He led his followers into what was clearly a personal dispute between members of the Barunay royal family, with decisive results.[28] The case of Rajid and the special relationship Sultan Saiful Rijal had with the Kadayan of Jerudong is more complex. It illustrates some of the subtleties and nuances of Malay ethnic identification in Brunei.

The pride in his Kadayan cultural heritage exhibited by Si-Kasim (or Orang Kaya Kasim; father of Si-Rajid – or Pangiran Tumanggung Rajid – and son of Sultan Saiful Rijal) and his refusal of a noble *citiria* title in favour of a much lower ranking title of Land Minister, accords completely with my own experience with the Kadayan. Informants would often say, of themselves: *tida maw* (*cari*) *pangkat* (we don't want or seek rank). Kadayan – both in ideology and in fact – exhibit a thorough-going egalitarianism in all aspects of their lives. No one would wish to set himself apart from, and especially over his peers. On the other hand, Kadayan also express a keen sense of appreciation for custom and tradition. It is not at all surprising that Kasim would brush aside the offer of a noble title from his older half-brother Sultan Hasan, and accept instead a traditional Kadayan office, believing this more appropriate to his chosen identity as a Kadayan.

While the case of Rajid might appear to confound this conclusion, it does not. After Rajid defeated Pangiran Tumanggung Raja Digayuh, Sultan Muhyiddin announced to the assembled state officials (*pambasarpambasar nagara*) that henceforth Rajid would be known as Pangiran Tumanggung Rajid, the fourth vizier of Brunei. It is the style and manner in which the Sultan made this award which may well have persuaded Rajid, preventing any possible refusal on his part. The use of the power of office in this way would make perfect sense in Brunei, if not in all societies.

At first glance this analysis would appear to have revealed a paradox in ethnic identifications. Sultan Saiful Rijal is Barunay. His son, Pangiran Anak Kasim is Barunay, but becomes Kadayan, as Si-Kasim, who later becomes Orang Kaya Kasim. Finally, Kasim's son, Si-Rajid, is Kadayan but becomes Barunay, as Pangiran Tumanggung Rajid (and, as Mohd. Jamil indicates, Pangiran Tumanggung Rajid had numerous noble descendants, some of whom are prominent in Brunei 1971: 85–86). But the paradox is only apparent, not real. To be a Kadayan is, above all, to participate in a way of life. There is no substantial difference whether one embraces it unknowingly, by accident of birth, as do most Kadayan born in Kadayan communities of Kadayan parents, or by conscious choice, as Kasim did. He, it must be remembered, had a choice (his father was a Barunay Sultan, his mother a Kadayan). Rajid likewise had, as it were, a choice; the choice, however, was made for him, by Sultan Muhyiddin.[29]

Ritual relationships and the status of the Kadayan in Brunei society

The traditional ritual relationships of the Kadayan to the Barunay, and especially the royal family, are intertwined with the relative status of the Kadayan in the overall social system of Brunei society. The Kadayan have long occupied a very low position of social prestige within the society at large. From the point of view of local Barunay cultural and legal theory, the Kadayan belonged – as did all members of Brunei society – to the Sultan, in the sense that all members of the society are the Sultan's subjects (*rayat*).

There are a number of traditional ritual relationships which have bound the Kadayan and the Barunay together. Many of these traditions have fallen away in the twentieth century, but the evidence for them is well-known. The importance of the Kadayan as makers and unmakers of Sultans has been discussed previously. Relationships between particular groups of Kadayan and members of the royal family were illustrated in the discussion of political relationships linking the Kadayan and Barunay.[30]

Another connection between these two Malay groups is their participation in the set of traditional ritual offices and titles awarded by the Sultan. This system of titles was probably the most complex and elaborate in the Malay world, if twentieth-century elaborations of it are any guide (see Yusuf 1958, 1975). The Brunei system of offices and titles is structured by ethnicity and social class.[31] The most important of these offices and titles are awarded only to Barunay nobles and Barunay aristocrats. According to Brunei custom and tradition (see Yusuf 1958: 42–45, 1975: 64–66), the four (now five) offices of Vizier (*wazir*) and the 60 *citiria* can be awarded only to nobles (*raja-raja*, or *pangiran-pangiran*); the 73 offices of minister (*mantri*) only to aristocrats (*awang-awang*). Traditionally three minister offices were awarded to Chinese [2] and Indians [1]; in recent years a few additional minister offices have been developed and awarded to Europeans. There are a dozen or so palace offices, the details of which are not clear, which are also awarded to Barunay. Kadayan, along with members of other non-Barunay ethnic groups, may receive only offices of Land Minister, of which there are an indefinite number, and Head Land Minister (*Kapala Mantri Darat*), of which there are four. These Land Minister offices have considerably lower rank and prestige than those of Minister awarded to Barunay aristocrats.

Thus the Kadayan had their own place in the traditional, ritual Brunei state, assigned by custom and history. While their position was a lowly one, beneath the ranks of the Barunay nobles (*pangiran-pangiran, raja-raja*), aristocrats (*awang-awang*), palace officials (*pagaway astana*), religious officials (*pagaway ugama*), and 'other' officials (*pagaway*), it was, in the form of their leaders holding Land Minister offices (along with Dusun, Tutung, and Belait Land Ministers), nonetheless provided for in important state rituals (see, for example, the listings in Brunei 1963: 29–33, 35–39; and in Yusuf 1975: 64–88, in which the Land Ministers are always listed last).[32] This pattern suggests that the Kadayan have long been considered to be part-and-parcel of Brunei society, not only by themselves but also by the Barunay.

Kadayan settlement patterns and ethno-historical orientation areas

The locations of the old territories to which Kadayan trace their ancestry further illustrate how they have been inextricably connected with the rest of Brunei society for a very long time. Informants commonly trace genealogical connections to ancestors in particular *nagri kadayan asli* (original Kadayan lands). For example, a person will claim to be, or be referred to as, an *urang salar* (a Salar person), or an *urang* Damuan (a Damuan person), meaning that the individual traces a substantial portion of his or her ancestry to the Salar *nagri* or the Damuan *nagri*. Because the relationships of individuals to these areas are now calculated genealogically, and because marriages have commonly occurred between individuals from different *nagri*, a person sometimes has connections back to more than one of these areas. Informants understand this complication and will often indicate that the majority of their ancestors came from one *nagri*, and other ancestors from one or more other areas.

These *nagri* spatially circumscribe the modem capital and the major traditional Barunay settlement (see Map 10.2). Both Malay groups were positioned planometrically in a circular pattern, with the Barunay at the centre; the Kadayan at the periphery. This structural alignment promoted and facilitated the relationships of economic, political, and social symbiosis. In earlier centuries the agricultural Kadayan were dispersed and spread out over the landscape, cultivating their swiddens. The non-agricultural Barunay were concentrated mainly in a large dense community at the centre, located around a sharp bend in the Brunei River, near its confluence with the Kianggih and Kadayan Rivers. One aristocratic informant indicated that in earlier times when Kadayan brought their goods down the Kadayan River, which drains the Berakas and Gadung nagri to the north, they had to stop off first at the house of the Orang Kaya DiGadung (a Barunay aristocrat, probably living in the Barunay village of Kampong Sungai Kadayan) to let him take what he wanted before they could proceed further to engage in trading and barter.

In modern Brunei these *nagri* do not appear to have any function other than serving as foci of orientation to the past.[33] Fragmentary information suggests that there could have been ritual differences between the different *nagri* in earlier times. For example, one woman, who had grown up in Salar, stated that people who descend from the Salar *nagri* have a taboo against eating the horseshoe crab (*bulangkas*). Her husband, also of Salar ancestry but not having grown up there, present at the time, was surprised and indicated that he had not known of this prohibition. Another area of possible ritual difference is found in particular details of Kadayan marriage ceremonial procedure, but data are too fragmentary to be more specific.

The original number of the ancestral nagri is uncertain. Most informants indicated there were at least seven (Salar, Berakas, Gadung, Damuan, Masin, Kasat, and Kianggih, see Map 2) but some suggested as many as twelve. Informants differ on the number in at least two ways, by employing synonymous references as well as cross-cutting inclusions for a number of areas. For example, Kianggih is also known as Subuk, and Salar as Timur. Gadung is said by some to include a half dozen villages in addition to Jerudong, and others distinguish a separate Jerudong *nagri* which does not include Gadung. For some, Kilanas and Lumapas are included in the Damuan area and for others they are each separate *nagri*, and so on. (The areas represented in Map 10.2 thus constitute a minimal core number of *nagri*.) These differences between informants over the number of *nagri* may well reflect the massive social and cultural change which has occurred in the last few decades in Brunei. As much traditional culture disappears, these ethnohistorical orientation areas are losing any raison d'être and fast becoming forgotten.

The territories of the *nagri* roughly approximate the areas included in the bounds of one or more drainage basins within each *nagri*. This definition of *nagri* boundaries accords with the geographical parameters of the traditional Kadayan agricultural system. In their system of swidden agriculture, villagers annually shift the location of their swiddens within the bounds of the drainage basin of a feeder stream flowing into a larger river. Currently many also cultivate permanent rice-fields, but these techniques were introduced only in the early years of British administration in the twentieth century.

The ethno-historical orientation area was probably never as important as the village as a unit of Kadayan social structure, and consisted, according to informants, of a set of consanguineally-related individuals who, except for those who might have married into another area, occupied a particular named territory (Salar, Berakas, etc.). It also seems likely that each of these areas may have been under the leadership of its own Land Minister (or possibly, in earlier times, *Mantri* Kadayan: cf. Sweeney 1968: 25), such as the Orang Kaya Basar Imas, who was the leader of the Kadayan of the Kianggih *nagri*, at Subuk, during the disputed succession to the Brunei throne late in the seventeenth century. All *Mantri Darat* were appointed by the Sultan of Brunei.

The significance of the Kadayan ethno-historical orientation areas is twofold. They supply sociological matrices within which individuals trace their ancestry and to which they orientate themselves historically. Spatially they circumscribe the main traditional settlement of the Bangsa Barunay, or Barunay ethnic group, and the Royal Court of the Sultanate, which has long been located at the modern capital of the country. The locations of these centuries-old *nagri* in a geographically strategic position around the traditional centre of power of the Brunei Sultanate is a further indication of the importance the Kadayan have played in the larger society of Brunei for a long time.

Conclusions

One consideration which purposely has been only touched on in discussion is the question of the relative positions of the Kadayan and the Barunay, the two native Malay-speaking ethnic groups of Brunei Darussalam, in the overall system of social stratification in the country. Before one can proceed to an examination of the various status and ranking relationships which have tended to set them apart, it is necessary first to note the economic, political, sociological, and demographic relationships which have linked these two ethnic groups together historically. This has been the aim of this discussion. The reasoning for taking this approach is as follows. The significance of the stratificational differences between the Kadayan and the Barunay – pronounced as they are – will become clearer when certain basic strategic questions of living are answered. Where does food come from? Who are to be counted as potential allies – or enemies – in times of difficulty? Who controls the neighbouring territory? If procedures along the lines of those adopted here are not followed, then there is a danger of failing to recognise important relationships of mutuality, and focusing instead on social structural disjunctures and the unequal aspects of status and rank differences. In such a case, especially in a radically plural society like Brunei, crucial aspects of inter-ethnic relationships could easily be missed.

To conclude that the Kadayan were traditionally a people subject to the Barunay (as opposed to everyone being 'subjects' of the Sultan) – and I separate this question from that which asks whether any other ethnic groups in Borneo were subject peoples of the Barunay – leads one towards certain uncomfortable analytical conclusions about this society. First, it is the 'subjects' who occupy and live in virtually all the immediately neighbouring territory of the society, as seen from the centre. Second, only the 'subjects' have, from the perspective of comparative ethnography, the expected food-producing economy for staple foodstuffs. Finally, individual members of the 'ruling' ethnic group, on occasion, decide to give up their position in that group and become members of a 'subject' people. All of these conclusions appear, to me, to be counter-intuitive. We simply do not expect a society to be organised in such a fashion.

Table 7.1 Summary of 20th-century censuses of Brunei Darussalam

	a	*b*	*c*	*d*[1]	*e*[2]	*f*[3]	*g*[4]	*h*	*i*[5]	*j*
	1906 est.	*1911*	*1921*	*1931*	*1947*	*1960*	*1971*	*1981*	*1986*	*1991*
Total Population	25,000	21,718	25,451	30,135	40,657	83,877	136,256	192,832	226,329	260,482
Indigenous	24,500	20,916	23,943	26,746	31,161	59,203	97,820	140,892	167,019	–
Malay	nr	nr	13,641	14,835	16,742	41,135	89,268	125,717	155,533	–
Barunay	12,000	11,554	nr	nr	nr	nr	nr	nr	nr	–
Other indigenous	12,500	9,362	10,302	11,911	14,419	14,068	8,552	15,175		–
Kedayan	7,000	4,931	4,734	5,871	6,726	4,291	nr	nr	nr	–
Murut	4,000	563	nr	290	296	nr	nr	nr	nr	–
Bisaya	nr	nr	nr	[0]	35	nr	nr	nr	nr	–
Dusun	nr	951	1,115	2,118	2,757	4,891	nr	nr	nr	–
Dali	nr	118	nr	nr	nr	nr	nr	nr	nr	–
Belait	nr	1,097	nr	446	721	nr	nr	nr	nr	–
Tutong	nr	1,667	2,391	2,733	2,431	nr	nr	nr	nr	–
Melanau	nr	nr	nr	[0]	86	318	nr	nr	nr	–
Iban	nr	nr	nr	453	1,330	3,900	nr	nr	nr	–
Land Dayak	nr	nr	nr	[0]	2	nr	nr	nr	nr	–
Punan	nr	nr	nr	[0]	29	nr	nr	nr	nr	–
Residuum	nr	35	35	nr	1,089	686	nr	nr	nr	–
Chinese	500	500	1,423	2,683	8,300	21,795	31,925	39,461	41,401	–
Indian	nr	44	38	377	454		2,162	5,919		–
Others	500	22	47	329	742	2,879	4,349	6,500	17,909	–
Javanese	nr	nr	–	165	237	nr	nr	nr	nr	–
European	nr	22	[36]	70	394	nr	nr	nr	nr	–
Residuum	nr	nr	–	[94]	111	nr	nr	nr	nr	–

Notes:

nr: not reported [ ]: interpolated from next succeeding census

[1]: Definitions of 'Indigenous', 'Malay', and 'Other Indigenous' differ; this census combines Brunei and British Malaya.

[2]: 'Other Indigenous' Residuum includes: 1 Kayan, 2 Kenyah, 1 Kelabit, and 2 Tatau.

[3]: 'In 1960 many of the "Other Indigenous" population were suspected to have been included in the "Malays"' (Brunei 1976: 6).

[4]: 'Malay – which consisted of the Malays, Kedayans, Bisayah, Dusuns, and Muruts. Also included were those who called themselves orang Brunei [Barunay], Belait, Tutong' (Brunei 1973: 34). 'In 1971 the definition of "Malays" was changed to indigenous populations of the Malay race which censuses' (Brunei 1976: 6).

[5]: '"Malay" includes Muruts and Dusuns' (Brunei 1989: 9).

Sources of demographic information: a: McArthur (n.d.); b: Chevallier (1912); c: Nathan (1922); d: Jones (1962); e: Vlieland (1932); f: Noakes (1950); g: Jones (1962); h: Brunei (1973); i: Brunei (n.d.); j: Brunei (1989); k: Anon. (1993).

It is more appropriate to analyse the relative positions between the Kadayan and the Barunay in the social structure of Brunei society by considering the panoply of their differences within the context of the theoretical model of the plural society, as D. E. Brown has done (1976). Then it becomes possible to consider the various positions of power, prestige, and – in a Weberian sense – social honour, to be a complex, intricate expression of perhaps the most important defining characteristic of a plural society. That is the fact that one ethnic group monopolises political power in the social system of the overall society. The evidence presented here and the arguments adduced point to the conclusion that the Kadayan and the Barunay were, in the past, symbiotic participants in a common economy; but – and this has not been discussed here – they were to a much lesser extent co-participants in a common system of social values, general orientation, and personal goals.

Acknowledgments

Field research in the village of Pyasaw-Pyasaw, Labu Valley, Temburong District, Brunei, 1968–71, was supported by National Institutes of Health Research Grant 1 TOL MH 11,231–01, and Wenner-Gren Foundation for Anthropological Research Pre-Doctoral Fellowship No. 2173, and was sponsored locally by the Dewan Bahasa dan Pustaka, Brunei. I would like to thank Donald E. Brown, George N. Appell, and William R. Roff for their readings of an earlier version of this paper which was presented at the 36th annual meeting of the Association for Asian Studies, Washington, DC, in March 1984.

Note on transcription. Italicised citations follow my phonemicisation of Brunei Malay (see Maxwell 1969, 1985; on the spelling 'Kadayan', see Maxwell 1970). It should be noted that the Brunei dialect of Malay has only three phonemic vowels, i, a, and u. The orthographic vowels <e> and <o>, therefore, have only phonetic significance, or reflect spelling conventions and are without phonemic significance. I have attempted to follow recent standardised conventions of the uniform spelling system for Malay and Indonesian, where possible (see, e.g., Anon. 1984). The spellings of place-names follow Brunei conventions.

Notes

1 This question is one in which I had a hand in raising. It developed during my field research in Brunei, when Don Brown asked me to comment on a draft of his dissertation, which he had graciously sent me and which greatly increased my understanding of the country and the society of Brunei, and he included my view of that time that 'the Kedayans should in some sense be considered a part of Brunei society' in the published version (see Brown 1970:16).

2 Brown is one of the few observers of Brunei who has paid careful attention to the relevance of the concept of 'plural society' to understanding the social system of the Sultanate (esp. 1976: 81–99, 181–197). The concept is an old one, perhaps first applied by the Dutch economist Boeke to try to understand the social and economic system of the Dutch East Indies in the decades preceding the Second World War (see Boeke 1953; Boeke and others 1961). J. S. Furnivall developed the concept further in his studies of Burma and the Netherlands Indies (1944, 1956). M. G. Smith developed the concept

even further in his studies of the British West Indies (1965a), Grenada (1965b), and the Hausa (1960, 1978). Brown then refined some of Smith's ideas (see, esp., Smith 1971b: 440–448) in referring to the 'radically plural society', of which Brunei is an example (Brown 1976: 83). Others have applied the concept to societies in Melanesia (Glick 1970), the Caribbean (Rubin 1960; Smith 1970), and Africa (Kuper 1970; Tuden and Plotnicov 1970). Smith (1971b) presents a useful summary of the concept of the 'plural society' and criticisms of it.

3 Brunei had of course been experiencing intermittent contact with Europeans, especially with the Portuguese and Spanish, throughout the sixteenth century after the visit of Antonio Pigafetta in 1521 (Pigafetta 1969; see Nicholl 1975). However, these contacts were sporadic and often highly fractious. They did not lead to any enduring linkages with the West. The number of visits to Brunei by Europeans appears to have dropped off dramatically in the seventeenth century (see also Brown 1970: 146–149).

4 I have followed primarily the account by Low written in 1875 as part of an official report to the British government (Brown 1969a), for two reasons. By 1875, Low had long experience in the area and was intimately familiar with many of the details of Brunei history (for example, Low 1848). Secondly, his account is relatively close, chronologically, to the events in question. However, the recent publication of correspondence of Sultan Muhammad Kanzul Alam and Pangiran Muda Muhammad Alam, sixteen Malay letters dating from 1821 and 1822 (Gallop 1995), suggests that the degree of turmoil in this period may have been a little overstated and that the history of this period may need re-examination.

5 This account refers only to the loss of territories north of Brunei Bay to European powers. Accounts of the loss of the areas north of Kimanis to the Sultanate of Sulu in the seventeenth century differ (see Brown 1969a).

6 All of Sarawak's Limbang District, located only a short distance to the south of the modern capital, was part of Brunei until it was seized by Sarawak's Raja Charles Brooke in 1890 (cf. Criswell 1971: 226; Tarling 1971: 415–417; Baring-Gould and Bampfylde 1909: 352; Brown 1968: 101, 1970: 154–155; Wright 1970: 201). The long-smouldering Limbang question has resurfaced a number of times since 1890: in 1895 (Brown 1968: 112–113), in 1901 (Ranjit Singh 1984: 94; Tarling 1971: 483–490), in 1904 (McArthur 1987: 138–144), in 1941 (Tregonning 1958: 88; Criswell 1971: 228; Turnbull 1989: 216), in 1962 (Observer 1970: 35) when Brunei's claim was officially revived (Turnbull 1992: 621), with considerable press coverage in 1970 (Stephen 1970; Correspondent 1970; Observer 1970), in late 1975 (Saunders 1994: 164–165), in 1977 (Ranjit Singh 1984: 204–205). I was sitting in the audience at the Dewan Bahasa dan Pustaka Brunei on 30 September 1970 when the then D. Y. T. M. Paduka Seri Begawan Sultan Sir Muda Omar Ali Saifuddin, who was delivering an address at the ceremonies celebrating the change of the name of the capital of Brunei from Bandar Brunei to Bandar Seri Begawan, following a discussion of the dangers of traffic accidents, abruptly punctuated his delivery with *Limbang berhak Brunei!* (Limbang rightfully belongs to Brunei!) and launched into an impassioned discussion of the rightfulness of Brunei's claim. This is a very passionate issue in Brunei, and, reportedly, still very much alive. Recently, however, 'both countries agreed to resolve their overlapping claims on Limbang through bilateral discussions without arbitration by a third party' (Anon. 1994: 92).

7 For example, Brunei's annual GDP per capita has fluctuated, in recent years, from B$56,979 in 1980 to B$23,400 in 1993, due to varying world prices for petrochemical products (Anon. 1994: 92). Saunders notes that in 1987 Brunei offered Indonesia a US$100 million loan, 'on very generous terms' (1994: 178).

8 Other ethnic groups are also referred to as 'Malay' in Brunei, but these are not natively Malay-speaking (Martin 1992: 108, quoted in King 1994: 178–179). These are speakers of Tutong, Belait, Dusun (= Bisaya), Murut (Lun Bawang), etc. who have adopted Islam and live in a Malay style (See notes to [Table 7.1]).

9 During 1968–71, I estimated the major concentration of Barunay communities (the water village – actually a series of 36 or more different villages – located in the Brunei River at Bandar Seri Begawan) to have a population of about 20,000. The 1971 Brunei census gives the population as 22,364, in 0.4 square miles (Brunei 1973: 31). This Barunay settlement which has existed continuously for nearly the last five centuries (Pigafetta 1969: 95) may have long been the largest traditional community built over water in the Malay world (see Brown 1970: 39–62).

10 The reasons why the Kadayan left what is now Brunei are not entirely clear. St. John reports that 'about a thousand of these men' went over to the island of Labuan to be farmers, but gives no reason why they left Brunei (1863: II, 295). Speaking of the Kadayan in 1890, Clutterbuck writes 'there must be some two thousand of them now settled in Labuan' (1891: 203). Hall reports that 'No people lived permanently on the island [of Labuan] when the Sultan of Brunei [Omar Ali Saifuddin II) ceded it to Queen Victoria a hundred and ten years ago' (1958: 10), i.e., on 24 December 1846 (Forbes 1848: 287–288); but Forbes, who visited Labuan in January 1847, writes of obtaining information from 'the natives residing at Labuan' (1848: 322). According to Baring-Gould and Bampfylde, 'Many of the peaceable Kadayans removed into the Limbang [Valley], having been driven from their homes, with the loss of all their property' (1909: 361 n.) for refusing to aid in an attack on rebels in Tutong and Belait Districts, sometime around the turn of the twentieth century. Other Kadayan, however, appear to have joined in this, or some other attack around the same time. Tarling notes that in (probably) 1901, 'Pg. Tajudin [a son-in-law of the Sultan (Hashim): Baring-Gould and Bampfylde 1909: 361) had attacked with 100 Dusuns and 250 Kedayans from Belait and killed four people from Birau, a Tutong tributary'. Writing in the fourth year of British administration in Brunei, Chevallier noted a decrease in the number of poll-tax paying citizens. 'The Kedayans are the most troublesome people in regard to this tax. A very large number of their people left the State in former days to escape the extortions of the Pengirans [nobles]' (Chevallier 1910: 2). In 1842, Mundy found a colony of some thirty Kadayan families, which had grown from an original six or seven male immigrants, living at a fishing station at Siru, located just to the west of Sematan in Sarawak's First Division (1848: I, 310). Rutter, writing eight decades later, records Kadayan scattered along the west coast of Sabah (ex-British North Borneo) and at Sipitang (1922: 52, 79–80). The 1947 Sarawak Census enumerated Kadayan living in the Census Districts of Kapit (1), Bintulu (335), Miri (2,671), Baram (7), Limbang (1,658), and Lawas (600) (Noakes 1950: 45–49).

11 In Brunei the definition of the cultural category 'Malay' is a complex and important issue. Locally the term Melayu has at least five different polysemous senses of meaning, which depend on particular combinations of religious, linguistic, ethnic, and legal criteria (see Maxwell 1980).

12 In discussing the results of the 1981 Census, Saunders says 'The impression is of a relatively small majority of ethnic Malays (excluding Kedayans, Dusuns, and other indigenous peoples) of about 55 per cent' (1994: 175). By 'ethnic Malays', Saunders clearly indicates the Barunay. The accuracy of his claim is open to question. If the Kadayan are excluded, I believe it is exceedingly unlikely that the 'ethnic Malays' would constitute 'a relatively small majority . . . of about 55 per cent'. Indeed, my own work leads me to suspect that if the Kadayan were excluded, the 'ethnic Malays' (i.e., Barunay) would very likely constitute less than 50 per cent of the population of Brunei Darussalam. During the period of my research in Brunei, I estimated there were at least 172 Kadayan villages, with 31 others identified by informants as mixed between Kadayan and at least one other ethnic group. I have no idea how many Kadayan villages there are in Sarawak, Labuan, and Sabah, but would estimate that there certainly would be at least 50, and probably more in these areas.

13 For example, I was told that the reason the Kadayan joined the Brunei Rebellion was that they wanted to join Malaysia (in 1963); on the other hand, I was told that it was

because they did not want to join Malaysia. Both statements were made by different, very knowledgeable and competent, Kadayan informants from Temburong District, where support for the rebellion has been said to have been the strongest (Harrisson 1963: 21; Smith 1963).

14 Curiously, St. John mentions that some 'gardeners' did live in one or more of the smaller Barunay villages at the capital around the middle of the nineteenth century (1863: II, 281), but does not elaborate. Nonetheless, the basic fact that the Barunay were not traditionally agriculturalists remains clear (see Maxwell 1980).

15 Adams actually refers to 'the Kianggi, an agricultural race' (Belcher 1848: II, 180), but other accounts make it clear that the people living in the middle and upper reaches of the Kianggih River were then – as they are today – Kadayan (Dickenson 1838: 183; Keppel 1846: I, 322). While it is not a common term, the Kadayan are still occasionally referred to as *urang* Kianggih.

16 It is actually quite remarkable that the authors of major works on Brunei are so silent as to where the capital obtained its foodstuffs, given the fact that the Barunay themselves, as far as is known, have never been food producers. Tarling reports a sago factory in Tutong in 1879 (1971: 265), and, discussing events in the Limbang Valley in 1889, mentions that 'most of the sago trade was carried on at Danau' (1971: 404), which is located nearly 25 km (about 15 air miles) south-west of the modern town of Limbang and about 30 km (nearly 20 air miles) south-south-west of the capital of Brunei, and very close to the modern border with Brunei's Tutong District. Horton notes that four sago factories in the capital had closed after the seizure of the Limbang Valley by Sarawak's Charles Brooke in 1890 (1987: 30), presumably because the supply of raw sago had been shut off. The majority of references to sago in the main sources on Brunei refer to export trade, and the revenue derived therefrom, but not to its local consumption as a food.

17 This Sultan, Omar Ali Saifuddin II, died on 18 November 1852 (Veth 1856: 487). Hugh Low states that 'He had been married to a lady, The Pengiran Isteri, a daughter of Pengiran Anak Bahar, and a niece of Raja Muda Hassim, but had been separated from her without leaving any family' (Brown 1969a: 148).

18 Today Berakas is a sub-district (mukim) of Brunei-Muara District (*dayrah*), encompassing, approximately, the drainage basin of the Berakas River, a tributary of the Kadayan River. The sub-district includes roughly 30 square miles (80 square kilometres) bordering the South China Sea. While in Brunei, I estimated that the Berakas sub-district contained about 19 villages, of which at least 8 were Kadayan settlements (Berakas, Lambak, Manggis, Salambigar, Serusop, Sungai Hancing, Timbunan, and Tilung); and 8 were Barunay (Anggerik Desa, Burong Pingai Berakas, Delima I. Delima II, Luagan Pulai, Orang Kaya Besar Imas, Palait, and Pulai B). Of the latter 8, 4 represent recent migrants from the main water settlement at the capital. (See Chevallier 1910: 6, 1911: 15–16 for early British concern to get the Barunay to leave the traditional settlements over water and take up residence on dry land.) The Barunay villages tend to be located very close to the main trunk road between the capital and the port town of Muara, located to the north-east. Kadayan villages are found both along this road as well as in the traditional rice-growing areas away from it.

19 Damuan is an area of Kadayan settlements just upstream of the traditional capital. It encompasses, approximately, the drainage area of the Damuan or Kilanas River, and includes much of the sub-districts of Sengkurong, in Brunei District, and Keriam, in Tutong District. I tabulated at least 18 villages for Kilanas – 14 as Kadayan and one as possibly Barunay; 25 villages for Sengkurong – 21 as Kadayan and none as Barunay; and 23 villages for Keriam – 16 as Kadayan and one as possibly Barunay. The present-day Kadayan villages of Mulaut and Tanjong are situated along the Tutong Road in Sengkurong. Apparently, there is no extant village of Damuan although the name is well-known, designating one of the Kadayan ethno-historical orientation areas. The

village of Pilong (Mundy's Pelang) was probably located somewhere near the Pilohong River (see Maxwell 1984a), a tributary of the Damuan or Kilanas River (United Kingdom 1962). I have been unable to locate Kabiran Batu.

20 I encountered no evidence of Kadayan knowledge of these events during my research with them. This research, however, was situated in the Temburong District, far away from the capital and the area under discussion. Informants there knew of Orang Kaya Basar Imas only as an important earlier Kadayan leader.

21 Noble class membership is passed patrifilially, that is from a noble father to his children. The marital or ethnic status of the mother does not affect the son being a noble, but it does affect which of the ranked sub-classes of nobles he or she falls into.

22 In public settings Kadayan are more politely referred to by a euphemistic synonym, such as *urang darat* (lit. land people, but actually an ethnonymic lexeme synonymous with the term Kadayan), or *anak kampung darat* (land villagers). While the public use of the term Kadayan is a sensitive issue in modem Brunei, the Kadayan routinely use it to refer to themselves without pejorative connotation, in intimate or informal sociolinguistic settings. When visiting a Kadayan village for the first time in Brunei, I never used the term 'Kadayan' in conversation until a villager had used it to me first. Then I felt quite free to use it, and never experienced any ill-feeling directed toward me for doing so.

23 The term *pangiran* indicates that he was a noble, and combined with *anak*, that he was the son of a Sultan but of a non-noble mother.

24 In the past the person-prefix 'Si-' designated not only a Kadayan, but any person in the society who was not a Barunay noble or aristocrat, including: other Barunay, Kadayan, Chinese, and members of non-Malay indigenous ethnic groups such as Tutong, Dusun, Belait, Murut, etc. This pattern was made obsolete in March 1964 by a decision of the Privy Council which extended the use of the terms *awang* (for males) and *dayang* (for females) to all persons who were not Barunay nobles or aristocrats, including foreigners (Anon. 1964: 1). Previously the terms *awang* and *dayang* were used exclusively to refer to Barunay aristocrats (see also Maxwell 1984a).

25 A *citiria* is any one of the 60 different traditional state offices, and titles, which the Sultan of Brunei may confer on a male noble (Yusuf 1975: 47–51).

26 Kadayan refer to a person with extraordinary strength as an *urang kuat*, which literally means 'a strong person', but the phrase *urang kuat* is a lexeme whose meaning cannot be conveyed by its literal meaning. It denotes a person who is strong, but who has abilities beyond the normal. Part of its connotation includes super- or preternatural capability, and the probability that this capacity is due to magical power. Si-Rajid's experience with the spirit in the cave would indicate that magic was part of his personal power. The great Brunei culture hero Awang Simawn was an *urang kuat* (see Maxwell 1984b, 1995: 184–186).

27 Kadayan have no dislike or fear of the dark. Other groups in Borneo, especially ones famed for waging war and taking heads, have a distinct dislike of travelling at night for any purpose (cf. Furness 1902: 169; Harrisson 1970: 83–85). Kadayan still hunt, fish and collect wild fruit at night.

28 The role played by the Suluk in this affair was certainly also very important, but, I believe, in the view of most people in Brunei, that of the Kadayan was most decisive. Low briefly summarises two different traditions – one Barunay and one Suluk – regarding what role they played in settling the dispute (Brown 1969a: 152–153).

29 One can speculate about whether circumstances such as these may hold the key to understanding some of the obscure named subclasses of Barunay nobles and aristocrats, such as *kadayan raja-raja* (raja-raja: 'nobles; the noble class'), *kadayan awang-awang*, and also *awang-awang kadayan* (*awang-awang*: 'aristocrats; the aristocratic class' – cf. hawang2 Kedayan, Sweeney 1968: 27). Kadayan informants were unable to shed any light on the meaning or significance of these terms, which is not at all surprising, given the pronounced Kadayan lack of interest in all distinctions of rank and status.

These designations are primarily Barunay distinctions, possibly marking the status of certain individuals as having Barunay noble or aristocratic fathers and Kadayan mothers. Other subdivisions within the Barunay aristocratic class are similarly obscure (cf. Brown 1970: 15).

30 There are other traditional ritual relationships of tribute, such as the presentation of newly- harvested rice, from the Kadayan to the Barunay, but these will require a separate analysis at another time.

31 Ordinarily (i.e., excepting such rare cases as those of the Kadayan just discussed), membership in Barunay social classes is based on ascription, not achievement, as is commonly the case in the West. Thus in Brunei there is no social mobility, in either direction, that is under the control of an individual, through his or her own personal efforts. An aristocrat can never become a noble; a noble can never become an aristocrat. The only way a person can be a noble is to have a father (genitor, not social father) who is a noble. Consequently, in Brunei the markers of wealth and social status are independent variables; in the West, especially in the United States, they are linked or coupled variables.

32 While I cannot substantiate the claim empirically, it is my impression that in recent decades the number of Kadayan Land Minister office-holders has probably exceeded the total of all Land Ministers belonging to other ethnic groups.

33 For example, in the village of Pyasaw-Pyasaw, many individuals traced their ancestry to the Salar *nagri*. According to villagers, this settlement was founded by a number of migrants to the Labu Valley from Salar, around the first decade of this century, probably to work as tappers on a rubber estate which had opened a few miles downstream from the present location of the village (cf. Owen 1910a: 6). It is not certain, however, that these were the first Kadayan in the Labu Valley. The British Consul-General for Borneo, Dr. Peter Leys, reported 50 Kadayan living in the Labu Valley during his visit there in 1885 (Anon. 1885: 5). Other Pyasaw-Pyasaw villagers trace relationships to Damuan, and a few to Kasat. Inhabitants of Karnpung Selanyau, in Sibuti sub-district of Sarawak's Fourth Division, appear to trace much of their ancestry to the Gadung *nagri*. This village was founded around the late 1920s and early 1930s by a number of families from a Kampung Selanyau in that area (Sather and Hatta 1974: 250, 265n.).

References

Abdul Latif Haji Ibrahim (1971) Variations and Changes in the Names and Locations of the Wards of Brunei's Kampong Ayer over the Last Century. *Brunei Museum Journal* 2 (3): 56–71.

Anon. (1878) Notes on Borneo: The Field, the Farm, the Garden: The Country. *Gentleman's Newspaper* 52 (1344): 413.

Anon. (1885) Diary of a Cruise with the British Consul-General Up the Tamburong and Labu Rivers in Brunei Bay, on a Visit to the Head-Hunting Muruts, Now in Rebellion against the Brunei Government. *North Borneo Herald and Official Gazette* 3 (7): 2–5.

Anon. (1964) Call Him Awang. *Borneo Bulletin* 12 (11): 1.

Anon. (1984) *Daftar Ejaan Rumi Bahasa Malaysia*. Kuala Lumpur: Dewan Bahasa dan Pustaka.

Anon. (1993) Brunei. In *Asia Yearbook 1994, a Review of the Events of 1993*. Hong Kong: Review Publishing Co, pp. 94–95.

Anon. (1994) Brunei. In *Asia Yearbook 1995, a Review of the Events of 1994*. Hong Kong: Review Publishing Co, pp. 91–92.

Baring-Gould, S. and C. A. Bampfylde (1909) *A History of Sarawak under Its Two White Rajahs 1839–1908*. London: Henry Sotheran.

Belcher, E. (1848) *Narrative of the Voyage of H.M.S. Samarang, during the Years 1843–46; . . . with Notes on the Natural History of the Islands, by Arthur Adams*. Published under the Authority of the Lords Commissioners of the Admiralty. 2 vols. London: Reeve, Benham, and Reeve.

Boeke, J. H. (1953) *Economics and Economic Policy of Dual Societies, as Exemplified by Indonesia*. New York: Institute of Pacific Relations.

Boeke, J. H. and others. (1961) *Indonesian Economics: The Concept of Dualism in Theory and Policy*. The Hague: W. van Hoeve (Selected Studies on Indonesia 6).

Brackman, A. C. (1966) *Southeast Asia's Second Front: The Power Struggle in the Malay Archipelago*. London: Pall Mall Press.

Brooke, Charles (1866) *Ten Years in Sarawak*. 2 vols. London: Tinsley Brothers.

Brown, Donald E. (1968) Two Colonial Office Memoranda on the History of Brunei by Sir Reginald Edward Stubbs. *Journal of the Malaysian Branch of the Royal Asiatic Society* 41 (2): 83–116.

Brown, Donald E. (1969a) Hugh Low on the History of Brunei. *Brunei Museum Journal* 1 (1): 147–156.

Brown, Donald E. (1969b) The Social Structure of 19th Century Brunei. *Brunei Museum Journal* 1 (1): 166–179.

Brown, Donald E. (1970) Brunei: The Structure and History of a Bornean Malay Sultanate. *Brunei: Special Monograph of the Brunei Museum Journal* 2 (2).

Brown, Donald E. (1976) *Principles of Social Structure: Southeast Asia*. Boulder, CO: Westview.

Brown, Donald E. (1978) Brunei in Comparative Perspective. *Sarawak Museum Journal* 26 (47): 135–160.

Brunei (1988) *Brunei Darussalam in Profile*. London: Shandwick, on behalf of the Government of Brunei Darussalam.

Brunei (1973) Jabatan Setia Usaha Kerajaan: Bahagian Ekonomi dan Perangkaan [1973]. In *Laporan Banchi Pendudok Brunei 1971: Report on the Census of Population 1971*. Bandar Seri Begawan: Star Press.

Brunei (n.d.) Kementerian Kewangan: Unit Perancang Ekonomi: Bahagian Perangkaan [n.d.]. In *Jadual-Jadual Rumusan Banci Penduduk Brunei 1981; Summary Tables of the Brunei Population Census 1981*. Bandar Seri Begawan: Jabatan Percetakan Kerajaan, Kementerian Undang-Undang.

Brunei (1989) Ministry of Finance: Economic Planning Unit. Statistical Division. In *Demographic and Social Section*. Brunei Darussalam Population Survey 1986. Bandar Seri Begawan: n.p.

Brunei (1963) Pejabat Pengetua Pegawai Adat Isti'adat [1963]. In *Ranchangan Istiadat Bertindek dan Berkhatan Yang Teramat Mulia Pengiran Anak Puteri Amal Umi Kalthum al-Islam dan Yang Teramat Mulia Pengiran Anak Puteri Amal Rakiah, Brunei Darussalam*. Kuala Belait: Brunei Press Berhad.

Brunei (1976) State Secretariat: Economic Planning Unit: Statistics Section [1976]. In *Brunei Statistical Yearbook 1974/75*. Bandar Seri Begawan: Star Trading and Printing Ltd.

Chevallier, H. (1910) *Annual Report on the State of Brunei for the Year 1909*. Singapore: Government Printer.

Chevallier, H. (1911) *Annual Report on the State of Brunei for the Year 1910*. Singapore: Government Printer.

Chevallier, H. (1912) *Annual Report on the State of Brunei for the Year 1911*. Singapore: Government Printer.

Clifford, H. (1902) A Dying Kingdom. *Macmillan's Magazine* 86: 106–114.

Clutterbuck, W. J. (1891) *About Ceylon and Borneo*. London: Longmans, Green and Co.

Correspondent (1970) Strip Tease (Brunei-Malaysia). *Far Eastern Economic Review* 70 (47): 7–8.

Criswell, C. N. (1971) The Origins of the Limbang Claim. *Journal of Southeast Asian Studies* 2 (2): 218–229.

Dickenson, J. T. (1838) Notices of the City of Borneo and its Inhabitants, Made During the Voyage of the American Brig Himmaleh in the Indian Archipelago, in 1837. *The Chinese Repository* 7 (3): 121–136, 137 (4): 177–193.

Forbes, F. E. (1848) *Five Years in China: From 1842 to 1847; with an Account of the Occupation of the Islands of Labuan and Borneo by Her Majesty's Forces*. Taipei: Ch'eng Wen, reprinted 1972.

Forrest, T. (1780) *A Voyage to New Guinea and the Moluccas, from Balambangan: . . . During the Years 1774, 1775, and 1776*. Second edition. Kuala Lumpur: Oxford University Press, reprinted 1969.

Furness, W. H. (1902) *The Home-Life of Borneo Headhunters, Its Festivals and Folk-Lore*. Philadelphia: J. B. Lippencott.

Furnivall, J. S. (1944) *Netherlands India: A Study of Plural Economy*. Cambridge: Cambridge University Press.

Furnivall, J. S. (1956) *Colonial Policy and Practice: A Comparative Study of Burma and Netherlands India*. New York: New York University Press.

Gallop, A. T. (1995) Malay Sources for the History of the Sultanate of Brunei in the Early Nineteenth Century: Some Letters from the Reign of Sultan Muhammad Kanzul Alam. In Victor T. King and A. V. M. Horton (eds.), *From Buckfast to Borneo: Essays Presented to Father Robert Nicholl on the 85th Anniversary of his Birth 27 March 1995*. Hull: Centre for Southeast Asian Studies, pp. 178–206.

Glick, P. B. (1970) Melanesian Mosaic: The Plural Community of Vila. In Jn L. Plotnicov and A. Tuden (eds.), *Essays in Comparative Social Stratification*. Pittsburgh: University of Pittsburgh Press, pp. 95–117.

Guillemard, F. H. H. (1886) *The Cruise of the Marchesa to Kamschatka & New Guinea; with Notices of . . . Various Islands of the Malay Archipelago*. 2 vols. London: John Murray.

Hall, M. (1958) *Labuan Story: Memoirs of a Small Island*. Jesselton: Chung Nam Printing Company.

Harrisson, T. (1959) Some Tasks of Research in Borneo. *Bulletin of the International Committee for Urgent Anthropological and Ethnological Research* 2: 76.

Harrisson, T. (1963) *Background to a Revolt, Brunei and the Surrounding Territory*. Brunei Town, Brunei: Light Press.

Harrisson, T. (1970) *The Malays of South-West Sarawak before Malaysia: A Social-Ecological Survey*. London: Macmillan.

Horton, A. V. M. (1987) Brunei 1904–1908: M. S. H. McArthur and the Foundation of the British Residential System. In A. V. M. Horton (ed.), *Report on Brunei in 1904*. Athens, OH: Ohio University Center for International Studies. Monographs in International Studies, Southeast Asia Series 74, pp. 1–73.

Hose, C. and W. McDougall (1912) *The Pagan Tribes of Borneo*. [Reprinted 1966]. 2 vols. New York: Barnes and Noble.

Jacob, G. L. (1876) *The Raja of Sarawak: An Account of Sir James Brooke, Given Chiefly Through Letters and Journals*. 2 vols. London: Macmillan.

Jesse, J. (1775) Substance of a Letter to the Court of Directors [of the East India Company, London], Dated July 20, 1775, at Borneo Proper. In R. Rost (ed.), *Miscellaneous Papers*

Relating to Indo-China. [Reprinted for the Straits Branch of the Royal Asiatic Society, 1886]. Vol. 1. London: Trubner, pp. 20–26.

Jones, L. W. (1962) *Brunei: Report on the Census of Population Taken on 10th August, 1960*. Kuching: Government Printing Office, Sarawak.

Keppel, H. (1846) *The Expedition to Borneo of H.M.S. Dido for the Suppression of Piracy*. 2 vols. London: Chapman and Hall.

Keppel, H. (1853) *A Visit to the Indian Archipelago, in H.M. Ship Maeander*. 2 vols. London: Richard Bentley.

King, V. T. (1994) What Is Brunei Society? Reflections on a Conceptual and Ethnographic Issue. *South East Asia Research* 2 (2): 176–198.

Kuper, L. (1970) Stratification in Plural Societies: Focus on White Settler Societies in Africa. In L. Plotnicov and A. Tuden (eds.), *Essays in Comparative Social Stratification*. Pittsburgh: University of Pittsburgh Press, pp. 77–93.

Kuper, L. and M. G. Smith (1971) Introduction to Part I. In L. Kuper and M. G. Smith (eds.), *Pluralism in Africa*. Berkeley: University of California Press, pp. 3–5.

Leigh, M. B. (1974) *The Rising Moon: Political Change in Sarawak*. Sydney: Sydney University Press.

Low, H. (1848) *Sarawak: Its Inhabitants and Productions*. London: Richard Bentley.

Low, H. (1880a) History of the Sultans of Bruni and of Their Descent, from Sultan Abdul Kahar to Sultan Jalil-ul-Jebar. *Journal of the Straits Branch of the Royal Asiatic Society* 5: 9–23.

Low, H. (1880b) List of the Mahomedan Sovereigns of Bruni, or Borneo Proper. *Journal of the Straits Branch of the Royal Asiatic Society* 5: 24–31.

Low, H. (1880c) Selesilah (Book of the Descent) of the Rajas of Bruni. *Journal of the Straits Branch of the Royal Asiatic Society* 5: 1–8.

Low, L. (1987) Brunei: Economy. In *The Far East and Australasia 1988*. London: Europa Publications Ltd, pp. 251–254.

Marryat, F. S. (1848) *Borneo and the Indian Archipelago*. London: Longman, Brown, Green, and Longmans.

Martin, P. W. (1992) Linguistic Research in Brunei Darussalam: A Review. In Dato Seri Laila Jasa Awang Haji Abu Bakar bin Hj. Apong (ed.), *Sumbangsih UBD: Esei-esei Mengenai Negara Brunei Darussalam*. Gadong: Akademi Pengajian Brunei, Universiti Brunei Darussalam, pp. 106–117.

Maxwell, A. R. (1969) Kedayan Ethno-Ornithology: A Preliminary Report. *Brunei Museum Journal* 1 (1): 197–217.

Maxwell, A. R. (1970) On the Various Spellings of the Word 'Kadayan'. *Brunei Museum Journal* 2 (1): 87–103.

Maxwell, A. R. (1980) Urang Darat: An Ethnographic Study of the Kadayan of Labu Valley, Brunei. Unpublished PhD thesis, Yale University.

Maxwell, A. R. (1982) *Lexical Evidence and Brunei Ethnohistory*. Paper presented at the Annual Meeting of the American Society for Ethnohistory, October, Nashville, TN.

Maxwell, A. R. (1983) Kedayan in the Shair Ken Tambuhan and Kadayan in Brunei. *Borneo Research Bulletin* 15 (2): 87–97.

Maxwell, A. R. (1984a) Kadayan Evidence for Word Medial *h* in Brunei Malay. *Borneo Research Bulletin* 16 (1): 3–12.

Maxwell, A. R. (1984b) Kadayan Personal Names and Naming. In E. Tooker (ed.), *Naming Systems: 1980 Proceedings of the American Ethnological Society*. Washington, DC: American Ethnological Society, pp. 25–39.

Maxwell, A. R. (1985) Kalupis: A Delicacy of Brunei. *Brunei Museum Journal* 6 (1): 75–88.

Maxwell, A. R. (1995) Who Is Awang Simawn? In Victor T. King and A. V. M. Horton (eds.), *From Buckfast to Borneo: Essays Presented to Father Robert Nicholl on the 85th Anniversary of his Birth 27 March 1995*. Hull: Centre for Southeast Asian Studies, pp. 179–206.

Maxwell, A. R. (1996) Headtaking and the Consolidation of Political Power in the Early Brunei State. In J. Hoskins (ed.), *Headhunting and the Social Imagination in Southeast Asia*. Stanford: Stanford University Press, pp. 90–126.

McArthur, M. S. H. (1987) *Report on Brunei in 1904*. A. V. M. Horton (ed.). Athens, OH: Ohio University Center for International Studies. Monographs in International Studies, Southeast Asia Series 74.

McArthur, M. S. H. (n.d.) Unpublished. Report of the State of Brunei for 1906. [Carbon Copy of 21 pp. Typescript, Bound in with Published Reports 1907–24 (vol. 1) in the Brunei Museum Library].

Mohd. Jamil Al-Sufri, Pehin Orang Kaya Amar Diraja Dato Seri Utama Awang Haji (1971–73) *Chatatan Sejarah Perwira2 dan Pembesar2 Brunei*. 2 vols. Bandar Seri Begawan: Dewan Bahasa dan Pustaka, Brunei.

Mohd. Jamil Al-Sufri, Pehin Orang Kaya Amar Diraja Dato Seri Utama Awang Haji (1991) Sultan Tengah (Sultan Sarawak Pertama dan Terakhir). *Sarawak Gazette* 118 (1518): 37–41.

Mohd. Jamil bin Khatib Hj. Awg. Omar, Hj. (compiler) (1963) *Salasilah Raja-Raja Brunei*. [1 Sheet]. Bandar Brunei: Jabatan Ukor.

Mundy, R. (1848) *Narrative of Events in Borneo and Celebes, Down to the Occupation of Labuan*. 2 vols. London: John Murray.

Nathan, J. E. (1922) *The Census of British Malaya (the Straits Settlements, Federated Malay States and Protected States of Johore, Kedah, Peris, Kelantan: Trengganu and Brunei): 1921*. London: Waterlow and Sons Ltd.

Nicholl, R. (1975) *European Sources for the History of the Sultanate of Brunei in the Sixteenth Century*. Bandar Seri Begawan: Brunei Museum.

Nihal Singh, S. (1971) *Malaysia – A Commentary*. New York: Barnes and Noble.

Noakes, J. L. (1950) *Sarawak and Brunei (the Colony of Sarawak and the British Protected State of Brunei): A Report on the 1947 Population Census*. London: Crown Agents for the Colonies; Kuching: Government Printer, Sarawak.

Observer (1970) The Limbang Strip. *Far Eastern Economic Review* 69 (52): 35.

Owen, J. F. (1910a) *Annual Report on the State of Brunei for the Year 1908*. Singapore: Government Printer.

Owen, J. F. (1910b) A Short Account of Native Industries in Brunei: Appendix. In J. F. Owen (compiler), *Annual Report on the State of Brunei for the Year 1908*. Singapore: Government Printer, 10.

Parnell, E. (1911) The Tribute Paid in Former Days to the Sultan of Brunei by the Then Dependent Province of Sarawak. *Sarawak Museum Journal* 1 (1): 125–130, reprinted in *Sarawak Gazette* 96 (1343), 1970: 9–11.

Pigafetta, A. (1969) *The Voyage of Magellan: The Journal of Antonio Pigafetta: A Translation by P. S. Paige*. Englewood Cliffs, NJ: PrenticeHall.

Pringle, R. (1970) *Rajahs and Rebels: The Ibans of Sarawak under Brooke Rule, 1841–1941*. London: Macmillan.

Ranjit Singh, D. S. (1984) *Brunei 1839–1983: The Problems of Political Survival*. Singapore: Oxford University Press.

Reece, R. W. H. (1982) *The Name of Brooke: The End of White Rajah Rule in Sarawak*. Kuala Lumpur: Oxford University Press.

Roorda van Eysinga, P. P. (1832) Berigt van Eenen Reiziger over Borneo Propre (Eigenlijk Borneo). In P. P. Roorda van Eysinga (ed.), *Verschillende Reizen en Lotgevallen*. Vol. 4. Amsterdam: Johannes van der Hey en Zoon, pp. 1–32.

Rubin, V. (ed.) (1960) *Social and Cultural Pluralism in the Caribbean*.Greenwich, NY: Annals of the New York Academy of Science, 83.

Runciman, S. (1960) *The White Rajahs: A History of Sarawak from 1841 to 1946*. Cambridge: Cambridge University Press.

Rutter, O. (1922) *British North Borneo: An Account of Its History, Resources and Native Tribes*. London: Constable.

Rutter, O. (ed.) (1935) *Rajah Brooke & Baroness Burdett Coutts*. London: Hutchinson and Co.

Sather, C. and Hatta Solhee (1974) Kampong Selanyau: Social and Economic Organization of a Kedayan Rice-Growing Village in Sarawak. *Sarawak Museum Journal* 22 (43): 249–266.

Saunders, G. (1994) *A History of Brunei*. Kuala Lumpur: Oxford University Press.

Smith, M. G. (1960) *Government in Zazzau, 1800–1950*. London: Oxford University Press.

Smith, M. G. (1965a) *The Plural Society in the British West Indies*. Berkeley: University of California Press.

Smith, M. G. (1965b) *Stratification in Grenada*. Berkeley: University of California Press.

Smith, M. G. (1971a) Institutional and Political Conditions of Pluralism. In L. Kuper and M. G. Smith (eds.), *Pluralism in Africa*. Berkeley: University of California Press, pp. 27–65.

Smith, M. G. (1971b) Some Developments in the Analytical Framework of Pluralism. In L. Kuper and M. G. Smith (eds.), *Pluralism in Africa*. Berkeley: University of California Press, pp. 415–458.

Smith, M. G. (1978) *The Affairs of Daura*. Berkeley: University of California Press.

Smith, R. T. (1970) Social Stratification in the Caribbean. In L. Plotnicov and A. Tuden (eds.), *Essays in Comparative Social Stratification*. Pittsburgh: University of Pittsburgh Press, pp. 43–76.

Smith, T. E. (1963) The Brunei Revolt: Background and Consequences. *The World Today* 19 (3): 135–138.

Stephen, I. (1970) The Limbang Claim: Brunei to Press for British Action. *The Straits Times*, 31 October, 2.

St. John, Spenser (1863) *Life in the Forests of the Far East; or Travels in Northern Borneo*. Second edition. 2 vols. London: Smith, Elder.

St. John, Spenser (1879) *The Life of Sir James Brooke, Rajah of Sarawak; from His Personal Papers and Correspondence*. Edinburgh: William Blackwood and Sons.

St. John, Spenser (1899) *Rajah Brooke: The Englishman as Ruler of an Eastern State*. London: T. Fisher Unwin.

Sweeney, P. L. Amin (1968) Silsilah Raja-Raja Berunai. *Journal of the Malaysian Branch of the Royal Asiatic Society* 41 (2): 1–82.

Tarling, N. (1971) *Britain, the Brookes, and Brunei*. Kuala Lumpur: Oxford University Press.

Tarling, N. (1978) *Sulu and Sabah: A Study of British Policy towards the Philippines and North Borneo from the Late Eighteenth Century*. Kuala Lumpur: Oxford University Press.

Tarling, N. (1982) *The Burthen, the Risk, and the Glory: A Biography of Sir James Brooke*. Kuala Lumpur: Oxford University Press.

Templer, J. C. (ed.) (1853) *The Private Letters of Sir James Brooke, K.C.B., Rajah of Sarawak, Narrating the Events of His Life from 1838 to the Present Time*. 3 vols. London: Richard Bentley.

Treacher, W. H. (1889–90) British Borneo: Sketches of Brunai, Sarawak, Labuan and North Borneo. *Journal of the Straits Branch of the Royal Asiatic Society* 20: 13–74, and 21: 19–121.

Tregonning, K. G. (1958) The Partition of Brunei. *Journal of Tropical Geography* 11: 84–89.

Tregonning, K. G. (1960) *North Borneo*. London: Her Majesty's Stationery Office.

Tregonning, K. G. (1965) *A History of Modern Sabah* (North Borneo 1881–1963). Second edition. Singapore: University of Malaya Press.

Tuden, A. and L. Plotnicov (eds.) (1970) *Social Stratification in Africa*. New York: Free Press.

Turnbull, C. M. (1989) *A History of Malaysia, Singapore, and Brunei*. Sydney: Allen and Unwin.

Turnbull, C. M. (1992) Regionalism and Nationalism. In N. Tarling (ed.), *The Cambridge History of Southeast Asia, II: The Nineteenth and Twentieth Centuries*. Cambridge: Cambridge University Press, pp. 585–645.

United Kingdom. Directorate of Overseas Surveys (1962) Brunei 1:50,000 with Part of Sarawak, Brunei Town 4111414. [Printed by the Ordinance Survey. Government Copyright].

Veth, P. J. (1854–56) *Borneo's Wester-Afdeeling, Geographisch, Statistisch, Historisch Poorafgegaan door eene Algemeene Schets des Ganschen Eilands*. 2 vols. Zaltbommel: Joh. Noman en Zoon.

Vlieland, C. A. (1932) *British Malaya (the Colony of the Straits Settlements and the Malay States under British Protection, Namely the Federated States of Perak, Selangor, Negri Sembilan and Pahang and the States of Johore, Kedah, Kelantan, Trengganu, Perlis and Brunei): A Report on the 1931 Census*. London: Crown Agents for the Colonies.

Walker, W. (1969) How Borneo Was Won: The Untold Story of an Asian Victory: The Round Table. *The Commonwealth Quarterly* 223: 9–20.

Wolters, O. W. (1967) *Early Indonesian Commerce: A Study of the Origins of Srivijaya*. Ithaca, NY: Cornell University Press.

Wolters, O. W. (1970) *The Fall of Srivijaya in Malay History*. Kuala Lumpur: Oxford University Press.

Wright, L. R. (1970) *The Origins of British Borneo*. Hong Kong: Hong Kong University Press.

Yura Halim (1951) *Pengiran Bendahara Menjadi Sultan, atau Mahkota yang Berdarah*. Brunei Town, Brunei: Pustaka Cesar.

Yura Halim and Jamil Umar (1958) *Sejarah Berunai*. Kuala Belait: Brunei Press.

Yusuf, P. M. (1958) *Adat Istiadat Diraja Berunai* [In Jawi]. Singapore: Azahari Press.

Yusuf, P. M. (1975) Adat Istiadat Diraja Brunei Darussalam. *Brunei Museum Journal* 3 (3): 43–108.

Figure 8.1 Donald Brown in his motorboat on the Brunei River, 1968

8 Living on water

Water settlements in Borneo*

Hans-Dieter Evers

Introduction

Donald Brown, upon arrival in Brunei in late 1966, insisted on living in Kampong Ayer, the traditional centre of the Brunei Malays or ethnic Bruneis. Many attempts have been made to resettle the local population on the mainland, but contrary to expectation, Kampong Ayer is still a flourishing water settlement, supported partly by local pride and sentiment and partly by tourist groups in line with heritage areas in Georgetown, Penang or China Town in Singapore.

Water settlements were and are still common along the rivers and coasts of Borneo, but as the following study shows, the water settlements along the Brunei River are by far the largest in extent and in number of inhabitants throughout the Indonesian, Malaysian and Brunei districts and provinces. Using remote sensing data, we measured the extent of water villages and estimated their number of households and inhabitants. Water villages (kampong ayer) cover an area of approximately 25 square kilometres, housing approximately 215,000 inhabitants. Though water villages are closely rooted in Malay customs and traditions, other communities have also moved in, making use of relatively cheap accommodation.

Borneo water villages

Borneo's coastal areas and river estuaries are subject to occasional heavy rainfall and flooding. Swamps and low areas, a few feet above sea level, are found not only along the coasts but also further inland. The coastal population has adjusted to these hydrological conditions and established settlements which are sustainable under these conditions. Considerations of security from floods, wild animals and human enemies has shaped housing and settlement patterns around Borneo and, indeed, in many other parts of Southeast Asia (Waterson 1993). Living on water has been one of the answers to coping with harsh geophysical conditions (Evers 2013). This has been a common practice among various Austronesian groups throughout Southeast Asia (Dumarcay 1987; Waterson 1990).

Malay houses have traditionally been built on stilts to raise living quarters off the muddy and often flooded ground. A cooling breeze could keep living quarters cool and insects away. Along the estuaries of rivers, houses were often built on the water, increasing safety and easy access to river transport. Water settlements are also found in other parts of Southeast Asia, such as in Cambodia, Vietnam (Biggs et al. 2009), Thailand, Singapore and elsewhere in Indonesia and Malaysia. Though Malays have undoubtedly been the most fervent builders of water villages, other local and migrant groups have also settled on water (Bideau and Kilani 2010). Water settlements were also constituent elements of 'hydraulic societies' as found in ancient China, and in Thailand, Cambodia and Vietnam (Evers and Benedikter 2009; Molle et al. 2009).

As the Malay kingdoms around Borneo had their centres of power, government and trade located at the estuaries of larger rivers (Boomgaard 2007), their 'capitals' were also built on water. Brunei Darussalam, Pontianak, Kutai and other Malay kingdoms had water villages (*kampung air/kampong ayer*) as their capital 'cities', but also other settlements were mostly Malay water villages or longhouses of other ethnic groups. With modernisation, urbanisation and economic development settlements sprung up on higher ground, often clustered around government offices or Chinese shop-houses. Water villages have in some areas disappeared, in others expanded with population increase. Our pilot study attempts to show the extent of water villages as typical Borneo settlements. We will also try to estimate the number of families and persons living in water villages. Based on remote sensing data, we provide a baseline study which can be used as a background to more detailed field research. Based on the very limited literature and our occasional field visits, we suggest that the ethnic composition of water villages has become quite diverse with growing social and geographical mobility and with the influx of migrant workers from neighbouring countries. With the motorisation of river traffic, even formerly remote water villages have become accessible from the newly emerging urban centres and have apparently grown in size.

Measuring water villages around Borneo

In order to measure the extent of water villages we have used remote sensing data, based on Google Earth and occasionally Landsat data. Polygons were drawn around the clearly visible water settlements around the coastline of Borneo, its major river estuaries and its islands and the number of houses counted (see Figure 8.1).

From the number of houses, a rough estimate of the population size could be calculated.

Our analysis yielded the following results

- We identified 84 major water villages on Borneo (Figure 8.2).
- Water villages occupy a total area of 24.52 square kilometres (Table 8.1).
- An estimated 43,025 houses and 215,000 people live in water villages around Borneo.

As smaller settlements and water villages on the upper reaches of Borneo's rivers were not counted, our figures probably underestimate the total number of people living in water villages.

Our baseline survey showed that water settlements are found all around the coastal areas of Borneo but with a concentration in the low-lying areas of South

Figure 8.2 Measuring the size of water villages (example from Labuan)

Source: Google Earth, November 2013.

and East Kalimantan. The largest water village was probably Kampong Ayer along the Brunei River (Jones 1997); it is the traditional heartland of the independent state and sultanate of Brunei Darussalam (Fanselow 2014; Kershaw 2002; King 1994). However, from an estimated population of 25,000 in 1981, it had declined to around 13,000 in 2011 (Khai Zem Mat Sani 2016; Wikipedia 2019), though this has since decreased further (see Haji Tassim bin Haji Abu Bakar, Chapter 9). This is partly due to the planned and newly constructed water village settlements, built by the Bruneian government since the 1980s, the increasing desire of young people to live on land with access to modern facilities (Ford 2018) and urban redevelopment, including the recently opened Sungai Kedayan Eco-Corridor, which displaced 500 residents from Kampong Ayer (Ain Bandial 2017). South and East Kalimantan contain vast low-lying areas, for which the construction of water villages is suitable or even mandatory.

Conclusion

As we could show on the basis of our survey, water villages are still an important form of settlement on Borneo. Our data open up a number of possible research

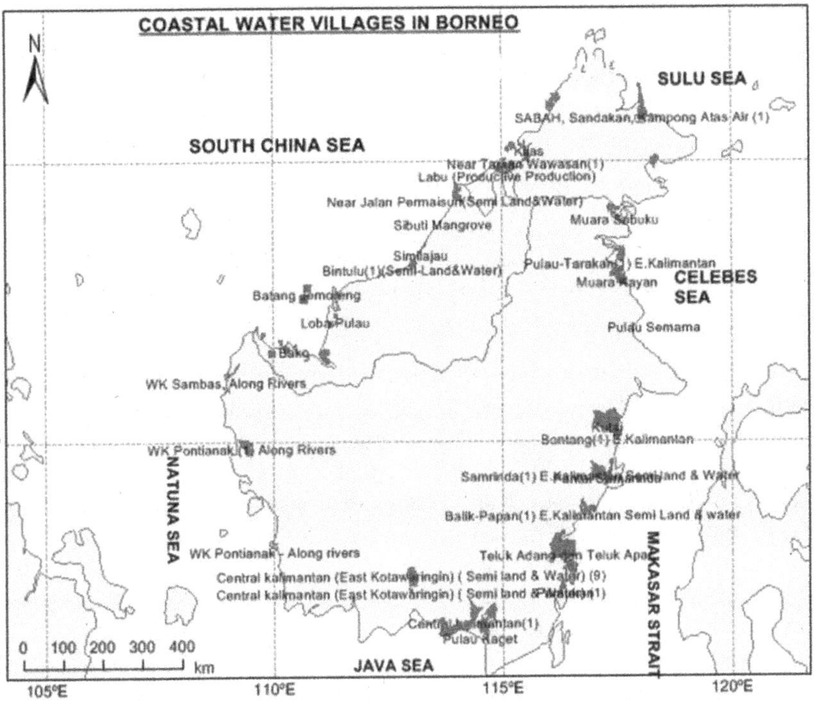

Map 8.1 Water villages around Borneo

Source: GIS data based on Google Earth, 2014.

Data analysis and map design: Hans-Dieter Evers and Khairi Latif (UBD)

Table 8.1 Size of water villages by state or province, 2013

State/Province	*Water villages (sq. km.)*
Brunei Darussalam	2.2
Kalimantan Tengah	2.0
Kalimantan Timur	6.4
Kalimantan Selatan	6.7
Kalimantan Barat	1.1
Sabah	5.8
Sarawak	0.4
Total	24.5

questions. As indicated earlier, houses on stilts and water villages are part of the housing tradition and physical culture of the Malays and other maritime- and riverine-oriented people. It remains, however, an open question as to who actually inhabits current water villages. Many migrant workers have moved into the

Table 8.2 Extent of water villages (sq. km.), Borneo

State/Province	*Water village area in sq. km.*
Brunei Darussalam	9%
Kalimantan Tengah	8%
Kalimantan Timur	26%
Kalimantan Selatan	27%
Kalimantan Barat	4%
Sabah	24%
Sarawak	2%

Source: Own estimates, based on Google Earth and author's field data.

water villages of Brunei Darussalam, particularly those from other parts of Asia, including Indonesia and the Indian subcontinent (Muhammad Faiz Zul Hamdi et al. 2017). Our field studies in East Kalimantan (Clauss et al. 1987; Evers et al. 1988; Evers and Gerke 1992) have shown that water settlements along the middle Mahakam River are mostly Kutai Malays, but other ethnic groups, like various Dayak groups, have also moved from the interior of Borneo to the coastal rivers and are found in water villages as well (Gerke 1997). The overall population dynamics of Bornean water villages is of special interest in light of the expected sea level rise due to climate change (Evers 2013). This will reduce dry land suitable for settlements and urban expansion, and may force an even more extensive construction of water villages on Borneo and elsewhere in Asia. Experience gained in centuries of 'living on water' will be a valuable asset that needs to be recorded.

Note

* This study was conducted within the research programme of the Institute of Asian Studies, while the author served as Eminent Visiting Professor of Universiti Brunei Darussalam between 2011 and 2014. A summary of the results was presented at the Inaugural Borneo Studies Network Meeting and Workshop, Universiti Brunei Darussalam in 2014 and published as 'Kampung Air: Water Settlements on the Island of Borneo' in *The Journal of the Malaysian Branch of the Royal Asiatic Society* 88 (1): 79–85. This is a revised version of the paper produced with the kind permission of the editor of the journal.

References

Ain Bandial (2017) Sungai Kedayan Eco-Corridor: A Piece of the BSB Masterplan Comes to Life. Available at: thescoop.co/2017/10/19/sungai-kedayan-eco-corridor-piece-bsb-masterplan-comes-life/ (accessed 14 August 2019).

Bideau, Florenz Graezer and Mondher Kilani (2010) La Patrimonialisation des Chinese Clan Jetties de Penang (Malaisie). De la Marge au Centre. In Francois Ruegg and Andrea Boscoboinnik (eds.), *From Palermo to Penang: A Journey of Political Anthropology*. Münster: LIT Verlag, pp. 311–329.

Biggs, David A., F. Miller, C. T. Hoanh and F. Molle (2009) Built Waterscapes: Environmental History and Development Politics in the Mekong Delta. In F. Molle, T. Foran and M. Käkönen (eds.), *Contested Waterscapes in the Mekong Region: Hydropower, Livelihoods and Governance*. London: Earthscan, pp. 203–226.

Boomgaard, Peter (ed.) (2007) *A World of Water: Rain, Rivers and Seas in Southeast Asian Histories*. Leiden: KITLV Press.

Clauss, Wolfgang, Hans-Dieter Evers and Solvay Gerke (1987) The Formation of a Peasant Society: Population Dynamics, Ethnic Relations and Trade among Javanese Transmigrants in East Kalimantan, Indonesia. *Indonesia* 46: 79–90.

Dumarcay, J. (1987) *The House in South-East Asia*. Singapore: Oxford University Press.

Evers, Hans-Dieter (2013) Living on Water in Borneo (Conference Presentation), Borneo Studies Network Inaugural Meeting and Workshop. Institute of Asian Studies, Universiti Brunei Darussalam, Gadong, 21–22 October.

Evers, Hans-Dieter (2015) Kampung Air: Water Settlements on the Island of Borneo. *Journal of the Malaysian Branch of the Royal Asiatic Society* 88 (1): 79–86.

Evers, Hans-Dieter and Simon Benedikter (2009) Hydraulic Bureaucracy in a Modern Hydraulic Society: Strategic Group Formation in the Mekong Delta, Vietnam. *Water Alternatives* 2 (3): 416–439.

Evers, Hans-Dieter, Wolfgang Clauss and Solvay Gerke (1988) *Population Dynamics, Ethnic Relations and Trade among Javanese Transmigrants in East Kalimantan*. Yogyakarta: Population Studies Center, Gadjah Mada University.

Evers, Hans-Dieter and Solvay Gerke (1992) The Culture of Planning: Transmigration Area Development in East Kalimantan, Indonesia. *International Sociology* 7 (2): 141–152.

Fanselow, Frank (2014) The Anthropology of the State and the State of Anthropology in Brunei. *Journal of Southeast Asian Studies* 45 (1): 90–112.

Ford, Pete (2018) Brunei's Troubled Heart. Available at: southeastasiaglobe.com/business-troubled-heart-the-story-of-kampong-ayer/ (accessed 14 August 2019).

Gerke, Solvay (1997) Ethnic Relations and Cultural Dynamics in East Kalimantan: The Case of the Dayak Lady. *Indonesia and the Malay World* 72: 176–187.

Jones, Andrew (1997) Urban Conservation Issues in Brunei Darussalam: The Case of Brunei's Water Villages. *Planning Perspectives* 12 (4): 457–475.

Kershaw, Roger (2002) *Monarchy in South-East Asia: The Faces of Tradition in Transition*. London and New York: Routledge.

Khai Zem Mat Sani (2016) Kampong Ayer Research. Available at: apb.ubd.ed.u.bn/kampong-ayer-research (accessed 14 August 2019).

King, Victor T. (1994) What Is Brunei Society? Reflections on a Conceptual and Ethnographic Issue. *Southeast Asia Research* 2: 176–198.

Molle, Francois, Peter P. Mollinga and Philippus Wester (2009) Hydraulic Bureaucracies and the Hydraulic Mission: Flows of Water, Flows of Power. *Water Alternatives* 2 (3): 328–349.

Muhammad Faiz Zul Hamdi, Norhidayah Abdullah and Diyana binti Narudin (2017) *Space, Place and Identity: How Migration Have [sic] Transformed Kampong Ayer*. Gadong: Institute of Asian Studies, Universiti Brunei Darussalam, Working Paper Series, No. 28.

Waterson, Roxana (1990) *The Living House: An Anthropology of Architecture in South-East Asia*. Singapore: Oxford University Press.

Waterson, Roxana (1993) Houses and the Built Environment in Island South-East Asia: Tracing Some Shared Themes in the Uses of Space. In James J. Fox (ed.), *Inside Austronesian Houses: Perspectives on Domestic Design for Living*. Canberra: Research School of Pacific Studies, The Australian University, pp. 220–235.

Wikipedia (2019) Kampong Ayer. Available at: en.wikipedia.org/wiki/kampong-ayer (accessed 14 August 2019).

9 Development, change and modernisation in Kampong Ayer over the last fifty years

Haji Tassim bin Haji Abu Bakar

Introduction

Situated on the Brunei River, for centuries Kampong Ayer was Brunei's capital and administrative, commercial, and manufacturing centre.[1] Spanish sources dating from the sixteenth century also indicate that it was an important centre for the dissemination of Islam and Malay culture to other parts of Borneo and some Philippine coastal areas (Nicholl 1975: 32; Iik Arifin Mansurnoor 1992: 150). The first contemporary eyewitness written description of this water city dates to 1521 in the account of Antonio Pigafetta, the Italian chronicler of Magellan's *Voyage around the World*. At the time of Pigafetta's visit, Brunei was probably at the zenith of its power and prosperity. This is reflected in his description, which portrays Kampong Ayer (which essentially was Brunei) as a large, sophisticated, and wealthy trading city with a splendid royal court (Nicholl 1975: 8–13). At this time in history, the population of Kampong Ayer was probably about 25,000 to 30,000 people (Asbol bin Haji Mail and Tassim bin Haji Abu Bakar 2016: 101), a figure that later eyewitness accounts also suggest for the middle of the nineteenth century (Brown 1970: 40).[2] By the beginning of the twentieth century, however, the population was just under 10,000 (Chevallier 1912: 11), a decline that was probably linked to the increasing economic problems the sultanate experienced during this period. From the early part of the twentieth century, Kampong Ayer went through a number of profound changes as Brunei began to develop as a modern country. The British Residential system, which was established in 1906, shifted the administrative centre of the country from Kampong Ayer to land and began to develop Brunei Town (Bandar Seri Begawan) as a commercial area. British Residents also encouraged the inhabitants of Kampong Ayer to move to the land, although they had little success, and it was only in the 1950s that a marked movement from water- to land-based housing began with the advent of various resettlement schemes. Over the years these resettlement schemes were expanded, which led to increasing numbers of people leaving Kampong Ayer, some of whom did so because their homes were lost to fires. An important consequence of this movement of people, together with the social and economic development of Brunei, has been the loss of various handicraft skills once practiced by Kampong Ayer's residents and often linked to specific villages that no longer exist.

Many residents, however, declined the opportunity to move away from Kampong Ayer, and it remains the home of some 13,000 people today, about 3 per cent of Brunei's total population. Kampong Ayer continues to represent a unique symbol of Brunei's past. At the same time, Kampong Ayer itself has been subject to increasing modernisation over the years as schools and police stations were built on water and modern amenities, such as running water and electricity, were supplied to its residents. From the 1980s, new and modern Kampong Ayer housing and villages were also constructed for residents who lost homes in fires, or wished to continue living on water. As part of Brunei's drive to attract more tourists, Kampong Ayer is also promoted as one of the sultanate's most important tourist attractions. This chapter discusses the various changes that have taken place in Kampong Ayer over the last century, focusing mainly on the period since the 1950s.

Changes in the names of Kampong Ayer villages and the loss of heritage

In his major study on Brunei published in 1970, in one chapter, titled 'Bandar Brunei – The Capital City', Donald Brown gives considerable attention to Kampong Ayer where he resided during his field research in 1967–1968 (1970: 39–62). In his work Brown refers to Spenser St. John's 1862 publication that mentions a number of the older and unique Kampong Ayer village names and notes that the names of many villages were based on the particular occupations of their inhabitants. For example, Kampong Pabalat (Fishing Net village) was inhabited by fishermen, Kampong Periuk (Brass Cooking Pot village) by brass workers, Kampong Terkoyong (Shell village) by collectors of pearl oyster, Kampong Peminiak (Oil village) by those who produced oil, and Kampong Padaun (Leaf village), by people who made roofing mats from nipah palm leaf. The names of other kampongs were derived from titles of nobles, such as Kampong Sultan Lama, Kampong Bendahara Lama, Kampong Pemancha Lama, Bakut Siraja Muda, Pengiran Kerma Indera Lama, Pengiran Tajuddin Hitam, and Setia Pahlawan, which were all inhabited by people of royal descent. These villages comprised noble families; they were important commercial areas but were also used as venues for major ceremonies and festivals. Other villages were named after their geographic locations, such as Kampong Sungai Kedayan (the village on the Kedayan River), where residents included several high noble officials as well as brass workers, goldsmiths, gold brocade producers and traders; others were Kampong Sungai Asam (the village of the Asam River), Kampong Pekan Lama, Kampong Sungai Pandan (the village of the Pandan River), Kampong Lurong Dalam, Kampong Lurong Sikuna, Kampong Sungai Si Amas, Kampong Ujong Kinik, Kampong Sungai Kebun, and Kampong Bukit Berumput (and see Maxwell, in Chapter 7).

Some of the kampongs that St. John mentions no longer exist today as they were abandoned or destroyed by fire. For example, in 1981 a huge fire broke out in Kampong Sultan Lama, close to where Sultan Hashim Jalalul Alam

Aqamaddin (1885–1906) is buried, that destroyed about three-quarters of the village. A second smaller fire followed and destroyed the kampong's remaining houses. As a consequence, all the inhabitants from this village were moved to land-based accommodation, with the majority being rehoused in the Kampong Perpindahan Mata-Mata Gadong housing area. In other cases, some of the villages have remained to the present, but their names have changed over time. These older names remain in the memory of Kampong Ayer's former and current residents, many of whom continue to use the names when referring to these kampongs rather than the modern ones. These include Kampong Masjid Lama (today, Kampong Pengiran Bendahara Lama), Kampong Yang Di-Pertuan Lama (today, Kampong Sultan Lama), Kampong Pekilong Muara, Kampong Setia Pahlawan, Kampong Pabalat (today, Kampong Saba), and Kampong Lurong Sikuna, a name that is derived from a type of schooner called *tambatan sekunyir*. These older names remain important for the descendants of the original inhabitants who now live in land-based housing, despite their never having lived on Kampong Ayer themselves. This is mainly because different Kampong Ayer villages had different levels of status, and being able to trace one's descent from one of the more high-status villages continues to be a mark of prestige in modern-day Brunei.

The development of Brunei's capital, Bandar Seri Begawan, and Brunei's modernisation in general, has also played a part in the demise of Kampong Ayer villages. In the 1950s, Kampong Sumbiling Lama and Kampong Bukit Salat were removed from the Sungai Kedayan area to the riverbank close to the Rangas Lama Bridge in order to facilitate the construction of the Omar Ali Saifuddien Mosque. More recently, the Sungai Kedayan Eco-Corridor project (later renamed Taman Mahkota Emas, The Golden Jubilee Crown Park), which was completed in October 2017, led to the removal of a number of Kampong Ayer villages. These included Kampong Sumbiling Lama, Kampong Bukit Salat, Kampong Sungai Kedayan A and B, Kampong Pengiran Pemancha Lama, and Kampong Ujong Tanjong. The residents of these villages were resettled on land in various housing schemes provided by the government.

In constructing the Taman Mahkota Emas, an aim was to show the identity and beauty of Bandar Seri Begawan and, through its historical themes, link the park to Brunei's Malay Islamic Monarchy philosophy and showcase the sultanate's cultural heritage. There are various historical informative panels in the park that relate to the history of Kampong Ayer's villages and their heritage.

Resettlement and the decline of handicraft manufacturing in Kampong Ayer

While many of Kampong Ayer's villages were once associated with specific economic activities and the production of handicrafts, this is no longer the case. This is a consequence of two main factors: the movement of people from water to land, and the social and economic modernisation of Brunei. The movement of people

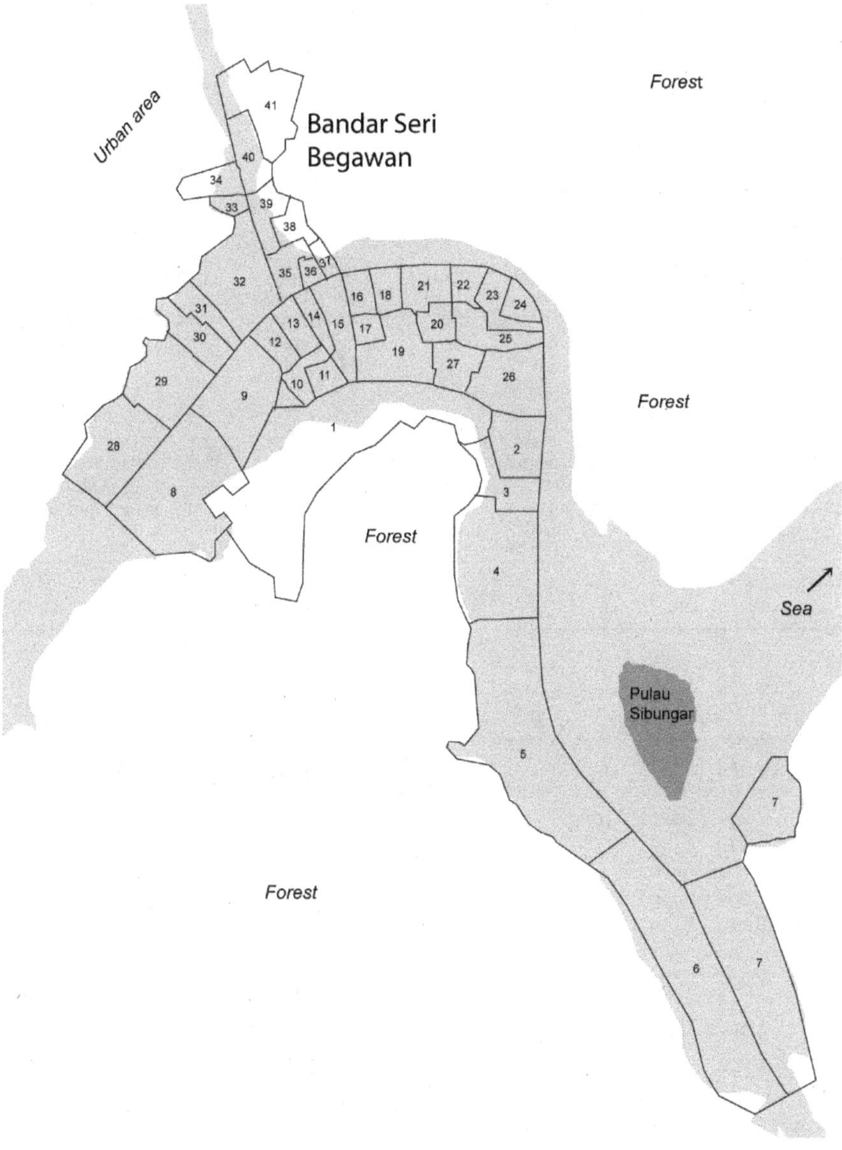

Map 9.1 Map of Kampong Ayer: Location of current kampongs and those that no longer exist

Key:

1. Kampong Sungai Kebun	2. Kampong Ujung Kelinik	3. Kampong Sungai Siamas	4. Kampong Setia 'A'
5. Kampong Setia 'B'	6. Kampong Bolkiah 'A'	7. Kampong Bolkiah 'B'	8. Kampong Burong Pingai Ayer
9. Kampong Lurong Dalam	10. Kampong Sungai Pandan 'A'	11. Kampong Sungai Pandan 'B'	12. Kampong Pandai Besi 'A'
13. Kampong Pandai Besi 'B'	14. Kampong Setia Negara	15. Kampong Pekan Lama	16. Kampong Bakut Pengiran Siraja Muda 'A'
17. Kampong Bakut Pengiran Siraja Muda 'B'	18. Kampong Bakut Berumput	19. Kampong Peramu	20. Kampong Setia Pahlawan
21. Kampong Lurong Sikuna	22. Kampong Saba Laut	23. Kampong Saba Tengah	24. Kampong Saba Ujung
25. Kampong Saba Darat 'A'	26. Kampong Saba Darat 'B'	27. Kampong Pekilong Muara	28. Kampong Tamoi Ujung
29. Kampong Tamoi Tengah	30. Kampong Pengiran Tajuddin Hitam	31. Kampong Pengiran Kerma Indera	32. Kampong Pengiran Bendahara Lama
33. Kampong Limbongan	34. Kampong Ujung Bukit	35. Kampong Ujong Tanjong	36. Kampong Kuala Peminyak
37. Kampong Pemancha Lama	38. Kampong Sungai Kedayan 'B'	39. Kampong Sungai Kedayan 'A'	40. Kampong Bukit Salat
41. Kampong Sumbiling Lama			

Table 9.1 Total population of Kampong Ayer today[3]

District and Mukim	*Total Population*	*Total by Homes*
Mukim Burong Pingai Ayer	1,586	248
Mukim Saba	748	134
Mukim Sungai Kebun	5,149	732
Mukim Peramu	835	153
Mukim Tamoi	1,594	231
Total	9,912	1,498

from Kampong Ayer to land has been a long, ongoing process that began in the early twentieth century and continues today. Moving people to land from Kampong Ayer was initially a policy of the early British Residents following the establishment of the Residential system in 1906 (Hussainmiya 1995: 17–18). The first British Resident, Malcolm Stewart Hannibal McArthur (1906–1908), considered conditions in Kampong Ayer to be unhygienic and believed that moving people to land would have a positive impact on their health. However, his, and subsequent British Residents', main reason for this policy was economic. The majority of Brunei's population lived on Kampong Ayer at the time and McArthur, in

Table 9.2 Basic facilities of Kampong Ayer today[4]

DISTRICT AND MUKIM	*BALAI IBADAT (religious hall)*	*SCHOOL*	*MOSQUE*	*BRIDGE(METERS)*	*JETTY*	*POLICE STATION*	*FIRE-STATION*	*COMMUNITYHALL*
Mukim Sungai Kebun	–	6	2	3769.5	18	–	1	–
Mukim Saba	1	2	–	1522	9	–	–	–
Mukim Peramu	1	1	–	1718	6	1	–	–
Mukim Burung Pinggai Ayer	1	2	1	3132.9	18	–	–	1
Mukim Tamoi	–	1	1	2387.4	11	–	–	–

his efforts to make Brunei economically self-sufficient, considered that economic development would be facilitated if people became engaged in land-based economic activities. This policy of McArthur and later Residents, however, had little success as the vast majority of Kampong Ayer's inhabitants showed little desire to undertake such a cultural and physical upheaval.

It was not until the 1950s that any significant movement of people to land began, although numbers were initially small. This was linked to the sultanate's First Five Year Development Plan (1953–1958) that allocated about 80 per cent of the BND$100 million budget to infrastructure development. This included a plan for the resettlement of Kampong Ayer with funding allocated to purchase land that could be used to build houses for those who decided to resettle (Cleary and Wong 1994: 80). In the years that followed, there was increasing resettlement from Kampong Ayer, reaching a peak in the 1980s. These larger movements were facilitated by the increased number of various relocation housing schemes, such as Kampong Lambak Kanan, Lambak Kiri, Rimba, Menteri, Katok, and Meragang. Fires also played a role in this movement. Most of the houses, or in many cases whole villages that were burnt down, were not rebuilt and their residents simply decided to move to land and not return.

Many of the residents who moved away from Kampong Ayer from the 1960s were skilled in various handicrafts, as well as various sea- and river-based activities. These handicraft skills, in particular various types of metalwork, were generally known to specific families who for generations had passed their knowledge on to their descendants. When such families moved from Kampong Ayer to land, most did not continue to produce these handicrafts and instead became engaged in other economic sectors, leading to a loss of knowledge. This was also compounded by a lack of raw materials for metal-workers in the 1960s (Siti Norkhalbi and Abdul Hai Julay 2006: 10).[5] Another important factor in the decline of handicraft production was increasing employment opportunities for the younger generations from the 1960s onwards in other economic sectors, in particular the civil service and the oil industry, both of which offered better pay and working conditions. As a consequence, many young people had less need, or desire, to learn the skills of their forefathers. As these movements of people to land increased and Brunei continued its modernisation process, funded by oil revenues, Kampong Ayer increasingly lost its position as an important centre of economic activity and gradually was reduced to a large residential area, with many of the remaining residents now making a daily commute to land-based jobs rather than working in their own villages.

Changes and modernisation of Kampong Ayer in the pre-independence period

Despite the prospect of better and modern facilities offered by land-based accommodation and Kampong Ayer's declining economic importance, many residents made the decision not to move from their traditional homes. This necessitated bringing some modernisation to Kampong Ayer, which was being increasingly left behind as Brunei rapidly developed from the 1960s. As part of this modernisation process, the government built a number of concrete bridges that connected some of the villages to each other, and also to the land. This began with bridge connections from Kampong Saba to Kampong Peramu, and were later extended to Kampong Lurong Dalam and Kampong Burong Pingai Ayer, and then from Kampong Bendahara Lama to Kampong Tamoi. These bridges had a further function in that they were used as the base for the installation of water pipes, and later electric cables, as part of Kampong Ayer's modernisation process to supply the residents with clean and fresh running water. Previously, residents had to use dugout canoes (*gubang*) or water taxis each day to travel to the land in order to collect fresh water for daily use, which was then kept in earthenware urns. A number of the wealthier residents also began to use generators to obtain an electricity supply.[6] For most of the residents of Kampong Ayer, access to electricity was made available only in the 1970s, when electric cables were installed along the bridges. To some extent this helped reduce the possibility of fires as residents no longer had to use gasoline lamps, candles, and kerosene lamps for lighting.[7] Access to electricity had a significant impact on the modernisation process as residents began to use electrical appliances, such as radios, televisions, refrigerators, fans, and washing machines. The government also built numerous *surau* (prayer rooms) and mosques for the residents to attend Friday prayer.

The lifestyle of Kampong Ayer residents in post-independence Brunei

Due to the government's modernisation efforts, Kampong Ayer underwent a major transformation from a traditional water village to an increasingly modern one. It was not, however, only the physical aspects of Kampong Ayer that changed. The lifestyle of its residents also went through profound changes. Development led to an increasing interest in and demand for material objects, and traditional ways of life began to erode as Kampong Ayer's residents began to catch up with other parts of Brunei. Residents began to place greater importance on the ownership of expensive and luxury items, including household furniture, as symbols of wealth. The majority also bought cars, which were parked in increasing numbers in specially constructed car parks close to various jetties.

Modern and luxurious trappings increasingly became the yardstick to measure the standard of life and status of a family. These residents also attempted to mould their lifestyles to reflect new occupations, whether working in the public or private sectors, and displayed their status accordingly. Some residents also began working as water taxi-drivers to supplement their personal income.

The development of new Kampong Ayer housing in post-independence Brunei

Following Brunei's attainment of full independence in 1984, the development approach for Kampong Ayer and its residents can be divided into three parts.

Firstly, the government continued to develop existing Kampong Ayer villages by improving existing amenities and infrastructure and providing more facilities. Secondly, the policy of relocating residents to land continued for those who wished to be resettled, and as a consequence more land-based housing sites were planned and developed on a larger scale. However, these new housing areas were not limited to Kampong Ayer residents but were open to all Brunei citizens. Thirdly, there was a new approach to Kampong Ayer development. This was to relocate residents from older Kampong Ayer houses and villages to new and modern houses and villages built on water and constructed in other parts of the river.

The relocation programme from older to modern Kampong Ayer housing began in 1993, funded by the Sultan Hassanal Bolkiah Foundation and built by private contractors who produced neat rows of modern houses.[8] Willing residents were relocated to the new villages, the first of which was called Kampong Bolkiah A, located at a suitable site in the Buang Sakar area of the river. Several years later another new village was developed, called Kampong Bolkiah B. These projects were essentially undertaken for the benefit of residents who had lost homes in fires but did not want to relocate to land. While it was open to other Kampong Ayer residents who desired more modern housing, many of those who moved to Kampong Bolkiah A and B were the victims of a major fire that burnt down houses in Kampong Peramu, Kampong Setia Pahlawan, and Kampong Saba Darat B in September 1992. This fire affected some 183 families, with 1,083 people losing their homes.

The driving force behind the development of Kampong Bolkiah A and Kampong Bolkiah B comprised Kebawah Duli Yang Maha Mulia Paduka Seri Baginda Sultan and the Yang Di-Pertuan Negara Brunei Darussalam, who established the Sultan Haji Hassanal Bolkiah Foundation. The first new village was officially opened on 22 August 1994. In both villages, the houses were equipped with basic amenities, such as electricity and telephones, and were connected to each other by concrete bridges. In these new villages, *surau*, police stations, schools, and shops were also built. In addition, a Brunei textile-weaving workshop was established to train women who lived in these new villages in order to develop cottage industries and maintain the Brunei tradition of woven fabric production (Yahya bin Haji Ibrahim 1996: 7–8).

Two types of modern houses were built in Kampong Bolkiah A: 21 single-story Type A units and 205 two-story Type B units. Most of the houses in this kampong were specifically reserved for people who were victims of fire and sold at the subsidised price of BND$26,000 for the Type A units and BND$33,000 for the larger Type B units. The people who moved to these houses were also given 20-year interest free housing loans, which meant that repayment costs were relatively low with Type A unit owners paying about BND$108 per month and Type B owners about BND$138 a month (YSHHB 1998).

The second Kampong Ayer housing project, Kampong Bolkiah B, was completed by the Sultan Hassanal Bolkiah Foundation in 1995 and situated in the waters of Berambang Island. Many of the residents of the houses in Kampong

Bolkiah B were also fire victims from Mukim Saba, which consisted of Kampong Sungai Kebun and Kampong Sungai Pandan. The price of the houses in Kampong Bolkiah B were slightly more expensive than Kampong Bolkiah A, mainly because the houses were of a higher standard. Only some 250 Type B units were built and priced at BND$38,000 each with interest free loan repayment set at BND$162 a month over a 20-year period (YSHHB 1998).

The development of new housing on Kampong Ayer has continued to the present. In 2012 the Kampong Ayer Upgrading Pilot Project was completed. This project had two main aims: to provide increasingly modern and safe housing for residents, and to give Kampong Ayer a more attractive appearance. This project transformed Kampong Lurong Sikuna in Mukim Peramu, located across from the Royal Wharf in Bandar Seri Begawan, through the construction of numerous new houses. While these houses still maintain a traditional appearance, they have concrete floors, and the wooden walls are flame resistant. As with Kampong Bolkiah A, Type A one-storey and Type B two-storey houses were built, with the former covering an area of 130 square meters and costing BND$65,000, and the latter an area of 198 square meters costing BND$90,000. Plans for the development of further new housing in Kampong Ayer were announced in 2018 by the Minister of Home Affairs, who stated that BND$45 million has been allocated for a further 157 new houses as part of a revitalisation project for the water village that may include the development of a number of floating restaurants and food stalls that will help to attract people from the mainland, including tourists (Brunei Bulletin 2018; The Scoop 2018).

While these modern houses are safer and more hygienic than traditional housing, there is some concern that these new developments will lead to a loss of cultural heritage if older housing styles continue to disappear. Indeed, there has been a greater emphasis on modernisation than conservation. As a result, some have called for traditional housing to be maintained for the sake of future generations (*The Brunei Times* 2015). Another development that has concerned some people in Brunei is the changing ethnic composition of some parts of Kampong Ayer. During the past two decades numerous migrant workers from other parts of Asia, such as India, Bangladesh, and Thailand, have moved into vacant Kampong Ayer houses, attracted either by the cheap rent or placed there by their employers (Azman Ahmad 2013: 108). This concern appears directly linked to the special place that Kampong Ayer holds in the sultanate's history and in the minds of the Brunei population. Perceived as being the birthplace of Brunei Malay culture, some feel that allowing non-Brunei Malays to live on Kampong Ayer will change its identity and lead to it losing its distinctive culture. Notably, however, a recent study in relation to Indonesian migrant workers living in Kampong Ayer suggests that this view appears to be held more by ex-residents of Kampong Ayer rather than remaining residents. The study indicated that Indonesian migrant workers living in Kampong Ayer have successfully integrated themselves into local communities, partly because they share a similar culture and the same religion (Muhammad Faiz Zul Hamdi et al. 2017).[9]

The future of Kampong Ayer

In recent years there have been moves to promote Kampong Ayer as a tourist attraction, as part of the government's drive to increase tourism revenue. As part of this drive, a Cultural and Tourism Gallery was established in Kampong Ayer in 2009 by the Brunei Tourism Board, with assistance from the national museum. The gallery aims to provide local and foreign visitors with an understanding of Kampong Ayer's past important political, social and economic role. The gallery includes examples of handicrafts that were once made there, handicraft demonstrations, periodic cultural performances, and a souvenir shop. Furthermore, a number of Kampong Ayer homestays have also been established in recent years. They are advertised on international travel sites.

While some have argued that heritage tourism can revitalise Kampong Ayer and the return of various handicraft specialisations, this will also require a more conservation-centred approach, along with the current modernisation programmes. It will also require efforts to discourage younger residents from moving away from Kampong Ayer. As Abdul Latif Haji Ibrahim (2012) recently wrote, it is migration that over the years has had the most detrimental effect on Kampong Ayer culture and lifestyle, and that a culture can only exist when there are people who practise it.

Nevertheless, the remaining Kampong Ayer community continues to play an important role in maintaining and continuing its cultural heritage for both their land-based relatives and foreign visitors. For example, Brunei Malay communities in Kampong Ayer continue to practice the *berdangsanak* way of life, which is not simply to show respect to elders in the community but is primarily concerned with experience, knowledge of Islam, and everyday customs and traditions. The practice of *melagau*, inviting guests and neighbours in the surrounding area to one's house, is also a cultural practice that remains strong in Kampong Ayer and helps to enhance relationships within the community, something that has become less common among the land-based Brunei Malay communities. Today, however, neighbours and guests are unlikely to be invited in a traditional manner but rather through modern technology, such as the phone and such social media as WhatsApp and Facebook messages. Invitation cards are still used for events such as weddings.

While Kampong Ayer will never regain its position as the sultanate's political and economic centre, it nevertheless remains the heartland of Brunei Malay culture and as such needs to be preserved for future generations. Continuing modernisation is both unavoidable and necessary. The existing community and relevant authorities need to cooperate and support each other in achieving the goal of developing Kampong Ayer while at the same time maintaining it as Brunei's most important cultural heritage.

Notes

1 Tom Harrisson's 1952–1953 excavations at Kota Batu indicate that people had been living continuously in coastal areas around the Brunei Bay area for about 2,000 years (1971: 96–106). However, there is currently no archaeological evidence of any external

trade or the development of a polity in this area before the tenth century (Druce 2016: 28–35).

2 Pigafetta estimated that the city was home to 25,000 fires, generally interpreted to mean families, which would put the population at over 100,000. This seems improbable and likely an error, as it would have needed large-scale food imports to feed such a population that would have been beyond the capabilities of the swidden farmers, particularly the Kedayan, living in the immediate hinterland. The late-sixteenth-century Boxer Codex gives a figure of 8,000 citizens living on Kampong Ayer, which Carroll suggests may refer to the number of family heads (1982: 3, 21 n.11). See also Tassim Bin Haji Abu Bakar (2013).

3 Source: statistics obtained by author from Mohammad Hasanhamuny bin Bakar (Penolong Pegawai Kerja Tingkat 1), during a briefing at the Kampong Ayer Section in the Bahagian Institusi Mukim and Kampong, Brunei and Muara District Office, 14 March 2019.

4 Source: Statistics obtained by author from Mohammad Hasanhamuny bin Bakar (Penolong Pegawai Kerja Tingkat 1), during a briefing at the Kampong Ayer Section in the Bahagian Institusi Mukim and Kampong, Brunei and Muara District Office, 14 March 2019.

5 On handicrafts, see also Tassim Bin Haji Abu Bakar (2018).

6 Information obtained through an interview by the author with Dato Paduka Dr. Haji Abdul Latif Bin Haji Ibrahim, a former resident of Kampong Lurong Sikuna, Kampong Ayer (interview on 15 March 2009).

7 Information obtained through an interview by the author with Haji Abdul Majid Bin Haji Tuah, a resident of Kampong Burong Pingai Ayer, Kampong Ayer (interview on 14 March 2009).

8 This was part of HM Sultan Hassanal Bolkiah's Silver Jubilee celebrations.

9 For further discussion on post-independence resettlement, see Tassim Bin Haji Abu Bakar (2016).

References

Abdul Latif Haji Ibrahim, Dato Paduka Haji (2012) *Kampong Ayer: Living Memory*. Brunei Darussalam: Pentagram Design Sdn. Bhd.

Asbol bin Hj Mail, Haji Awang and Haji Tassim bin Haji Abu Bakar (2016) To Live on Water: Life Style of the Kampong Ayer Community during the British Residency Period, 1906–1941. In Ooi Keat Gin (ed.), *Brunei: History, Islam, Society and Contemporary Issues*. Abingdon, Oxon: Routledge, pp. 100–122.

Azman Ahmad (2013) The Constraints of Tourism Development for a Cultural Heritage Destination: The Case of Kampong Ayer (Water Village) in Brunei Darussalam. *Tourism Management Perspectives* 8: 106–113.

Brown, D. E. (1970) Brunei: The Structure and History of a Bornean Malay Sultanate. *Brunei: Special Monograph of the Brunei Museum Journal* 2 (2).

Brunei Bulletin (2018) Kampong Ayer to Get B$45-Million Facelift, 13 March. Available at: https://borneobulletin.com.bn/kampong-ayer-to-get-b45-million-facelift/.

The Brunei Times (2015) 20 May. Available at: https://btarchive.org/news/national/2015/05/20/preserve-kg-ayers-iconic-look.

YSHHB (1998). *Buku Majlis Sempena Memperingati 5 Tahun Penubuhan Yayasan Sultan Haji Hassanal Bolkiah*. Bandar Seri Begawan: YSHHB.

Carroll, John S. (1982) Berunai in the 'Boxer Codex' [with Commentary]. *Journal of the Malaysian Branch of the Royal Asiatic Society* 55 (20): 1–25.

Chevallier, H. (1912) *Annual Report on the State of Brunei for the Year 1911*. Singapore: Government Printer.

Cleary, Mark and Shuang Yann Wong (1994) *Oil, Economic Development and Diversification in Brunei Darussalam*. London: Macmillan.

Druce, Stephen C. (2016) The 'Birth' of Brunei: Early Polities of the Northwest Coast of Borneo and the Origins of Brunei, Tenth to Mid-Fourteenth Centuries. In Ooi Keat Gin (ed.), *Brunei: History, Islam, Society and Contemporary Issues*. Abingdon, Oxon: Routledge, pp. 20–44.

Harrisson, Tom (1971) Deep Level Carbon Dates from Kota Batu, Brunei (95 B.C. 1300 A.D.). *The Brunei Museum Journal* 2 (3): 96–107.

Hussainmiya, B. A. (1995) *Sultan Omar Ali Saifuddin III and Britain: The Making of Brunei Darussalam*. Kuala Lumpur: Oxford University Press.

Iik Arifin Mansurnoor (1992) Brunei Sebagai Sebuah Pusat Jaringan (Network) Intelektual Islam di Asia Tenggara. In Dato Seri Laila Jasa Awang Haji Abu Bakar bin Haji Apong (ed.), *Sumbangsih UBD: Esei-esei Mengenai Negara Brunei Darussalam*. Gadong: Akademi Pengajian Brunei, pp. 148–163.

Muhammad Faiz Zul Hamdi, Norhidayah Abdullah and Hazimatul Diyana binti Narudin (2017) *Space, Place, and Identity: How Migration has Transformed Kampong Ayer (Brunei)*. Universiti Brunei Darussalam/Institute of Asian Studies, Working Paper No. 28.

Nicholl, Robert (1975) *European Sources for the History of the Sultanate of Brunei in the Sixteenth Century*. Bandar Seri Begawan: Brunei Museum.

The Scoop (2018) Floating Restaurants, Food Stalls Proposed to Revitalise Kampong Ayer, 13 March. Available at: https://thescoop.co/2018/03/13/floating-restaurants-food-stalls-proposed-revitalise-kampong-ayer/.

Siti Norkhalbi Haji Wahsalfelah and Abdul Hai Julay (2006) *Sejarah Sosio-Budaya Kraftangan di Brunei Darussalam: Barangan Logam dan Kain Tenunan*. Seminar Sejarah Sosial dan Ekonomi Brunei, Faculty of Arts and Social Science, Universiti Brunei Darussalam, Gadong, 14–15 November.

Tassim bin Haji Abu Bakar, Haji (2013) Sejarah Awal Petempatan Kampong Ayer di Brunei Zaman Tradisi Sebelum 1906. In *Kerajaan-kerajaan Melayu dan Hubungannya dengan Kesultanan Brunei*. Bandar Seri Begawan: Brunei History Centre.

Tassim bin Haji Abu Bakar, Haji (2016) Perkembangan Rancangan Perpindahan Negara Brunei Darussalam Pasca Merdeka: Satu Dasar Kebajikan Negara. In *Brunei Merdeka: A Collection of Articles to Commemorate the Celebration of 30 Years of Independence in Brunei Darussalam*. Bandar Seri Begawan: Sultan Haji Hassanal Bolkiah Foundation and the Brunei History Centre.

Tassim Bin Haji Abu Bakar, Haji (2018) The Residents of Kampong Ayer, 1906–1940: The Activities of Pengalu, Padian, and Handiwork. *Tawarikh, International Journal for Historical Studies* 9 (2): 151–158.

Yahya bin Haji Ibrahim, Pehin Siraja Khatib Dato Paduka Seri Setia Haji Awang (1996) *Beberapa Aspek Mengenai Rumah dan Perumahan Di Kampong Ayer*. Paper presented at the International Symposium on Kampong Ayer organised by the Academy of Brunei Studies, Universiti Brunei Darussalam, Gadong, 6–9 September.

10 Prospects and challenges of heritage tourism at Kampong Ayer (water village) in Brunei Darussalam

Shafi Noor Islam

Introduction

Kampong Ayer is an area of Brunei's capital city Bandar Seri Begawan, which is located near Brunei Bay in Brunei Darussalam. The geographical location of Brunei Bay extends approximately 40 kilometres from east to west, whilst from south to north it is around 23 kilometres wide. It is a unique element of the cultural landscape that in 1980 consisted of 42 named stilt villages built along the banks of the Brunei River. By 2016 the number of villages had been reduced to 34, and the number has since fallen on account of the development of the Eco-Corridor. There are now around 10,000 inhabitants still living above water in Kampong Ayer (see Haji Tassim bin Haji Abu Bakar in Chapter 9). Kampong Ayer is culturally and historically the most prestigious, as well as the largest water settlement in the Southeast Asian region. It was formerly the capital of the Brunei Empire. According to the UNESCO (United Nations Educational, Scientific and Cultural Organisation) criteria of heritage site selection Kampong Ayer fulfils some of them. Considering the physical characteristics, traditional buildings and housing pattern, geological processes and cultural and natural activities, Kampong Ayer could be considered for submission as a UNESCO World Heritage Site (WHS) (Wikipedia 2019). The tangible and intangible cultural heritage of Kampong Ayer is still reflected in its exceptional cultural and historical qualities.

The present status of tourism in Kampong Ayer is not particularly significant, but there are some opportunities for the development of 'water tourism'. One of the planning objectives of the development of the Eco-Corridor within the territorial boundaries of the water village is to increase tourism activities in Kampong Ayer and the adjacent areas of Bandar Seri Begawan. However, Kampong Ayer is losing its natural landscape and cultural identity, which is the main challenge of tourism development and the sustainability of the livelihoods of residents there.

The objectives of this chapter are to understand and analyse the universal cultural value, heritage status and tourism activities at Kampong Ayer within the framework of UNESCO World Heritage Site selection. The study examines the opportunities and challenges of tourism development and better management and conservation policies of Kampong Ayer. The study is based on primary and secondary data.

Brunei's monarchy and its cultural heritage have been steadfastly upheld to this day. The country's royal heritage can be seen especially in the Brunei Muara District. In the 15th century, the sultans began to build Brunei into a powerful seafaring kingdom based at Kota Batu, downstream from the present site of Bandar Seri Begawan (Yogerst and Lloyd 1994). The period that followed is considered the nation's 'Golden Age', when Brunei extended its authority over a far greater geographical area than it occupies today, including much of coastal Borneo (a term which is actually an early European derivation of the name Brunei), and some coastal areas of the Philippines, including the Sulu archipelago, Palawan, Mindoro and Manila Bay. During this period there was a flourishing trade with China, Java, Malacca and other parts of island Southeast Asia. The 'Golden Age' is linked to the name of Sultan Bolkiah (r. late 15th and early 16th centuries), who is often credited with Brunei's expansion during this period (Kershaw 2001; Abdul Latif Haji Ibrahim 2005). The first recorded eyewitness account of Kampong Ayer also dates to this period, left in 1521 by Antonio Pigafetta, who noted that 'the city is entirely built in salt water, except the houses of the king and certain chiefs' (Nicholl 1975: 10).

Following a long period of decline, in 1888 Brunei became a British protectorate, and in 1906 a British residential system was introduced (Borneo Bulletin Yearbook [BBY] 2014). Brunei was eventually granted internal self-government in the 1959 Anglo-Brunei Agreement, and later that year Sultan Omar Ali Saifuddien promulgated the nation's first written Constitution on 29 September 1959. In 1967, the current Sultan, His Majesty Sultan Haji Hassanal Bolkiah Mu'izzaddin Waddaulah, was made the 29th ruler of Brunei Darussalam, leading the nation to achieve its independence in 1984. The Sultan declared Negara Brunei Darussalam as a sovereign, democratic and independent Malay Muslim Monarchy (*Melayu Islam Beraja*) administered according to the teachings of Islam (Abdul Latif Haji Ibrahim 2005; Borneo Bulletin Yearbook [BBY] 2014). Bandar Seri Begawan, formerly Brunei Town, was declared as the new capital of the country.

The geographical location of the case area

Brunei Darussalam comprises four districts: Brunei-Muara, Tutong, Belait and Temburong. The total land area is 5,765 square kilometres, with an estimated population of some 445,449 (as of 1 January 2019). As Brunei is located on the north-west shoreline of Borneo, its approximate 161-kilometre coastline faces the South China Sea (Abdul Latif Haji Ibrahim 2005; Borneo Bulletin Yearbook [BBY] 2014, 2015; Islam et al. 2014).

Brunei Darussalam is located within the tropical and sub-tropical region. Historically, Borneo is a place of geomorphic, anthropogenic and cultural and linguistic diversity (Tyler 2004). It is also a diverse country in historical terms derived from the country's links across the South China Sea and the Indian Ocean (Borneo Bulletin Yearbook [BBY] 2014, 2015).

Historical geography of Kampong Ayer

Since the establishment of a British Residency in 1906, there have been attempts to resettle residents from Kampong Ayer to dryland. However, there was little movement of people away from the water village until the 1980s, following significant efforts made by the Brunei government. At the same time, Kampong Ayer residents were also provided with amenities and facilities in order to modernise the sprawling settlement of villages of different sizes and shapes (Maps 10.1, 10.2). While there were 42 named villages listed in 1980 (Map 10.1), the number has been progressively reduced since then. By 2016 only 34 were recorded (Map 10.2, and see Haji Tassim bin Haji Abu Bakar in Chapter 9).

Data and methodology

The primary data used here on Brunei heritage was gathered from field studies in Bandar Seri Begawan. A field investigation was also carried out in Kampong Ayer where formal interviews were undertaken with the water village's inhabitants. During the field investigation a special discussion was arranged with the

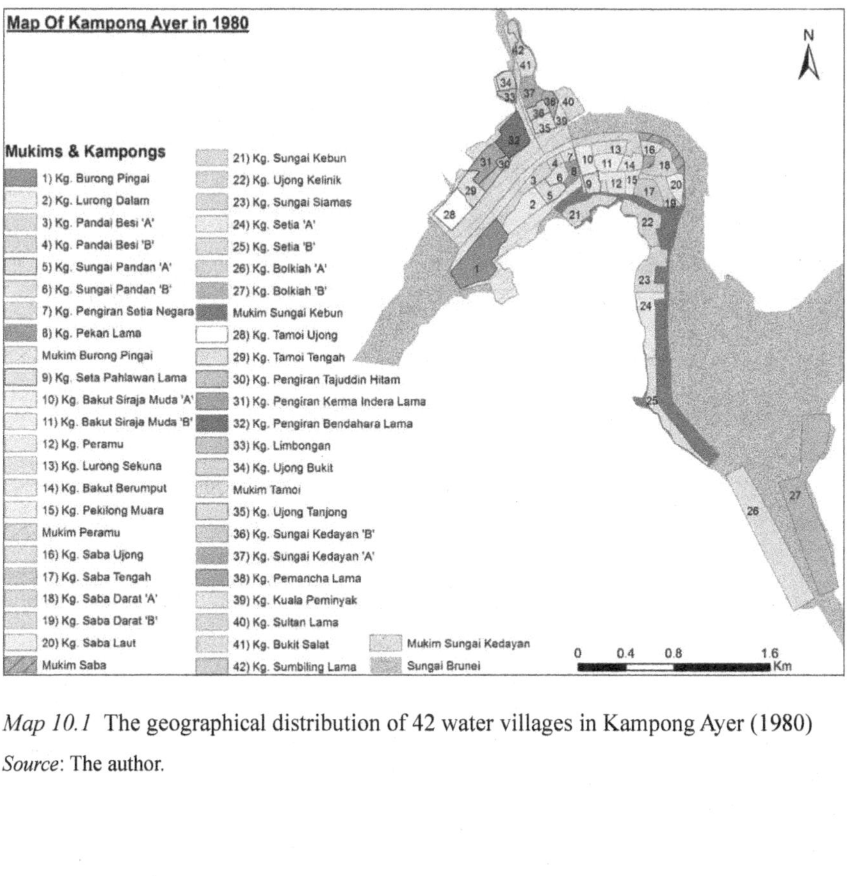

Map 10.1 The geographical distribution of 42 water villages in Kampong Ayer (1980)

Source: The author.

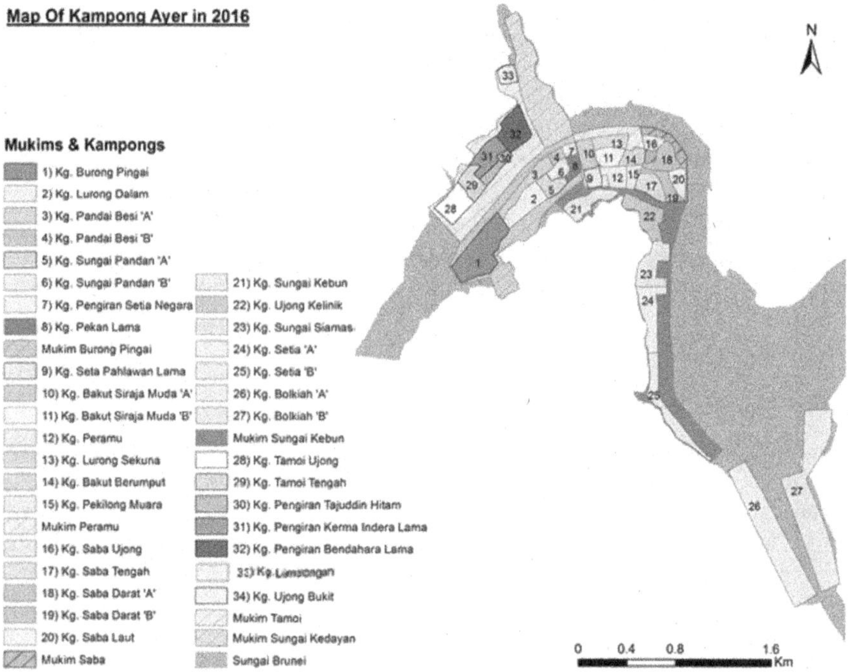

Map 10.2 The geographical location and distribution of 34 water villages in Kampong Ayer (2016)

Source: The author.

students of Universiti Brunei Darussalam (UBD) and the residents of Kampong Ayer for recording primary information on culture and heritage. A further field investigation was later undertaken by 58 students and the author of this chapter in Kampong Ayer and mosques in Bandar Seri Begawan. In addition, interviews were undertaken with researchers at UBD. Secondary data and information were collected from the UBD library, international organisations including UNESCO and IUCN (International Union for Conservation of Nature), and relevant academic publications. Besides this geomorphological and anthropological study, information was gathered through informal discussions with inhabitants in Kampong Ayer for benchmark data collection. Complete enumeration of the households in the research, covering the land-holding pattern, tenancy, occupation, demographic character, literacy and so on was also collected in 2015. The secondary data inputs were obtained from publications of government agencies, NGO reports and research organisations in Brunei. The data were analysed and imaged using Excel and Visio 32 software which were also used to develop the management plan for the sustainability of cultural heritage conservation in Brunei.

Public perception of tourism and cultural heritage

The term 'tourist' refers to an individual who travels for pleasure, for leisure and out of curiosity. Humankind has always had the desire to travel, visit exotic places and encounter different cultures (Hitchcock et al. 1993). On the other hand, according to Macintosh and Goeldner, 'tourism may be defined as the sum of the phenomena and relationships arising from the interaction between tourists, business suppliers, governments, and hosting these tourists and other visitors' (1986: 1).

Cultural and natural heritage are not renewable or irreplaceable. Nor are they the property of any one nation; they belong to humankind. Any heritage loss, through destruction or disappearance, is thus a loss for all humanity. Some expressions of heritage can be considered as of outstanding universal value and as such require special protection against the dangers of modernisation and economic development. The public concept and perception of natural and cultural heritage has been internationalised by UNESCO and its definitions of what is of 'outstanding universal value'. The scenic values of Kampong Ayer provide some of the unique aspects of the water village.

In an attempt to reduce this vulnerable situation for world heritage and to ensure the proper identification, protection, conservation and preservation of the world's irreplaceable heritage, the member states of UNESCO adopted in 1972 the World Heritage Convention. Up to July 2019, 193 countries had joined the UNESCO Convention; meanwhile, 1,121 World Heritage Sites had been identified (Cultural 869, Natural 213, Mixed 39; Wikipedia 2019). Currently, there is no designated WHS in Brunei, nor any on the Tentative List. On the basis of the UNESCO conference in 1972, the criteria were established for both cultural and natural site selection, though these have been modified and rearranged since then (UNESCO 1972; King 2016). UNESCO recognised the increase in threats to the world's cultural and natural heritage and began efforts to preserve humankind's irreplaceable assets of 'outstanding universal value' (UNESCO 1999). The Convention is designed to complement heritage conservation programmes at the national level and provided for the establishment of a World Heritage Committee and a World Heritage Fund. Both the committee and the fund have been in operation since 1976. The following definitions and concepts should be acknowledged and applied in management options (UNESCO 1999, 2008). The UNESCO definition of cultural heritage (1972) has been recognised and ratified based on the following criteria:

- *Monuments*: architectural works, works of monumental sculpture and painting, elements or structures of an archaeological nature, inscriptions, care dwellings and combinations of features, which are of outstanding universal values from the point of view of history, art or science.
- *Groups of buildings*: groups of separate or connected buildings which, because of their architecture, their homogeneity or their place in the landscape, are of outstanding universal value from the point of view of history, art or science.

- *Sites*: works of man or the combined works of nature and man, and areas including archaeological value which are of outstanding universal value from the historical, aesthetic or anthropological point of view.

In addition, UNESCO defines intangible heritage as

> embracing all forms of traditional and popular or folk cultures i.e. collective works originating in a given community and based on tradition. These creations are transmitted orally or by gesture, and are modified over a period of time through a process of collective reaction. They include oral traditions, customs languages, music, dance, ritual, festivals, congress, traditional medicine and pharmacopoeia, the culinary arts and all kind of special skills collected with the tools and aspects of their culture.
>
> (UNESCO 2019)

Tourism in Kampong Ayer

Tourism is one of the sectors that can assist in developing economic activities in Kampong Ayer as well as sustaining its cultural heritage. Despite being an important tourist site, Kampong Ayer is already in danger of losing its cultural heritage with rapid urbanisation, the migration of its population to resettlement sites on land and foreign workers coming to live there (Azman 2013). The number of tourists coming to Brunei is, however, steadily increasing each year, and this creates a need for socio-economic tourism activities, such as cultural heritage tourism, that could help conserve Kampong Ayer.

Tourism is a socio-economic phenomenon that contributes to the economic development of a country and can help increase employment and revenue generation. In 2015, the UN World Trade Organization stated that travel and tourism globally generated US$1.5 trillion in export earnings. Tourism in Brunei is an emerging economic sector that currently contributes 2% of the country's GDP; this is expected to increase each year. The number of tourist arrivals at the international airport in 2018 was 278,136, a notable increase on the figures for 2017 and 2016 which respectively were 258,955 and 218,809 visitors. According to the Tourism Development Department, Brunei (2018), compared to 2016 when Brunei achieved only a 0.8% increase in tourist arrivals on the previous year, in 2017 the increase was 18.3%. This increase is important for the preservation of Brunei's heritage, as Kampong Ayer is one of the country's major tourist sites. Nevertheless, UNESCO status would help preserve and protect this unique cultural and natural heritage, given the pressures which tourism might bring, among other pressures of modernisation to which it is subject.

In this section, I will look at the current level of tourism in Kampong Ayer followed by recommendations for cultural conservation through tourism activity. Table 10.1 shows the number of tourists who visited the Tourism Gallery at Kampong Ayer.

Table 10.1 The number of tourists visiting Kampong Ayer Tourism Gallery by region from January 2018 to March 2019

Year	*Southeast Asia*	*East Asia*	*Europe*	*Australia/ New Zealand*	*America*	*Others*
2018	1612	478	355	67	148	71
2019	2044	705	472	67	126	118
Total	3656	1183	827	134	274	189

Source: Field Survey, April 2019.

Table 10.2 The total and average number of tourists visiting Kampong Ayer Tourism Gallery, 2018–2019

Year	*Total number of tourists visiting Kampong Ayer Tourism Gallery*	*Average number of tourists within three months*
2018	2731	910
2019	3532	1177

Source: Field survey, April 2019.

Table 10.3 Total number of monthly tourists in Kampong Ayer from January to March 2019

Months	*Total number of tourists visiting Kampong Ayer Tourism Gallery by month*
January 2019	1188
February 2019	1260
March 2019	1044

Source: Field survey in April 2019.

The number of visitors to the Kampong Ayer Tourism Gallery could be obtained only from January to March 2019. The statistics demonstrate that tourists visiting the Gallery came mainly from Southeast Asia, especially from within Brunei, followed by Malaysia, then East Asia, Europe, America, Australia and New Zealand. Table 10.2 shows that a total number of tourists visiting the Kampong Ayer Tourism Gallery from January 2018 to March 2018 and from January to March 2019.

Therefore, from January to March 2018, the average number of tourists is 910, while an average of 1177 tourists visited the Gallery from January to March 2019. Table 10.3 shows the total monthly number of tourists who visited in 2019.

The data confirm the growing number of tourists in 2019, with a 29% increase from the previous year. An advantage of Kampong Ayer is that it is easily accessible, located as it is near the heart of Bandar Seri Begawan where there are other popular tourist sites, such as the Sultan Omar Ali Saifuddien Mosque, The Royal Regalia Museum, and The History Centre. In 2009, the Brunei Tourism Development Department established the Kampong Ayer Cultural and Tourism

Gallery for tourists to gain a better understanding of the history and livelihoods of Kampong Ayer. A local resident, Dayangku Kemariah Pg Haji Duraman, has also enhanced tourism in Kampong Ayer by providing a homestay/Airbnb, the well-known Kunyit 7 Lodge (2019). Launched in April 2015, and located just a boat ride from the Yayasan Sultan Haji Hassanal Bolkiah Complex, Kunyit 7 Lodge has already hosted guests from more than 40 countries, ranging from the United States to Switzerland, as well as Romania, Portugal and Spain. An old dwelling on stilts, it has four rooms that can accommodate up to 12 guests at one time. Dk Kemariah also organises guided tours and serves guests locally made snacks and sweetmeats, tea and soft drinks at her lodge and undertakes a walking tour in her village and surrounding villages. At the same time she helps the local community businesses by promoting the local products to the tourists visiting Kampong Ayer. If required she will also take tourists on a boat trip to the upper Brunei River to experience the local riverine environment and to see the proboscis monkeys in the wild. The lodge is her late grandfather's home and has sentimental and nostalgic value. After she took over the house in 2014 from her uncle, she decided to renovate it. She also stated that the reason that she opened the homestay was to give her family members, including her sons, nephews and nieces, the opportunity to do business while at the same time serve the community. Furthermore, she wishes to promote Brunei and the uniqueness of Kampong Ayer and its heritage. The tourists who stay here have the opportunity not only to experience the local lifestyle in Kampong Ayer, but also to get to know the history, culture and heritage of Kampong Ayer. By opening the lodge, it also helps Kampong Ayer's cottage industries, such as prawn cracker-making and handicrafts near to her lodge, and it increases business of local water taxis as the only way to get there is by boat. Therefore, it is having a positive impact on the socio-economic development of the local people of Kampong Ayer.

Opportunities and challenges of tourism development in Kampong Ayer

In the past the residents always had relationships which were family-oriented and residentially close. When there was an event, the residents would gather together in one house and help each other in terms of providing food, arranging chairs on the balcony of the house and collectively undertaking tasks that needed to be done (*bergotong-royong*). Now, many family members have moved from Kampong Ayer to housing schemes on land due to fire hazards and pollution (Seneviratne 1999). This has resulted in more migrants moving into Kampong Ayer because the house rental is cheap. Yet there remains a strong core of local residents.

Today, the majority of local Kampong Ayer residents interviewed were self-employed as fishermen and water taxi operators, while others engaged in homestay accommodation, trading, food processing, carpentry, construction work and handicrafts. Furthermore, a study by UNISSA in 2014 found that 46% of the local population in Kampong Ayer earned less than BND $1000 and 43% had no fixed income. In other words, there was considerable poverty in Kampong Ayer

(Rabiatul Kamit 2014; and see Muhammad Faiz et al. 2017). Tourism development in Kampong Ayer could help to ameliorate these local socio-economic conditions. Although the handicraft traditions of Kampong Ayer have declined, the Brunei government has supported the continuation of handicraft production in the Brunei Arts and Handicraft Training Centre, located across the river from Kampong Ayer (with its workshops in Kiulap). Tourism development in Brunei which integrates the water village into heritage trails, including the Arts and Handicraft Centre, the Royal Regalia Museum, The History Centre, the Malay Technology Museum, the Maritime Museum, the Istana Darussalam, the Archaeological Park and the Mausolea of Sultan Hassanal Bolkiah and Sharif Ali and the experience of journeying along the Brunei River, could provide the basis for a World Heritage Site. Kampong Ayer has its own natural beauty where, in spite of the changes, in certain of its landscapes still has the feel of a 'Venice of the East'. The newly-created Eco-Corridor also has a part to play in this integrated tourism experience.

The challenges of Kampong Ayer in the context of World Heritage Sites

At present Kampong Ayer from a structural point of view is not ready to be considered as a World Heritage Site, although some site selection criteria can possibly be met. There are no initiatives for the development and publication of a tourist map of Kampong Ayer and the Brunei River and its associated cultural sites, though a heritage trail in Kampong Ayer has recently been introduced. These considerations should be given priority by the government authorities responsible for deciding whether or not Kampong Ayer and its environs meet UNESCO requirements (UNESCO 2014).

Some of the elements of cultural heritage of Kampong Ayer have already disappeared or will do so in the near future, though the government has preserved some of these traditions in its museums and in its support for handicraft production. Nevertheless, the reasons for these threats, to which we have already referred, will not disappear and will likely accelerate. These include processes of modernisation, economic development and the resulting pressures on Malay traditional culture. The younger generation in Brunei has become less interested in practising the legacy of the older generation. Migration has transferred substantial populations from Kampong Ayer to the mainland with the provision of better housing development and wider job opportunities in the government sector. The market demand for traditional handicraft products has also declined in competition with imported and mass-produced goods.

The traditional social-cultural-economic complexes which comprised the *padian* (women boat vendors) and *pengalu* (suppliers of goods to the *padian*) have disappeared. No women are willing to be *padian* nor men to be a *pengalu* as they prefer to earn a consistent income by working on land, particularly in the government sector. Furthermore, the government has built a special covered market over the main river from Kampong Ayer at Kianggeh and a fish market for the people where they can be sited in one place and sell their products. It provides a convenient forum for both seller and buyer, and provides a modestly priced alternative for fruit and vegetables in competition with the modern supermarkets.

There are also specific infrastructural problems in relation to tourism development on Kampong Ayer. For example, there are no danger or warning signs to indicate potentially dangerous areas on walkways and bridges. The removal of litter and rubbish in the water village is not properly handled and thus causes unpleasant smells as well as being unsightly, which is not conducive either to the everyday lives of the residents or to the attraction of tourists. In addition, there are no street lamps which can be seen around the water villages, which could potentially lead to accidents at night for both inhabitants and tourists.

Conclusions

The Kampong Ayer water village catchment area is an area of cultural importance and national cultural identity (Borneo Bulletin Yearbook [BBY] 2014, 2015). Some of these important sites, both within and in the adjacent areas of Kampong Ayer, have the potential to be considered as a UNESCO WHS and as arenas for tourist development. But we have to add a qualifying statement: that the modernisation of Kampong Ayer, the government's resettlement policies, the reduction of its population and the introduction of migrant workers will probably not meet the approval of UNESCO. We have to consider a broader policy of cultural tourism and the integration of Kampong Ayer within this strategy. Kampong Ayer must be an important element in a wider vision of the cultural and historical importance of Kota Batu and the Brunei River, the original seat of the Brunei sultanate.

References

Abdul Latif Haji Ibrahim, Haji (2005) Culture and Counter Cultural Forces in Contemporary Brunei Darussalam. In Edwin Thumboo (ed.), *Cultures in ASEAN and the 21st Century*. Singapore: NUS Press, pp. 22–34.

Azman Ahmad (2013) The Constraints of Tourism Development for a Cultural Heritage Destination: The Case of Kampong Ayer (Water Village) in Brunei Darussalam. *Tourism Management Perspectives* 8, October: 106–113.

Borneo Bulletin Yearbook [BBY] (2014) *Brunei 2035 Development, Education and Health: Seeds of Success*. Bandar Seri Begawan: BBY.

Borneo Bulletin Yearbook [BBY] (2015) *The Guide to Brunei Darussalam 2015*. Bandar Seri Begawan: BBY.

Hitchcock, Michael, Victor T. King and Michael J. G. Parnwell (eds.) (1993) *Tourism in South-East Asia*. London: Routledge.

Islam, S. N., R. Karim, A. N. Islam and S. Eslamian (2014) Wetland Hydrology. In *Handbook of Engineering Hydrology*. Vol. 3. New York: CRC Press/Taylor and Francis, pp. 119–34.

Kershaw, Roger (2001) Brunei, Malay, Monarchical, Micro-State. In J. Funston (ed.), *Government and Politics in Southeast Asia*. Singapore: Seng Lee Press, pp. 1–35.

King, Victor T. (ed.) (2016) *UNESCO in Southeast Asia: World Heritage Sites in Comparative Perspective*. Copenhagen: NIAS Press.

Kunyit 7 Lodge (2019) Kunyit Lodge Brunei. Available at: facebook.com/Kunyit-7-Lodge-1669520159933934/ (accessed 17 November 2019).

Macintosh, Robert Woodrow and Charles R. Goeldner (1986) *Tourism: Principles, Practices, Philosophies*. New York: Wiley.

Muhammad Faiz Zul Hamdi, Norhidayah Abdullah and Hazimatul Diyana binti Narudin (2017) *Space, Place and Identity: How Migration have (sic) Transformed Kampong Ayer (Brunei)*. Gadong: Institute of Asian Studies, Universiti Brunei Darussalam, Working Paper Series, No. 28.

Nicholl, Robert (1975) *European Sources for the History of the Sultanate of Brunei in the Sixteenth Century*. Bandar Seri Begawan: Brunei Museum.

Rabiatul Kamit (2014) Poverty Still Rife in Kampong Ayer. Available at: btarchive.org/news/national/2014/09/30/poverty-still-rife-kampong-ayer (accessed 17 November 2019).

Seneviratne, Kalinga (1999) Culture-Brunei: Old Water Village Drowning in Modern Problems. Available at: ipsnews.net/1993/03/culture-brunei-old-water-village-drowning-in modern-problems (accessed 17 November 2019).

Tourism Development Department, Brunei, Ministry of Primary Resources and Tourism (2018) Statistics, 2014–2018. Available at: tourism.gov.bn/SitePages/statistics.aspx (accessed 18 November 2019).

Tyler, Rodney (2004) *Brunei Darussalam: The Making of a Modern Nation*. Bandar Seri Begawan: R. Tyler.

UNESCO (United Nations Educational Scientific and Cultural Organization) (1972) *Convention Concerning the Protection of the World Heritage Cultural and Natural Heritage*. Paris: UNESCO World Heritage Centre.

UNESCO (United Nations Educational Scientific and Cultural Organization) (1999) *World Heritage Centre, Report 1999/3*. Paris: UNESCO World Heritage Centre.

UNESCO (United Nations Educational Scientific and Cultural Organization) (2008) *Policy Document on the Impacts of Climate Change on World Heritage Properties*. Paris: UNESCO World Heritage Centre.

UNESCO (United Nations Educational Scientific and Cultural Organization) (2014) *Brunei Darussalam: UNESCO Country Programming Document 2013–2016*. Bandar Seri Begawan, organised by UNESCO Jakarta in Bandar Seri Begawan.

UNESCO (United Nations Educational Scientific and Cultural Organization) (2019) *What Is Intangible Cultural Heritage?* Paris: UNESCO World Heritage Centre.

Wikipedia (2019) World Heritage Site. Available at: en.wikipedia.org/wiki/World_Heritage_Site (accessed 17 November 2019).

Yogerst, J. and R. Ian Lloyd (1994) *The Golden Legacy-Brunei Darussalam*. Bandar Seri Begawan: Syabas.

Figure 11.1 From left to right: Donald Brown in cara Melayu; Carrie Brown with hawker (*padian*) at the ladder to their house in Kampong Ayer; Donald and Carrie in the Brunei Museum; and Donald and Carrie on the ladder to their house in Kampong Ayer, with on-looking neighbours, all 1967

11 Epilogue

Brunei studies: 50 years and more

Donald E. Brown

Brunei Studies is now an established and productive academic field: witness the contents of this book and volume 1. Just over fifty years ago the foundations had already been laid: in Brunei, the establishment both of the Brunei Museum (Muzium Brunei) and the Language and Literature Bureau (Dewan Bahasa dan Pustaka). Each of these institutions was already productive, the Dewan more internally focused, the Museum with both national and international aims, owing in no small measure to its first Director, Pengiran Dato Paduka Haji Shariffuddin bin Pengiran Metali, to whom an enormous vote of thanks is due and to whom the first volume has been dedicated. The Museum supported and published my socio-cultural-historical overview of Brunei, and related studies by the anthropologists Allen Maxwell and Linda Amy Kimball, along with the historian Nicholas Tarling, were underway or very soon to follow.

Although very little known in the wider world, a parochial Brunei Studies existed long before fifty years ago, in the writings of Bruneians themselves on their own history and on the nature of their society and culture. Although those writings are comparatively few, they are indispensable in the attempts of all scholars to facilitate the study of Brunei that now exists.

The current centre of Brunei Studies is Universiti Brunei Darussalam (UBD), some of whose faculty are contributors to and editors of the two volumes. UBD has an Academy of Brunei Studies, hosts the Secretariat of the Borneo Studies Network, and supports a Chair in Borneo Studies in the Institute of Asian Studies. Abroad there is a Brunei Research Center at the Guangxi University for Nationalities, Nanning, Guanxi, China. A very substantial portion of publications on Brunei have flowed from research conducted by scholars outside of Brunei, perhaps especially from the United Kingdom, given its long-term engagement in Brunei affairs, but also importantly from the work that was undertaken by American social scientists in the late 1960s and early 1970s. Since then local and expatriate scholars at UBD have contributed immeasurably to our store of knowledge on Brunei and the wider Borneo.

A major topic of interest in Brunei Studies in recent decades, reflected in contributions to the two volumes, is the national ideology referred to as MIB (*Melayu Islam Beraja*). The terms refer to the ethnic category of Brunei Malays, their Islamic religion and their monarchical government. Absolute monarchy is rare in the modern world and so generates considerable academic commentary both in and outside of Brunei. The ethnically plural nature of Negara Brunei Darussalam is a continuous topic of interest in Brunei Studies, but specifically Islamic issues of contention have tended to be confined to scholarship outside of Brunei.

While there may be better examples, Brunei Studies has contributed to wider academic issues in at least two ways in which I was involved. On the one hand, my reflections on the Bruneian sense of history led me to a wider hypothesis about the nature of society and the sense of history, and my use of the term 'society' led Victor T. King to espouse a wider conception of the term, forcing greater attention to the causes and effects of relations between one people and their neighbours. Allen Maxwell also entered that exchange. There is now a considerable literature by a variety of scholars that refers to Brunei for the comparisons it provides on a variety of topics of interest throughout the world.

A deficiency of Brunei Studies is the study of and insight into Brunei's political life. Decisions and laws are made by the Sultan. But how does he arrive at his decisions? Whom does he consult? What sort of pressures does he face? Insightful public discussions of such matters are decidedly limited in Brunei as compared to more politically open societies. This was much the case when I did my fieldwork in Brunei, and seems much the case in more recent times. Rumours flew then but open and public discussions of the issues were minimal, except by outsiders, whose access to accurate information was and is limited precisely because they are outsiders.

There is still much to do and say in Brunei Studies. Its robust future is assured, and I count myself privileged to have taken part in developing our understanding of Brunei's history, society and culture.

Index

Note: Page numbers in **bold** indicate a table and page numbers in *italics* indicate a figure. Page numbers followed by 'n' indicate a note on the corresponding page.

abai (Dusun term for Brunei Malays) 107
Abdul Aziz Juned 52
Abdul Hamid, Shaikh 39n11
Abdul Harun Majid: *Rebellion in Brunei* (2007) 23, 25
Abdul Jalilul Akbar, Sultan 126
Abdullah Ja'afar 40n19
Abdul Latif Haj Ibrahim, DP Dr Haji 14, 162, 163n6
Abdul Mubin, Sultan 126–127
Abdul Rahman, Tunku 27, 28, 33–36, 37
Abell, Sir Anthony 26, 28, 30, 40n19, 41n42
Abu Bakar, Sultan (Johore) 31
Achmad Zaidi 25, 39n14
Adams, A. 136n15
adat (Malay customs) 55
Adau Gayoh (Dusun harvest festival) 85
Ahmad Boestamam 27, 28, 40n27, 41n38
Ahmad Tajuddin, Sultan 52
Ajeerah Najib, Siti 78, 79
alai gayo (Dusun communal dwelling) 92, 95, 97, 100–102, 105, 109nn10–11, 110nn13–14, 111n19; not regarded as an *alai awad* (longhouse) 93; site as identity 93
Alak Betatar, Awang 10
alan suguton (benefactor to rely on) 94
alat-alat kebesaran diraja (royal regalia) 54
Alliance Party (Malaya) 27
Al-Muhtadee Billah, Crown Prince Haji (b 1974) 15, 17, 19
American Association of Asian Studies 19n
Amin Abdul Aziz 54
Andar Amou bin Yuan, OK 105, 112n30
animism 10, 16, 91, 104
apical ancestor (Dusun) 94–95
aqidah (doctrine) 52, 56
Aqidah Control Unit (1986–) 53, 57
archaeological evidence 162–163n1
Ari, OK Temanggong 112n29
Arir, OK Laksamana 105, 112nn29–30
Arts and Handicraft Training Centre 173
Asiyah az-Zahra Ahmad Kumpoh 53–54, 109n7
awang 137n24
awang-awang (aristocrats) 128, 138n31
ayau (military means) 107
Azahari, Shaikh A. M. 2, 21–45; Arab ancestry 25, 26; birth of PRB 27–28; at Bogor 25, 36, 39, 43n75; business undertakings 24, 30; death in exile (2002) 36; delegation to Colonial Office (1957) 30, 32, 42n50; did not launch 1962 rebellion himself 23; early career 25–27; education 25; faith in magical amulets 43n75; goals might have been advanced better by forming branch of UMNO 28; imprisonment (1953) 27; nominated by Sultan to Legislative Council 31–32; 'not a communist' 34; place of birth 25, 39n10; PRB leader 27–39, 41–43; speeches 28, 41n43; 'string of failures' (1957) 30; supporters 27–28; veterinary science 25
azimat (talisman) 56

babulang (cockfighting) 111n22
Badaruddin Othman (MoRA) 53
Badarudin, Pengiran (*fl.* 1845) 124
Bahai 52
Bahasa Mengenali Bangsa (Language Identifies Race/Ethnicity) (RTB series) 83

balian pengiaw (chief priestesses) 96, 96–97, 98, 110–111n18
Bampfylde, C. A. 123, 135n10
Bandar Seri Begawan 5, 9, 134n6, 154
Baram 106, 112n33
Baring-Gould, S. 123, 135n10
Barisan Buroh Bersatu Brunei (BULF) 32, 42n58
Barisan Sosialis (Socialist Front, Singapore) 34, 35, 37, 42n62
Belait District 90, 91, 93, 106, 108n1, 109n7, 122, 135n10
Belait ethnic group 3, 10, 71; census figures 70, **132**; in or out of mainstream 67–72; *menteri darat* 129; *puak jati* 67
Belait language 72–74, 79, 134n8; distinct from Brunei Malay 68; ethnolinguistic vitality ratings **78**; 'language shift' to Pan-Brunei Malay *77*; recent developments 84–86
Belcher, Sir Edward 124
Berakas 124; Kedayan villages 136n18
berdangsanak way of life 162
bergotong-royong (mutual aid) 172
Bernstein, J. H. 109n7
'big man' (Dusun) 94–95
Birau (Tutong tributary) 135n10
Bisaya language 72–74, 79; dialect of Dusun language **73**; distinct from Brunei Malay 68; ethnolinguistic vitality ratings **78**; 'language shift' to Pan-Brunei Malay *77*; recent developments 84–86
Bisayas: akin to Dusuns of Brunei/NBD 90, 95, 99–100, 103, 105, 106, 108n2, 111n22
Bisayas (Brunei) 10, 69, 71, 108n3, 122, **132**; in or out of mainstream 67–72; *puak jati* 67
black magic: bureaucratised representations 55–58
Boeke, J. H. 133n2
Bolkiah, Sultan 166
bomoh (supernatural healers) 49, 60, 62–63; arrests (2004–2005) 57; 'good' versus 'bad' 56–57; role (protection against sorcery) 55; state's classificatory power 55–64; stigma 57
Boothby, Sir Robert 42n60
Borneo 8; water villages 4, 5, 146–151
Borneo Bulletin 10, 35, 41n35
Bourdieu, P. 49, 50, 64
Boxer Codex 163n2
Brackman, A. C. 24
Braighlinn, G. 72
British Borneo Federation proposal 9, 33
British Malayan Petroleum Company 26
British Residency (1906–1959) 5, 8–9, 21, 26–33, 38, 42n45, 123, 152, 156, 158, 166, 167
Brooke, Rajah Sir Charles 8, 134n6, 136n16
Brooke, Rajah Sir Charles *Vyner* 8, 120
Brooke, Rajah Sir James 8, 117, 118–119, 124, 125
Brown, Carrie C. 5, *176*
Brown, Donald E. (b 1934) vii, 1–6, 55, 56, 57, *176*; 'Brunei society' issue 4, 67, 92; 'careful attention to plural society' 133–134n2; 'conquest state' 107; 'deep elements' 104; 'domestic versus foreign accounts' of Brunei 47, 64; 'gap between ideal and actual' 111n20; on membership of a social group 110n12; minority ethnic groups 85–86, 108–109n4; shifting identities in Brunei 71–72; social stratification 109n4
Brown, D. E.: article: 'Inter-Hierarchical Commissions' (1973) 4, 91, 105
Brown, D. E.: book: *Principles of Social Structure* (1976) 99–101, 133
Brown, D. E.: monograph: *Brunei: Structure and History* (1970) 1, 21; chapter on Kampong Ayer 153
Brown, D. E.: personal: based at Kampong Ayer 5, 146, 153; doctoral dissertation 21, 133n1; doctoral fieldwork 54; grasp of history 21–22; listener 64; in motorboat on Brunei River (1968) *145*;
BRUFICO (Brunei Film Company) 27
Brunei (Negara Brunei Darussalam from 1984): agreement with UK (1959) 22, 35; basic facts 7–8; British protectorate (1888) 8; 'common economy' 133; 'example of radically plural society' 117, 134n2; independence (1984) 1, 9, 36; 'Malaysia' commission (1962) 31; population (2011, 2017) 71; post-colonial cultural transformation 54; relations with Spaniards 8; religious 'purification' of culture 47, 49, 63; state of emergency (1962–) 9, 36; succession disputes 118; system of territorial control 105; transformations (recent) 1–6; wealth 13, 120, 134n7
Brunei Annual Report (1906–) 68; (1956) 27
Brunei Arts and Handicrafts Training Centre 5
Brunei Bay 119, 121, 134n5, 162n1, 165

Brunei Chinese community 16, 59, 69, **132**; estimated size (2017) 71; traditional offices bestowed by sultans 129
Brunei citizenship 69; 'good citizenship' 51, 53
Brunei Constitution (1959) 3, 9, 10, 11–12, 50, 68, 70, 79, 85; Amendments (2004) 11, 12; democratic replacement required (1962) 35; 'instrument of colonialism' 31; provisions 31, 36; *puak jati* 67; six-year gestation period 29–30; 'three-corner tussle' 29–31
Brunei Empire 8, 10, 11, 67, 165, 166
Brunei history i, 1, 2, 6, 8–9, 21, 22, 29, 35, 47, 68, 119–120, 178 reasons for sultanate's decline (by C19) 123; trade patterns 123–124; *see also* Dusun oral history
Brunei Malay language 3, 67–89, 133; definitions 72; dialect of Malay **73**, 79; differentiated from Standard Malay 72; ethnolinguistic vitality ratings **78**; language shifts 76–78; peak of linguistic hierarchy 78; use by RTB 83
Brunei Malays ('Barunay'; 'Bruneis') 3, 9–10, 118; absorption of other indigenous groups 71–72; census category introduced only in 1941 70; census figures 70, **132**; economic activities 121–122, 136n14; food supplies 122, 136n16; monopoly of political power 133; *puak jati* 67; rebellion (1962) 24; term appeared in census of 1947 70
Brunei Malays ('Bruneis') versus non-Bruneis 4, 91, 102, 104, 107
Brunei Museum 3, 177
Brunei National Archives 23
Brunei National Democratic Party (BNDP) 15
Brunei Nationality Enactment (1961; later 'Act') 3, 34, 69
Brunei People's Party *see Partai Rakyat Brunei* (PRB)
Brunei Rebellion (1962) 2, 9, 15, 21–45; causes 24; Cold War context 2, 24, 28–29, 34, 37, 38–39; course 22–24, 39nn1–6; critical files still in embargo 23, 39n3; failure 36; 'froze' democratic process 24; impact on Brown's researches 2; Kedayan involvement 121, 135–136n13; labels 24; literature survey 23–25, 39; overseas military support (failure to materialise) 37; post-facto justifications 23; sensitivity 21, 22; sources 23
Brunei River 5, 129
Brunei society 4, 67, 68, 101, 108, 178; place of Kedayans 117–144; status of Kedayans 128–129, 138nn30–32
Brunei State Council 29
Brunei Studies 6, 177–178
Brunei Town 5, 22, 27; Catholic mission school 25; *see also* Bandar Seri Begawan
Brunei United Labour Front (BULF) 32, 42n58
Bukits (Bisayas): census figure (1921) 70; label for Dusuns (1958) 108n1
bulangkas (horsehoe crab) 130
bureaucratic meaning-making 48–50, 63
Bureaucratisation of Islam (BoI) 46–66
Burgess, A. 41n40
Burhanuddin, Dr 27, 28, 41n37

Carroll, J. S. 163n2
caste 106
censuses 69–72, **132**; (1921) 70; (1981) 135n12; (2001) 70–71
ceteria (*citiria*) 126, 128, 137n25
Chanin, E. 23
Chevallier, H. 122, 135n10
China/PRC 12, 34, 37, 177
Christians 10, 16
Clandestine Communist Organisation 34
Clifford, Sir Hugh 120
Clutterbuck, W. J. 135n10
Cobbold Commission 31
Cochrane, Rear-Admiral Sir Thomas 124
cockfights 127
colleges or councils (Smith) 95–96
colonial records: British 21, 23; Spanish 152
Coluzzi, P. 78
communism 25, 26, 32, 34, 37
corporate groups 95–96, 102, 103; *waris* group 99–101
corporations 95–96; corporation aggregate 102–103; corporation sole 102
culture 1, 6, 12, 15, 47, 49, 54, 63, 82, 84, 85, 92, 97, 101, 104, 107, 130, 152, 161, 162, 168–170, 177, 178

dagang serah (forced trade) 112n29
Damuan River: Kedayan villages 125, 129, 136–137n19
Darah Kedayan (Kedayan Blood) 83
Darusysyifa' Warrafahah (2007–) 58–63

dato (title) 4, 90, 94
Dato di-Gadong (title) 105, 112n29
Day of Judgement 46, 54
Dayang Buncu 104, 111nn26–27
Demang Lebar Daun 12–13
derato (Dusun deities) 96–99, 103, 104, 108n3, 110n18, 111nn23–27
deviancy 3, 49, 52, 54–55, 57
deviant-declared practices 58–63
Dewan Bahasa dan Pustaka (Language and Literature Bureau) 81, 134n6, 177
Director of Curriculum Development (DCD) 80
District Councils 22, 29, 35; electoral college for Legislative Council 31, 34, 42n66
Druce, S. C. i, vii, 1–6
dukun (traditional healer) 96
dunia ghaib (invisible world) 60
Dusun *adat* 94, 96, 98, 99
Dusun ancestral sites 93, 109n10
Dusun language 72–74, 79; distinct language (from Brunei Malay) 68; ethnolinguistic vitality ratings **78**; lack of writing system 108n3; 'language shift' to Pan-Brunei Malay *77*; recent developments 84–86; same as 'Bisaya' 134n8; UBD Borneo languages programme 81–82; use in RTB news broadcasts (early 1980s) 83
Dusun oral history 92, 103–106, 111–112
Dusun social group 94
Dusun social identity 92–96, 109–110
Dusun social organisation 3–4, 109n7, 109n9
Dusun society: 'acephalous' 92; administrative mechanisms (separation of authority and power) 97–98; everyday-defined social reality 90–116; integration into organisational structure of Brunei sultanate 90–116; links to coastal trade networks 93; management of social affairs 96–98; modernisation via economic changes 104–105, 109n7; power ('religious' versus 'secular') 98, 99, 110n17; separation of 'leadership' and 'authority' 98–99
Dusuns (Brunei) 3, 9, 69; akin to Bisayas of Limbang 90, 95, 99–100, 103, 105, 106, 108n2, 111n22; categorised as *puak jati/rakyat jati* 67, 108n1; census figures 70, **132** (current estimate 90); 'colonised by Brunei sultans' 111n27; distinct from Sabah Dusuns 90; exonym 106; found in middle reaches of Tutong and Belait Districts 108n1; Islamisation in coastal areas 91, 109n7; labelled as 'Bisaya' in *BAR 1906* 108n1; in or out of mainstream 67–72; *menteri darat* (land chiefs) 4, 90–116, 129; 'never considered themselves part of sultanate' 107; 'not traders' 106; oral sources 91, 92; religion 111n23; tax payments 106, 112n31
dwibahasa (bilingual) education policy 77

economic diversification 7, 16, 17, 19, 85
education 13, 77; institutional support for minority ethnic languages 79–81
Eickelman, D.: 'objectification of Muslim consciousness' 48, 63
elderly people 56–57
elders (minority communities) 4, 86
elites 17, 19
English language viii, 12, 25, 27, 40n27, 77, 80, 82, 84, 118
epistemic exchange 47, 64
ethnic classification 67–72; 'thorny problems' (Brown) 68
ethnic identity 69, 71–72, 78
ethnolinguistic groups: nomenclature changes 68
ethnolinguistics 3; minority indigenous groups 3, 67–89; vitality ratings **78**
Evers, H.-D. vii, 5, 146–151
everyday life 47, 49; *see also* Shamsul Amri Baharuddin
exorcism 49, 50, 59–60
exports and imports 13

Farage, S. 49, 50, 64
fatwas 53, 54
Firdaus Haji Abdullah 41n33
fish and fishing 27, 41n34, 106, 109n7, 121, 135n10, 137n27, 153, 172, 173
food 4, 98, 103, 131, 163
Forbes, F. E. 135n10
Furnivall, J. S. 133n2

Gadong/Gadung 130, 138n33, 154
gangguan (disturbances by *jin*) 59–60
gerakan bawah di tanah (underground movement) 27
Gilbert, J. O. 28, 30
Goeldner, C. R. 169
Google Earth 147, *148*, *149*
Gorvett, J. 17–18
gubang (dugout canoes) 159, 163n6
Gunn, G. C. 72

Hahn, H-P. 48
Hales, H. 40n16
Hall, M. 135n10
hamlets 95, 109–110n11
Hanna, W. A. 23
Hapidz Laxamana 32
Haron Din 58, 61, 62
Harrison, R. 110n11
Harrisson, T. 69, 108n1, 117, 121, 122; excavations at Kota Batu 162n1
Harun bin Mohd Amin (Harun Aminurrashid) 28, 40n27, 41n36
Hasan, Sultan 120, 126, 127
Hashim/Hasyim, Sultan 111n21, 112nn29–30; burial place 153–154
Hassanal Bolkiah, HM Sultan 1, 9, 50; accessibility 15–16; decision-making process 178; Darusysyifa' 64–65n3; full title 7; independence *titah* (1984) 10, 50; on MIB 10–11; ministerial posts 15; power 11–13; Vision 2035 programme 61
Hasyim, PM (*fl.* 1840s) 136n17
hegemonic discourse 49, 54
herbs 56, 59, 61, 62
Herzfeld, M.: part played by symbols 49–50, 63
Hidup, H. B. 32
hikayat 104
Hinduism and Hindu influence 12, 94, 103
histeria (hysteria) 59, 60
HMS *Hazard* 125
HMS *Samarang* 124
Hong Kong 37
housing 5–6, 13, 146, 149, 152–154, 158, 165, 172, 173; new (at Kampong Ayer) 159–161
Hussainmiya, B. A. viii, 1, 2, 21–45; interview with Azahari (1994) 39n12; self-censorship of interviewees 23; *Sultan Omar Ali Saifuddin and Britain* (1995) 23, 40n19
hydraulic societies 147

Iban 3, 7–8, 10, 16, 55, 86, **132**; language 81–82; longhouses 93; regarded as 'non-indigenous' to Brunei 67, 68, 70; *tuai rumah* 95
Ibrahim Ali Omar Shah, Sultan 120–121
Ida'an Dusun 110n16
identity 14–15, 48, 50, 51, 69, 71–72, 78, 92–96, 109–110
Iik Arifin Mansurnoor 52
ilmu sihir (sorcery) 126
Imas, OK Besar (Si-Imas) 126–127, 130–131, 137n20, 137n28
Indians **132**; traditional office bestowed by sultans 129
Indic elements 54
Indonesia 25–26, 33, 34, 40n23, 134n7
Institut Tahfiz Al-Quran 60
intermarriage 68, 76
'internal conquest' idea 104
invulnerability 54, 55, 56
Islam 9, 103; bureaucratisation 3, 46–66; official religion 10
Islamic bureaucracy: exclusive right to publish about Islam 52
Islamic discourse: centralisation 52–53
Islamic orthodoxy (state-enforced): hybrid pathways 3, 46–66
Islamic Party of Malaysia 58
Islamic Religious Council (MUIB: *Majlis Ugama Islam Brunei*) 46, 52, 53, 64n1
Islamic scholars: 'by definition civil servants' 52
Islamisation 46–47, 52, 64

Jais Karim 27, 41n28
Jamil al-Sufri, Pehin 128; *8 Disember: Dalangnaya Siapa?* (2003) 25; full titles 44, 142; *Liku–Liku Perjuangan* (1992) 25, 39n9
janang (Bisaya title in Limbang) 90
Japanese era in Brunei (1941–1945) 9, 25, 32, 41n36, 70
Jassin Affandi 38, 42n50; Yassin bin Affendi 32
Java 25, 57
Jerudong 125, 130
jilama gayo ('big men') 94
jin 55, 57, 59, 61, 64–65n3, 126, 137n26
jin kafir (infidel *jin*) 59
JMBRAS 5, 150n*
Johor 23, 30

Kalimantan: water villages 148, *149*, **149–150**
Kalimantan Utara 32
Kambar bin Mandi (*penghulu*) 112n30
kampong (village): 'new territorial concept' to Dusun 93
Kampong Ayer (KA) 2, 5–6, 67, 106; bridge-building 159; Brown's place of residence during fieldwork 5, 146, 153; changes and modernisation (pre-independence) 158–159; consumerism 159; destruction by fire 5–6, 153–154,

158, 159, 160, 172; development, change, modernisation (1970–2020) 152–164; facilities **157**, 159, 160, 163n4; future 162; handicrafts (decline) 5, 158, 163n5, 172–173; heritage tourism (prospects and challenges) 165–175; historical background 152–153, 162–163nn1–2; kampongs that no longer exist *155–156*; location of current kampongs *155–156*; loss of heritage 153–154, *155–156*, 161; migrant workers 161; naming system of individual wards 153; new housing 159–161, 163n9; population (current estimate) **156**, 163n3; population decline 5, 148; poverty 172; 'probably largest water village in Borneo' 148 ('largest traditional Malay community built over water' 135n9); removal of villages to facilitate large-scale construction works 154; resettlement policies 5, 136n18, 146, 152–160, 167, 172–174; symbolism 153; village names (changes) 153–154, *155–156*

KA: Cultural and Tourism Gallery 162, 170, **171**, 171–172

KA: Kampong Bolkiah A 160, 161

KA: Kampong Bolkiah B 160–161

KA: Kampong Lurong Sikuna 153, 154, *155–156*, 161

KA: Kampong Saba: *puak sakai* 67–68

KA: Kampong Sungai Kedayan 130, 153

KA: search for UNESCO WHS status 165–175; cultural heritage 169–170; data and methodology 167–168; geographical location of case area 166; historical geography 167; infrastructural problems 174; map of KA (1980) 167, *167*, (2016) 167, *168*; opportunities and challenges 172–174; public perception of tourism 169–170; tourism in KA 170–172; tourist numbers (2018–2019) **171**

KA: Sultan Omar Ali Saifuddien [III] Mosque 154, 171

KA Malay language (Balandih) 72, 74–76; dialect of Standard Malay 73; shift to 'Pan-Brunei Malay' *77*; 'variety of Brunei Malay' 68

Kampong Bebuloh 90

Kampong Danau 106

Kampong Lumut 106

Kampong Rambai 112n29

Kampong Ranau (Sabah) 110n11

Kampong Sungai Damit Pemadang 102, 109n11, 110n13, 112n29

Kampong Sungai Liang 106

Kampong Tanjung Maya 105

Kampong Telisai 106

Kampong Ukong 102, 106, 108n2, 112nn29–30; *alai gayo* 93, 109n11; apical ancestor 95, 110n13

Kasim, Pengiran Anak (son of Sultan Saiful Rijal) 125–126, 128; assumed name 'Si-Kasim' 126, 127; bestowed *menteri darat* title (*Orang Kaya*) 126; refusal of *ceteria* title 126, 127

kaunseling (counselling) 57–58, 61

KA Upgrading Pilot Project (2012) 161

Kayans 68, 106, 107, 112n32

kebal (invulnerable) 56

Kedayan language 72–77; dialect of Standard Malay **73**, 79; ethnolinguistic vitality ratings **78**; recent developments 84–86; shift to Brunei Malay 74–76; shift to 'Pan-Brunei Malay' *77*; use by RTB 83; 'variety of Brunei Malay' 68

Kedayan River 129–130, 153

Kedayans (Kadayans) 3, 4–5, 10, 69; agricultural communities (distribution) 120–121, 122, 135n10; Brunei historical traditions 125–128, 137–138; census figures 70, **132**; disparagement 126, 137n22; egalitarianism ('we do not seek rank') 127; ethno-historical orientation areas 129–131, 138n33; farmers 163n2; historical origins 'unclear' 121; importance as food producers 122; in or out of mainstream 67–72; makers and unmakers of sultans 123, 128; no dislike or fear of dark 137n27; 'one of least-known peoples of Borneo' 121; *puak jati* 67; rice-farmers 117; ritual relationships 128–129, 138nn30–32; settlement patterns 129–131, 138n33; spelling issue 133; status in Brunei society 128–129, 138nn30–32; 'substantial proportion of Malay component of Brunei's population' 121, **132**, 135n12; titles bestowed by sultans 128–129, 138n31; *urang Kianggih* 136n15

Kedayans: and Brunei Sultanate 121–125, 135–137; economic relationships 121–122, 123, 136nn14–17; political relationships 123–125, 136–137

Kedayans: Kedayan and Barunay 120–121, 134–135; nineteenth-century Brunei 118–120, 134nn3–7; place in traditional

Brunei society 117–144; problem 117–119, 133–134; source material (paucity) 118
Keesing, R. 97, 100
Kemariah PH Duraman, Dku 172
kepala menteri darat 4, 90, 105, 112n29, 129
Keppel, H. 124
kerasukan (possession) 59
keris 57
Kershaw, E. M. 74, 76, 77, 109n7
Kershaw, R. 72
ketua kampong (village headman) 4, 29, 51, 90, 103, 109n5, 110n15, 111n19
Khrushchev, N. 37
khurafat (forbidden superstition) 55
Kianggeh 130–131
Kianggeh market 173–174
Kianggeh River 136n15
Kilanas 130
Kimanis 134n5
Kimball, L. A. 177
King, V. T. i, viii, 1–6, 97, 103, 105, 178
kinship 96, 110nn11–13
knowledge: bureaucratisation 48; production 50–51, 64
Konfrontasi 24, 36, 121
Kota Batu 166, 174
kubur keramat ('powerful graves') 54, 55, 57
kucing emas (golden cats) 54
Kunyit 7 Lodge 172
Kutai 147, 150

Labuan 25, 32, 39n10, 40n27; example of water village *148*; Kedayan migrants 120, 135n10
labur gayo ('Great Deluge') 103, 111n23
language shift 74–78, 83–84; at dialectal level 75–76; at language level 76–78; lexical changes 75; phonetic changes 75
language shift process 77, *77*
languages of minority ethnic groups: decline (reduction in linguistic diversity) 74–81; director of curriculum development 79–80; education system 79–81; gloomy outlook 74; institutional support 79–84; Language and Literature Bureau 81; marginalisation 74, 76, 78, 79–81; officially labelled 'Malay dialects' 3, 67, 68, 72–74, 79, 83, 84; proper writing system absent 80; recent developments 84–85; RTB 82–84; UBD's Borneo languages programme 81–82
Lee Kuan Yew 35, 36
Legislative Council 9, 12, 31–32, 35–36, 38; composition (1962) 43n70; indirect elections (1962) 34, 42n66
legitimacy 13, 14, 16, 62
lengkap (complete) 50
Lévi-Strauss, C. 99
Leys, P. 91, 109n8
Liaw Yock Fang 12–13
Limbang 106, 110n15, 112n29, 112n33, 120, 122, 134n6, 135n10, 136n16; rebellion (1962) 22; *see also* Bisayas (Limbang)
Lim Cheng Choo, Dato Temenggong 43n70
Lim Chin Siong 36, 37
Lingenfelter, S. G. 93
Linton, P. M. (Brunei Shell Petroleum Company) 43n70
lobok organisation 99–100
Local Councils Enactment 42n47
'local globalisation' 84
London: Public Record Office 1, 21, 23
London-Cornell project 1
longhouses 93, 147
Low, H. 118, 134n4, 136n17, 137n28
lubok (family rooms in *alai gayo*) 93
Lumut 91, 109n7

McArthur, M. S. H. 108n2, 122, 156–158
MacDonald, M. 28
Macintosh, R. W. 169
Mackie, J. A. C. 21, 24
McLellan, J. viii, 3, 67–89
magical amulets 37, 43n75
Maine, Sir Henry 102
Majlis Mesyuarat Di-Raja (Privy Council) 31
Majlis Mesyuarat Kerajaan (Executive Council) 31
Majlis Mesyuarat Menteri-Menteri (Council of Ministers) 30
Majlis Mesyuarat Negeri (Legislative Council) 31–32
Makam di Luba (a royal grave) 57
makhluk Allah (creation of Allah) 62, 65n3
'Malay': definition issue 135n11
Malayan Communist Party (MCP) 34
Malayan People's Socialist Front 41n33
Malay ethnicity 9–10
Malay Islamic Monarchy *see* MIB
Malay language: national language 10, 79
Malay race: definition in Brunei Constitution (1959) 70; definition in

Brunei Nationality Enactment (1961) 69; usage in censuses (1971, 1981, 1991) 71
Malays 12–13
Malaysia 120; Brunei's refusal to join (1963) 9, 24, 33–36, 42–43; support for Brunei exiles 36
Malik, Prince 60
Malinowski, B. 99
Manila 8, 37
marriage 96, 98
Martin, P. W. 74, 76, 79
Masaru Emoto 62, 65n4
masuk Melayu 68, 102, 104
Maxwell, A. R. viii, 4–5, 72, 117–144, 177, 178; note on transcription 133
Means, G. P. 24
media 46–47, 60, 75, 77
melagau (inviting neighbours to one's house) 162
Melaka sultanate 8–9
Melanau 7–8, 16, 86, **132**; regarded as 'non-indigenous' to Brunei 68
Melanesia 94–95, 110n13, 134n2
Menon, U. 25
menteri besar (chief minister) 30, 31, 32
menteri darat (land chiefs) 4, 68, 86, 90–116, 126, 130–131; administrative mechanism 101–103, 111nn20–22; 'commission' rather than 'office' 101; not a hereditary post 101; 'power' and 'authority' 102; power limited by Dusun custom 98–99
menteri laut ('sea' chiefs) 4, 90
Metcalf, P. 103, 107, 112n33; *Life of Longhouse* (2010) 106, 112n33
MIB (Malay Islamic Monarchy): concept 9–10; 'exclusively defined' by government 51; genesis 10–11; national ideology 2, 3, 7, 13, 14–15, 46, 47, 50, 177–178; possible moral responsibility to support minority ethnic languages 84; three pillars 'integral to one another' 14; variables from within, challenges from without 16–18
MIB Concept Committee (1986) 50
MIB firewall 46, 48, 53–55, 63; undesired external elements 54
MIB publishing (systematic, 1994–) 51
MIB State 63, 64; bureaucratised Islam and classificatory power 50–52, 61
MIB Supreme Council (*Majlis Tertinggi MIB*, 1990–) 50–52, 53; 'five-year working plans' 51, 63; Secretariat 10, 16, 20, 50–51, 64n*
MIB workings 11–16; character 13–14; identity 14–15; power 11–13; sustainability 16; viability 15–16
middle class 17, 19
Ministry of Education: Director of Curriculum Development (DCD) 79; perceives ethnic languages as dialects of Malay 79
Ministry of Religious Affairs (MoRA) 52–53, 56, 61; vision and mission 53, 63
minority ethnic groups 3; ethnolinguistics 67–89; 'not natively Malay speaking' 134n8; shifts in identity 71–72
Mohamed Bolkiah, Prince 23; *Remember, Remember: 8th of December* (2007) 25
Mohammad [read as 'Muhammad'], Shaikh (brother to Azahari) 40n16
Mohammad Hasanhamuny bin Bakar 163n3
Mohd Manggol bin Dato Manggol (b. *c.* 1930) 27, 40–41n27
Mohd Yusof bin Pengiran Abdul Rahman, PH ('Yura Halim'): *Adat Istiadat Brunei* (1958) 108; *Mahkota Yang Berdarah* (1951) 127
monarchy 7–20
Mosque Affairs Department 53
mosques: Friday prayer sermons 53, 55
mudawi (medical practitioner) 59
Muhammad, Prophet 11, 12, 14, 56
Muhammad, Sultan 10, 13
Muhammad Alam, PM (Raja Api) 119, 134n4
Muhammad Ali, Sultan 127
Muhammad Hadi bin Muhammad Melayong 9, 51
Muhammad Jamalul Alam I, Sultan 119
Muhammad Jamalul Alam II, Sultan 112n29
Muhammad Kanzul Alam, Sultan 119, 124, 134n4
Muhammad Najib Noorashid 82, 85
Muhammad Tajuddin, Sultan 119, 124
Muhyiddin, Sultan 125, 126–128
Müller, D. M. viii, 2–3, 46–66; MIB generation 52, 55
Mundy, R. 124, 135n10, 137n19
Murut (Lun Bawang) language 68, 72–74, 79, 134n8; distinct from Brunei Malay 68; ethnolinguistic vitality ratings **78**; 'language shift' to Pan-Brunei Malay 77; recent developments 84–86
Muruts (Lun Bawang/Lun Dayeh) 3, 10, 71; census figures (and other estimates)

69–70, **132**; in or out of mainstream 67–72; *puak jati* 67, 69
musa'id (assistant medical practitioner) 59
Muslims 8, 10, 53, 55, 57, 58, 71

Nanning: Guangxi University (China) 177
National Army of North Kalimantan (TNKU) 23, 33, 34, 37, 39n2; arsenal 36–37
national curriculum 79–80
National Education Policy 77, 79–81
national identity 14–15, 50, 51, 72
national ideology *see* MIB (Malay Islamic Monarchy)
nation-state 3, 15, 46, 49, 63, 91
Negara Kesatuan Kalimantan Utara (NKKU) 23–24, 38, 40n27
Negara Zikir (nation that always remembers Allah) 61
neo-colonialism 24, 34, 39
Nikman, Sheikh 41n30
nobles 128, 137n21
Noor Azam Haji-Othman vii, 3, 67–89
Norafan Zainal 52
North Borneo 8, 24, 28, 120
Nothofer, B. 68, 72–74, 79
Nur Alam, Raja 119
Nuttall, Dr W. L. F. 40n16, 40n20

oil and gas industry 7, 13, 37–38, 50; price-volatility 17
Omar, Pengiran Di-Gadong (fl. mid-C17) 127
Omar Ali Saifuddin I, Sultan 119
Omar Ali Saifuddin II, Sultan 119, 124, 135n10; flight from capital and trust in Kedayans (1846) 125; widow (un-named) 122, 136n17
Omar Ali Saifuddin (Saifuddien) III, Sultan (r. 1950–1967; later Seri Begawan Sultan) 1, 2, 22–26, 134n6; ascendancy 36; and Azahari 38, 43n78; 'could control rain' 57; formation-of-Malaysia issue 35, 38; Islamic religious bureaucracy 52; opposition to Borneo Federation idea 33; resistance to power-sharing 29–31
Ooi Keat Gin vii–viii, 2, 7–20
orang darat 108n4
orang kaya (OK) 4, 90, 94
Orang Kaya Di-Gadong 130
orang pandai ('good' *bomoh*) 56–57, 61
Othman Mahmud, Shaikh 23
Owen, J. F. 122

Pacific War (1941–1945) 8–9, 25, 32, 41n36, 70, 120
padian (women vendors in boats) 173, *176*
pagun abai (Dusun term for Kampong Ayer) 107
pagun sawat 111n23
Palembang 12, 25
panakod ceremony 95, 96, 102, 110n15, 111n22
Pan-Bruneian Malay language (Noor Azam) 3, 67, 74–76, *77*, 77, 84
Pangiran Tumanggung Raja Digayuh 126, 127
pangkalan (riverine sites) 93
panglima (Bisaya title in Limbang) 90
Pan-Malayan Islamic Party 41n37
Partai Komunis Indonesia (PKI) 34
Partai Rakyat Brunei (PRB) 2, 9, 22; aspirations not met by Constitution (1959) 30–31; Congresses (1958) 32, (1961) 34; formation (1956) 28; manifesto (1956) 28; road to rebellion 33–36, 42–43
Partai Rakyat Malaya (PRM) 27, 28, 41nn33–34; Azahari's attempt to form branch in Brunei (1955) 27
Partindo (Indonesia Party) 34
pegawai istana (palace officials) 129
pegawai ugama (religious officials) 129
pembantu perawat (assistant medical practitioner) 59
pemujiaan (worshipping) 56
Penan (Punan) 3, 7–8, 10, 16, 86, **132**; regarded as 'non-indigenous' to Brunei 67, 68
pengalu: boat-rowing trader 106, 107; suppliers of goods to *padian*) 173
penghulu 29, 90, 103, 110n15, 111n19, 112n30
pengiran anak: meaning of title 137n23
Pengiran Di-Gadong (title) 105, 112n29
pengiran-pengiran (nobles) 128, 129, 138n31
penyuru (tax gatherers) 90–91, 109n6
Peranio, R. D. 93, 94, 95, 99, 110n12, 111n22
perawat (medical practitioner) 59
perbomohan ('*bomoh*-ism') 55
Philippines 8, 34, 134n3, 152
Pigafetta, A. 134n3, 152, 163n2, 166
plural society 117–118, 133, 133–134n2, 178
Poedjosoedarmo, G. R. 75
poisoning: 'classic *bomoh* tool' 59

police 26, 27, 41n28
Portuguese 8, 134n3
Poulgrain, G. 23, 25, 39n6, 39n12, 40n18, 42n63
power 11–13
power-knowledge nexus 49, 52, 61
PowerPoint 62, 63
Pretty, E. E. F. 26
Pringle, R. 109n8
puak jati (indigenous groups) 3, 67–68
puak sakai 67, 68
Pudarno Binchin vii, 3–4, 90–116
pulau (Dusun hamlet) 93
Pulau Cermin 127
punyit or *pungit* people (Kedayan) 107
Pusat Da'wah Islamiah 53
Pusat Sejarah Brunei (Brunei History Centre) 25, 39n4

Rabinah Uja 78
Raeburn, W. 30
raja gayo ('great' kings) 111n25
raja-raja (nobles) 128, 129
Raja Tengah (Tangah) 120–121
Raja Yang Prihatin/Pemedulian (Caring Monarch) 50
Rajid bin OK Kasim *see* Si-Rajid
ranggau (form of sorcery) 55
rank 127, 131; Kedayan lack of interest 137n29
Religious Council and Kadi Courts Act (RCKCA) 52, 53, 57, 64n1
religious freedom: 'more constrained than in neighbouring countries' 46
religious syncretism 54
Revolutions: China (1911) 12; Iran (1978–1979) 17; Siam (1932) 12
rice 93, 94, 103, 105, 111n23, 111n26, 122
rice-cult beliefs 91
rice tribute 138n30
rohani/emosi (spiritual/emotional [treatment field]) 59, 60
Rosenberg, P. 76
Russell [initial/s n.a.] 110n15
Rutter, O. 135n10

Sabah 90, 93, 122; water villages *149*, **149–150**
Saging bin Ebaah, Dato Pemancha 95, 102, 103, 106, 110nn13–14, 112n30; 'charismatic authority' 102, 111n21; founder of Kampong Ukong 105
sago 122, 136n16
Sahlins, M. D. 94–95, 110n13
Saiful Rijal, Sultan 128; special relationship with Kedayan of Jerudong 125, 127
St John, S. 68, 110n16, 122, 124, 136n14, 153
Salar 129, 130, 138n33
Saleha, Pengiran (consort of Sultan Muhammad Kanzul Alam) 119
Salleh, Pehin H. M. 32, 40n19, 41n35
Sarawak 28, 120, 122; British protectorate (1888) 8; Brooke era 119–120; Kedayan residents (1947) 135n10; local councils 29; water villages *149*, **149–150**
Sarawak United People's Party (SUPP) 24, 34, 35, 37
Saunders, G. 15–16, 134n7, 135n12
Sejarah Melayu 12
Selkirk, Lord 24, 43n78
Semaun/Simawn, Awang: an '*urang kuat*' 137n26
Sercombe, P. G. 77–78
sesat (deviant) 49
Sha'er Awang Simaun/Syair Awang Semaun 54; *puak sakai* 68
Shafi'i Sunni Islam 46, 50, 53, 64n1
Shafi Noor Islam viii, 6, 165–175
Shamsul Amri Baharuddin: 'authority-defined social reality' 92, 104–105, 106, 108; 'everyday-defined social reality' 92–93, 104–105, 108
Sharia-compliant healing 3, 58–63
Sharia Criminal Procedure Code (SPCO, 2013) 53, 57–58, 64n2
Shariffuddin bin Pengiran Metali, Pengiran DP Haji 177
sihir (sorcery) 55
Si-Imas 126; *see also* Imas, OK Besar
Si-Kasim 128; *see also* Kasim, Pengiran Anak
Sileh Yutong 111n26
SIL Speech Analysis System 75
Singapore 23, 24, 36
'Si-' prefix 126, 137n24
Si-Rajid (Rajid bin OK Kasim) 125–128, 137n26; promoted Pengiran Temenggong 127–128
siram ditaan (epic Dusun tales) 90, 92, 103–106, 108n3, 111–112; demonstrate Dusun egalitarianism 103–104, 111n26; incorporation of Malay characters 111–112n27; singers 104
SITC Perak 40n27, 41n36
S. M. & Sons 41n30
Smith, Brigadier E. D. 24

Smith, M. G. 95–96; lineage relations 102; notion of corporateness 101; plural society concept 133–134n2; separation of 'authority' and 'power' 97–98
social class 128, 138n31
social imaginaries 3, 55–58
social media 16, 75, 162; Facebook 56
social reality *see* Shamsul Amri Baharuddin
social status 92, 110n11, 111n26, 131, 138n31; Kedayan in Brunei society 128–129, 138nn30–32; Kedayan lack of interest 137n29
social stratification 68, 103–104, 107, 131
social structure 117, 131, 133; and history 1
sorcery 55, 59, 126
Southeast Asia: Malay maritime economy 123–124
South East Asia Research 5
Spanish attack on Brunei (1578) 125
Sri Tri Buana 12–13
Standard Malay language 72, 73, 76, 77, 82–83, 84
Starner, F. L. 38
state classificatory power 3, 46, 47, 48–52, 55–64
State Mufti 52, 53, 60–61
state power 46; symbols 57
stigma 3, 57, 74
Stockwell, A. J. 22, 23, 25, 31, 36
Subuk 130–131
Sukarno, President 22, 25
sultan (theory): possessor of magical powers (Brown) 65n3; *ulil amri* (leader of believers) and *khalifah* (Allah's vice-regent) 12, 14, 53, 65n3
Sultan Hassanal Bolkiah Foundation 160, 163n8, 171
Sulu 8, 134n5
Sumijah Alias 75
Sungai Kedayan Eco-Corridor 148, 154, 165, 173
Sungai Liang 91, 109n7
supernatural counterforces 53–55
Syarif Ali (Sharif Ali), Sultan 14, 166, 173
syirik (sin) 55
symbolic capital 50
symbolic power 49, 52; Syariah punishments 53
symbolism 49–50, 54, 63, 159

taboo 22, 130
tafrijiyah ('4444 prayers') 62
Ta'if (Ḥijāz, South Arabia) 14
takhta (throne) 8
tamarok 90, 94, 96, 97, 108n3; 'ritualised religious activity' 105
Tarling, N. 21, 135n10, 136n16, 177
Tasek Merimbun (ASEAN Heritage site) 85
Tassim bin Haji Abu Bakar, Haji vii, 5–6, 152–164
taxation 13, 29, 91, 101, 105
Temburong 42n66
Tentera Nasional Kalimantan Utara (TNKU) 23, 33, 34, 37, 39n2; arsenal 36–37
tetuwo (Dusun council of elders) 92, 95–96, 103, 110n16, 111n22; functions 96; public authority and personal 'power' 96–99, 110–111
tetuwo suguton (elder persons to follow) 94
Tey Tsun Hang 11
Tingang, OK Panglima 109n11, 112n29
tiri (genealogical layer) 110n13
titah 51
titles: bestowal 'structured by ethnicity and social class' 128
tourism 6, 84, 85, 146, 153, 162; definition 169; prospects and challenges 165–175
Tourism Development Department (2005–) 85, 170
trade 8, 107, 147
trade unionism 26, 32, 42nn57–58
tukang sihir (sorcerers) 55
tulin land 105, 112n29
tumuakar or *dulang pagar* (trays of food) 111n22
Tutong District 85, 90, 91, 93, 105, 106, 108n1, 109n7, 112n29, 122, 135n10, 136n16
Tutong language 72–74, 79, 81–82, 134n8; distinct from Brunei Malay 68; ethnolinguistic vitality ratings 78; 'language shift' to 'Pan-Brunei Malay' *77*; recent developments 84–86; Tutong-Malay dictionary (1991) 81
Tutong Town 105
Tutongs 3, 10, 69, 71; census figures 70, **132**; in or out of mainstream 67–72; *menteri darat* 129; *puak jati* 67

UMNO 27–28
UNESCO 165–175; cultural heritage of 'outstanding universal value' 169; definition of 'intangible heritage' 170
UNESCO, cultural heritage criteria: groups of buildings 169; monuments 169; sites 170

UNESCO: World Heritage Sites 6, 169
UNISSA 172
United Kingdom 22, 35, 177; Colonial Office 30, 32, 33, 42n5; intelligence services 22–23; 'neo-colonialism' 24
United Nations 36, 38
United North Kalimantan State (NKKU) 23–24, 38, 40n27
United States 138n31, 177
Universiti Brunei Darussalam (UBD) 168; Academy of Brunei Studies (*Akademi Pengajian Brunei*, 1990–) i, 11, 50–51, 177; Borneo languages programme 81–82, 84, 85; Institute of Asian Studies i, 177
Urang Darat (land people, i.e. Kedayans) 67, 137n22
urang kampung darat (land villagers) 137n22
urang kuat (person with extraordinary strength) 137n26
ustaz (teacher) 56, 57
Utusan Melayu 27

Vasil, R. K. 41n33
village: terminology 109n11
village headmen *see ketua kampong*
voluntary incorporation 102

Wacquant, L. J. D. 49, 50, 64
waris (Dusun descent group) 94–103, 107, 108, 109n11, 110n12, 110n15; as corporate unit 99–101; meanings (Dusun social group or Dusun descent group) 94
water-crystal photography 3, 62, 63
water taxis 159, 172
water villages (Borneo) 4, 5, 146–151; largest by far in NBD 146; map *149*; measurements 147–148; number, population, area 146, 147, **149–150**; purpose 146–147; remote sensing data 5, 146, 147
wazir (viziers) 31, 128
Weber, M. 100–101, 111n20, 133
welfare state 15, 16, 17, 18
White, D. C. 39n12, 40n16, 43n70
Wolters, O. W. 94
women 96, 99, 130
Woodward [initial/s n.a.] 110n15
World Heritage Committee 169
World Heritage Convention (1972) 169
World Trade Organisation 170

Yasun binti Yaba 112n30
Yawang Kabincuan 104, 111nn26–27
younger generations 11, 25, 26, 40n20, 52, 55, 75, 97, 148, 173, 158, 162; language shift 76–78
Yusop Damit, Dr Haji 43n80
Yusuf, Pengiran: trust in Kedayans 124

Zahari, Syed 36
Zaini Haji Ahmad, Haji 28, 32, 33, 38, 39n4, 40n16, 42n47, 42n50; *Pertumbuhan Nasionalisme di Brunei* (1989, rev. 2004) 23, 25, 39n4
zakat (alms) 50, 52
Zariani Abdul Rahman 39n12